The Life and Ministry of

William J. Seymour
and a history of the Azusa Street Revival

The Life and Ministry of

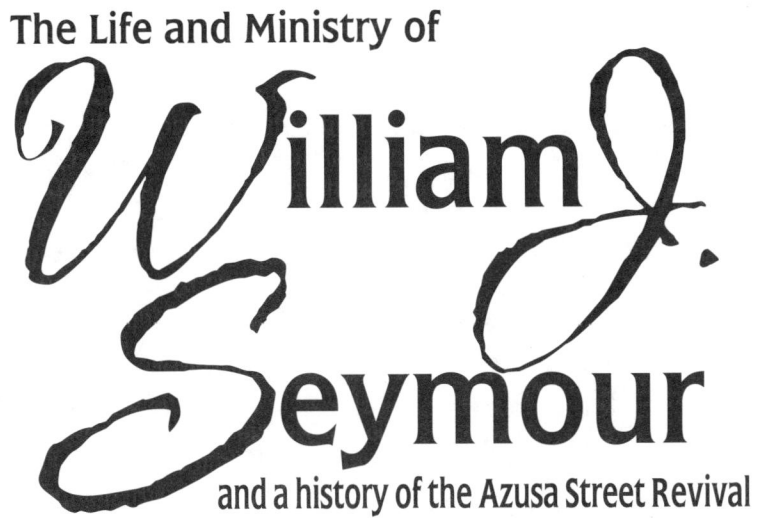

William J. Seymour

and a history of the Azusa Street Revival

THE COMPLETE AZUSA STREET LIBRARY
Volume 1

Dr. Larry Martin

CHRISTIAN LIFE BOOKS
THE PUBLISHING ARM OF RIVER OF REVIVAL MINISTRIES, INC.
PENSACOLA, FL 32516

Copyright © 1999 & 2014 by Larry Martin

ISBN 0-9646289-4-5
Library of Congress Catalog Number : 99-76361

All rights reserved. Reproduction in whole or part without written permission from the publisher is prohibited.

Printed in the United States of America.

CHRISTIAN LIFE BOOKS
P.O. Box 36355
Pensacola, FL 32516

www.azusastreet.org
www.drlarrymartin.org
www.pentecostalgold.com
www.jesus-is-the-answer.com
info@azusastreet.org

Dedication

**Dedicated to the memory of Rev. David A. Roper
(1906 - 1991)**

A pulpit pounding, pew jumping, holiness preaching Pentecostal pastor. He was used by God to build a great church in Comanche, Oklahoma. Under his anointed leadership my parents accepted the Fatherhood of God, the Lordship of Jesus Christ and the Power of the Holy Spirit. He was my first pastor. He whimsically prophesied my call to the ministry and dedicated me to God. He prayed for me.
His works follow him.

William Joseph Seymour
Signature on Transfer of Right of Way to
Iberia, St. Mary, and Eastern Railroad Company of Louisiana
Franklin, Louisiana
October 24, 1912

Contents

Foreword 9
Preface to the Series 11
Prologue 17

1 The Message–A New Pentecost 21
2 The Background–Life in Southern Louisiana 31
3 The Roots–The Seymour Family 47
4 The Sojourn–Seymour in the North 65
5 The Divine Appointment–Seymour and Parham 87
6 The City–Los Angeles, California 101
7 The Preparation–Hunger for God 119
8 The Result–Holy Ghost Outpouring 139
9 The Place–Old Azusa 155
10 The Beginning–The First Weeks 165
11 The Revival–Heaven on Earth 177
12 The Pilgrims–Williams, Mason, and Cashwell 209
13 The Commission–Into All the World 227
14 The First Challenge–Opposition 247
15 The Second Challenge–Division 267

16 The Apostolic Ministry–Seymour's Travels   301
17 The End–Disapointment and Death   323

Epilogue   351
Index   355
List of Illustrations   371
About the Author   377

Foreword

As a minister of the gospel, nothing stirs the cords of my soul like revival. In my library, I have a vast selection of books. When I need a spiritual boost, of course, I go to God's Word. But, when I approach my voluminous library, I inevitably go to the revival section. I am instantly inspired, challenged to greater holiness, and motivated to go after God for greater anointing.

Through the years, one of my heroes has been, William J. Seymour, the leader of the Azusa Street revival in Los Angeles. I would eagerly pick up any material I could on this humble servant that God used in such a mighty way. In his book, **The Life and Ministry of William J. Seymour**, Dr. Larry Martin handles his biography with reverence, care, and respect. I believe the Holy Spirit will use this book to disassemble wrong motives in our lives as Christians and help us lay a new foundation as men and women of God, based on humility and utter dependence on God.

When I read after someone, I want to know a little about their credentials and their integrity. Dr. Larry

Martin is not only a personal friend, but a man with a heart for revival. His rich history as an ordained minister, revival evangelist, Bible college president, and board member of a well-known Pentecostal denomination, qualifies Larry to speak into the lives of those hungry for fresh anointing.

Pastor John A. Kilpatrick
Former Pastor,
Brownsville Assembly of God
Pensacola, Florida

Preface to the Series

The twentieth century Pentecostal/charismatic movement was born on the first day of this century, January 1, 1901, in Topeka, Kansas. For several months, the fledgling faith slept like a babe in a crib. Then for a couple of years she crawled around in Kansas, Missouri and Texas. In April 1906, Pentecostalism stood to her feet in a dilapidated old mission at 312 Azusa Street in Los Angeles, California. Once standing, the movement swiftly ran around the world. Nearly one hundred years later she is still running as revival fires fall fresh on a hungry church.

This series of books is about the Azusa Street revival that started it all. It is not conjecture or hearsay. These are primarily eyewitness accounts. Although the witnesses lie silent in the grave, their testimonies live to speak to a new generation.

There are two reasons why I have collected and published these materials. First, before any of these testimonies are further scattered or forgotten, I want to establish a record for the future. A record that is available not only in libraries and archives, but accessible to all Spirit-filled believers, clergy, and laymen who want to relive their heritage. The Pentecostal/charismatic church must never forget what happened at 312 Azusa Street.

Secondly, I pray that the reading of these dramatic stories will create a hunger in the hearts of the people of God. Although the

United States is experiencing revival, many would argue that we have seen nothing that equals the power of the Azusa meeting and the impact it had on the world. The church must pray for a fresh outpouring for a new millennium.

I started this project with the assumption that I would publish one book, erroneously believing that few witnesses would be available. This single volume has grown into a series of books covering practically every aspect of the Azusa outpouring.

I have attempted to leave the record intact as much as is possible. In some cases, I have condensed and to a very limited extent I have corrected misspelling (especially proper names and usually following a parenthetical note) and punctuation. I have also changed the grammatical style (quotation marks, etc.) of some writers for the sake of consistency. In no instance did I add or subtract anything that changed the accuracy of the witnesses' accounts.

I pray that my desire to present the original accounts as they were written will not cause any to be offended. Blacks are generally referred to as "colored" and some other language might not be considered appropriate by today's standards. Please remember that what is not acceptable today was the norm 100 years ago. As you read, you will find that in most cases, the same language was used by both blacks and whites. In no case is it my desire to offend. In fact, my prayer is that once again the children of God might worship together as one, regardless of race, ethnicity, or affiliation. The "color line" that disappeared at Azusa Street can still be washed away by Jesus' precious blood.

Nearly a century and a half ago, Thomas Phillips struggled to write a history of the Wales revival of 1859. He wrote, "The difficulty has been to select and abridge, and so to arrange the materials as to avoid sameness and repetition on the one hand, and incompleteness on the other." Facing the same decision, I am sure I have erred on the side of "sameness." Although many witnesses described the same events or circumstances, I felt that despite the repetition, each person should be allowed to tell their own story in their own words.

The first book is a biography of William J. Seymour and a history of the Azusa revival. This book is essential to understanding the Azusa story. In the next three volumes, I included the testimonies of the true believers. Another volume contains the bitter words of Azusa's harshest critics. It seemed to me there would be no other way for a truly interested reader to share the full Azusa experience without tasting the bitter as well as the sweet. I have included a book on William H. Durham, Frank Bartleman's books, sermons preached at the mission and Seymour's *Doctrines and Discipline*. When finished, I pray the series will adequately tell the Azusa Street story.

Although the series will be comprehensive, it will not be complete. Thousands of people were blessed at the mission, but unfortunately their testimonies were never recorded or else they have been lost. These include some of the better known, like Canadian R. E. McAlister, E. W. Kenyon, and many more whose testimonies are known only to God and perhaps a small circle of surviving relatives.

For example, while researching an early leader in the Pentecostal Church of God, Harold Collins, I learned that his father, a Pentecostal pioneer in Oklahoma, was ordained at "old Azusa." George G. Collins had been a hired hand on the famous 101 Ranch. Who could have guessed he, too, was one of the thousands of Azusa pilgrims?

I am sure there are also many eyewitness accounts that are not yet available to me. If any reader is aware of any additional testimonies, I would appreciate having them for inclusion in future publications.

It is important that I repeat a paragraph from the preface of my previous work, **The Topeka Outpouring of 1901**, "As you read, you will notice minor variations and contradictions in the stories. This should not be surprising. As with witnesses to any event, different people will have a slightly different view or memory of the occurrence. If four people standing on each corner of an intersection viewed an automobile accident, each would describe the crash from their own perspective. Please do not let these minor contradictions be a stumbling block. The most important thing is that these marvelous events did occur and they started a mighty revival that has swept the world."

I am grateful to the guardians of our history for their diligence, without which this work would be impossible. I am grateful for the help provided by the following church, parachurch or denominational archives: The Flower Pentecostal Heritage Center (where I received most of my help); Ohio District Assemblies of God; Christ for the Nations; The Church of God Archives, Cleveland, TN; The Church of the Nazarene Archives; The Church of God Holiness; The Aostolic Faith Church, Portland; The Apostolic Faith Church, Baxter Springs; The Historical Center of the United Pentecostal Church; The International Pentecostal Holiness Church Archives; The International Church of the Foursquare Gospel; The Pentecostal Assemblies of the World; The Gospel Missionary Union; The United Methodist Church Archives; The Southern Baptist Church Archives; and The Church of the Assumption, Franklin, LA.

Librarians at the following schools also assisted me in my search for materials: Southwestern Assemblies of God University, The Assemblies of God Theological Seminary, The Holy Spirit Research Center of Oral Roberts University, Christian Theological Seminary, Heritage Bible College, Anderson University, DePauw University, Ozark Christian College, Missouri Southern State College, Hood Theological Seminary, Union University, Columbia International University, University of South Carolina, Mt. Pleasant College, William Jewell College, and Southwest Baptist University.

Editors of these periodicals helped with research: **The Los Angeles Times, Grace and Glory, The Texas Bar**, and **The Pentecostal Evangel.**

The staff members and volunteers at the National Archives in Washington, DC and College Park, MD and the branch office in Kansas City were all helpful. I am also grateful for the help I received from state archives in Missouri, Indiana, California, Texas, Mississippi, and Louisiana and the court clerk's office in St. Mary Parish.

I received assistance from public libraries in Los Angeles; Franklin, VA; Terre Haute, IN; Evansville, IN; Indianapolis; St. Louis; Kansas City, KS and MO; Independence, MO; Cape Girardeau, MO; Springfield, IL; Chicago; Cleveland; Cincinnati; Columbus; Dunn, NC; Jackson, MS; Mobile, AL; Houston; Memphis; Franklin, LA; New Orleans and Baton Rouge. The research department at Joplin's Public Library provided me with dozens of sources through interlibrary loan. Their capable help was invaluable.

Assemblies of God archivist Glenn Gohr's valuable assistance has greatly enhanced all of my projects. Glenn knows practically everything about early Pentecostal history and is generous in sharing what he knows. If he doesn't know it, he knows where to find someone who does. He has given me dozens of profitable leads. Glenn and I have traveled together searching for material and communicated hundreds of time through letter, telephone, and email. Every church history writer should be blessed with a friend like Glenn. I could not have written this book without his help.

Vinson Synan, Sherry Sherrod Dupree, Wayne Warner, Joyce Lee, Art Glass, Ruth Foster, Lucas Wegmann, J. Ramsey, James Corum, Vivian Deno, Richard Crayne, Smith Haley, Judith Dodd, James L. Dodd,III, David Cloud, John Hall, Calvin Durham, Thomas R. Williams, Ruth Foster, Dean Osterberg, Lary Goss, Johnny Cunningham, Sandra Bass, Jerry Jett, and John Worrell also provided information. Darrol Pierson shared a priceless folder on the Indianapolis "Gliggy Bluks." I have talked with dozens, if not hundreds, of people, many of whom should probably be mentioned, but my memory often fails me. No omission is intentional and any oversight would gladly be corrected in future additions. Although I have never met them, this work owes a great debt to Cecil M. Robeck and Douglas J. Nelson, the premier Azusa Street scholars.

I located and interviewed two of Seymour's relatives, Lucile Seymour and Donald Jones. Seymour is the widow of Van Seymour, son of Jacob Seymour, William's brother. Jones is the son of Jacob's daughter. Although they had little information to share, I am thankful for their cooperation.

A special thanks also goes to the many who provided me with articles, other materials and photographs with permission to reprint. Although every name is not mentioned here, I have attempted to give credit in the appropriate places. The series is better because of their generosity. Thank you to the men of God who took time from their busy schedules to write forewords for the series.

My further appreciation goes to Anita Montgomery, Glenn Gohr, Rhonda Walton, David Dillon, and Dan Dillon for editorial readings and comments. I am also grateful to David Coleman for an excellent illustration for the cover and Raymond Cook for the chalk portraits. John Mallinak did an excellent job designing the covers. His sister, Lauri Stone, added the special touch that made everything "just right."

It seems my friends at MPH always give extra effort to see that the books are top quality. Thank you to Brian Ramos, Harold Thompson, Carrie Oakes, Tammy Christie, and Greg Harvey.

A special thank you also goes to the members of my family, who have supported me as months of painstaking work turned into years. Thank you, T. J. and Summer for traveling with me, and when necessary, letting me travel alone. Thank you for your prayers and love.

Finally, let us all pray that the love, humility, tears, hunger, and Pentecostal power that were the spirit of Azusa will visit us again. Our world, our nation, our churches need Holy Ghost revival.

Larry Martin
Pensacola, Florida

Prologue

William Joseph Seymour
Larry Martin Collection
(Chalk portrait by Raymond Cook)

Brother Seymour was recognized as the nominal leader in charge. But we had no pope or hierarchy. We were "brethren." We had no human program. The Lord Himself was leading. We had no priest class, nor priest craft. We did not even have a platform or pulpit in the beginning. All were on a level. The ministers were servants, according to the true meaning of the word. We did not honor men for their advantage, in means or education, but rather for their God-given "gifts."

Brother Seymour generally sat behind two empty shoe boxes, one on top of the other. He usually kept his head inside the top one during the meeting, in prayer. There was no pride there.

Frank Bartleman
How Pentecost Came to Los Angeles

Now, just a word concerning Bro. Seymour, who is the leader of the movement under God: He is the meekest man I have ever met. He walks and talks with God. His power is in his weakness. He seems to maintain a helpless dependence on God and is as simple-hearted as a little child, and at the same time is so filled with God that you feel the love and power every time you get near him.

William H. Durham
The Apostolic Faith
February-March, 1907

I do not believe that any other man in modern times had a more wonderful deluge of God in his life than God gave to that dear fellow... God was in him.

John G. Lake describing Seymour in a sermon.
"Spiritual Hunger"

The writer has not a single doubt but that Brother Seymour has more power with God, and more power from God, than all his critics in and out of this city. His strength is in his conscious weakness, and lowliness before God; and, so long as he maintains this attitude, the power of God will, no doubt, continue to flow through him.

A.S. Worrell
Gospel Witness, reprinted in **The Apostolic Faith**
February-March, 1907

The Apostolic Faith Mission
Larry Martin Collection
(Water Color by David Coleman)

1 *The Message:* A NEW PENTECOST

The words "Azusa Street" have become synonymous with the origin of the 20th Century Pentecostal Revival. From the Apostolic Faith Gospel Mission at 312 Azusa Street, Los Angeles, California, the fire of Pentecost swept the world; yet, the flame did not begin at Azusa Street. Like an Olympic runner with a torch, William Joseph Seymour brought the flame to Los Angeles from Houston, Texas. The same fire had been carried to Houston by Charles Fox Parham, the founder of the Apostolic Faith.

Parham was born June 4, 1873, in Muscatine County, Iowa.[1] When he was five, his family moved to Kansas where Parham spent most of his life. As a child, Parham experienced many debilitating illnesses including

---

[1] James R. Goff, *Fields White Unto Harvest: Charles F. Parham and the Missionary Origins of Pentecostalism* (Fayetteville: University of Arkansas Press, 1988), 18.

encephalitis and rheumatic fever.[2] These unfortunate confrontations with pain, and even death, would greatly impact his adult life.

Parham felt an attraction to the Bible and a call to preach, even before his conversion at age thirteen. He began conducting revival meetings in local Methodist churches when he was fifteen.[3] In 1890 he started his formal ministerial training at Southwest Kansas College.[4]

A year later, Parham turned his back on God and on the ministry. Deciding that he preferred the income and social standing of a physician, he began medical studies.[5] Soon his rheumatic fever returned and it did not seem that Parham would recover.[6] After trusting God for his healing, the pain and fever that had tortured his body for months immediately disappeared. However, the healing was not yet complete. Months of inactivity had left Parham a virtual cripple. His ankles were too weak to support the weight of his body, so he staggered about, walking on the sides of his feet. In December 1891, Parham renewed his commitments to God and the ministry, and he was instantaneously and totally healed.[7]

Parham served a brief term as a Methodist pastor, but left the organization after a falling out with his ecclesiastical superiors.[8] He then became loosely

---

[2]James R. Goff, "Charles Fox Parham" in Stanley M. Burgess and Gary B. McGee, eds, *Dictionary of Pentecostal and Charismatic Movements* (Grand Rapids: Zondervan Publishing Co., 1988), 660.
[3]Goff, *Fields*, 27.
[4]Goff, "Charles," 660.
[5]Goff, *Fields*, 28.
[6]Goff, *Fields*, 28-29.
[7]Goff, *Fields*, 29.
[8]Robert M. Anderson, *Vision of the Disinherited: The Making of American Pentecostalism* (Peabody: Hendrickson Publishers, 1979), 49.

affiliated with the Holiness movement ᴡ
from the Methodists late in the nineteenth
never returned to structured denominationa

On December 31, 1896, Parham married Eleanor Thistlethwaite, a devout Quaker.⁹ The young couple worked together in the ministry, conducting revival campaigns in several Kansas cities. Influenced by a number of successful faith healers, Parham's Holiness message evolved to include an ever-increasing emphasis on divine healing. Eventually, Parham arrived at the belief that the use of medicines was forbidden in the Bible.¹⁰

In the summer of 1898, the aspiring evangelist moved his family to Topeka and opened Bethel Healing Home. For almost two years, the home served both the physical and spiritual needs of the city. Included in the services that Parham's ministry offered were an infirmary, a Bible institute, an adoption agency, and even an unemployment office. Parham also published a religious periodical, **The Apostolic Faith**. In only a few years, this would become the first Pentecostal journal.¹¹

After suffering a nervous breakdown in September 1899, Parham entered a period of study and personal introspection. He considered the theological positions of John Alexander Dowie, A.B. Simpson, Benjamin Hardin Irwin and others as he molded his own religious belief.¹²

In the summer of 1900, Parham took a sabbatical from the healing home to embark on a spiritual

---

⁹Goff, *Fields*, 38.
¹⁰Goff, *Fields*, 39.
¹¹Goff, *Fields*, 41-46.
¹²Goff, *Fields*, 49-56.

odyssey throughout the northeastern United States. For three months he visited some of the most prominent ministries in the nation. None had a greater impact on his theology than Frank W. Sandford of Durham, Maine.[13]

Like all Wesleyan Holiness believers, Parham taught that sanctification was a second work of God's grace. But when he was introduced to Sandford's teaching and the Fire Baptized Holiness movement, he began to enlarge his theology to include an experience beyond sanctification. This "third blessing," as Parham began to understand it, was a personal baptism in the Holy Spirit, identical to that which the church fathers received in the second chapter of Acts. This baptism, Parham believed, would empower Christians for the last-days harvest of souls.

Along his spiritual journey, Parham also developed some extreme, unorthodox doctrines. For example, he taught the total annihilation of the wicked.[14] His teachings on white superiority also included Anglo-Israelism, a cultic doctrine which argues that Anglo-Saxons are the ten lost tribes of Israel.[15] He also believed that interracial marriages caused the flood of Noah's day.[16]

When the preacher returned to Topeka early in the fall of 1900, he found that the colleagues he had left in charge of the healing home had staged a religious *coup d'etat* gaining control of the facility.[17] Not deterred by

[13] Goff, "Charles," 660.
[14] Charles F. Parham, *The Everlasting Gospel* (Baxter Spings: Apostolic Faith Bible College, n.d.), 111-117.
[15] Charles F. Parham, *Kol Kare Bomidbar: A Voice Crying in the Wilderness* (Baxter Spings: Apostolic Faith Bible College, n.d.), 105-108.
[16] Charles F. Parham, "God's Plan of the Ages" *Gospel of the Kingdom* (April 1910), 1.
[17] Gordon Lindsay, *They Saw It Happen: The Dramatic Story of Men of God Who Were Greatly Used in the Pentecostal Outpouring of the Twentieth Century* (Dallas: Christ for the Nations, 1983), 14.

their disloyalty, in October, Parham reloca[ted to an] elaborate, fifteen-room house in Topeka. The misfortunes of the home's original builder l[ed] residents to give the castle-like structure the d[ubious] nickname "Stone's Folly." With thirty-four stu[de]..ts, Parham began Bethel Bible College, a Bible school that would emphasize the Holy Spirit baptism.[18] Parham was especially interested in the way the experience related to missionary activities.

Parham said, "Our purpose in this Bible school was not to learn things in our head only, but have each thing in the Scriptures wrought out in our hearts."[19] All students (mostly mature, seasoned gospel workers) were expected to sell everything they owned and give the proceeds away so each could trust God for daily provisions. From this humble college, a theology was developed that would change the face of the Christian church forever.

After a study of the book of Acts, the students entered a time of prayer and waiting on God. On January 1, 1901, Agnes Nevada Ozman, a thirty-year old student, received the baptism in the Holy Ghost with the evidence of speaking in a language she did not know (known as glossolalia).[20] In the days following, Parham and a number of other students received the experience and spoke with tongues.

---

[18] Goff, *Fields*, 61-65.

[19] Charles F. Parham and Sarah E. Parham, *Selected Sermons of the Late Charles F. Parham and Sarah E. Parham* (Baxter Springs: Apostolic Faith Bible College, n.d), 75.

[20] There are conflicting stories about exactly how and when Agnes Ozman received the Holy Ghost Baptism. These are beyond the scope of this article. For the accounts of the eye witnesses to the incident, including Ozman, see Larry Martin, ed., *The Topeka Outpouring of 1901* (Joplin, MO: Christian Life Books, 1997).

Most church historians agree that the episode at Stone's Mansion initiated the modern Pentecostal revival. This is not to suggest that this was the first modern incident of tongues speaking. In fact, from the time of the Apostles until today there have been occasions when believers, caught up in the Spirit, spoke in tongues. The Huguenots in France and Irvingites in England both shared the experience. The great revivals of Wesley, Finney, and Moody were sometimes accompanied by manifestations of spiritual gifts.[21]

By the latter nineteenth century, there had been numerous occurrences of speaking in tongues. Confirmed reports came from Minnesota, North Carolina, Texas, and Tennessee in the decade before Parham's group received their baptism in the Holy Ghost.

Yet, the experience at Bethel College was unique. Parham and his students reached the theological conclusion that speaking in other tongues was the scriptural evidence of the Holy Spirit baptism. Earlier, tongues had been viewed as a demonstration of the Spirit similar to weeping, shouting, or shaking. Parham's group received the baptism with evidential tongues while earnestly seeking the experience.[22] Unlike his predecessors, Parham taught that those who did not speak in tongues had never received the fullness of the Holy Spirit.

The young preacher soon accompanied a team of evangelists who went forth from Topeka to share what Parham called the "Apostolic Faith" message. Unfortunately, their earliest attempts at spreading the news

---

[21] These experiences are well documented. See Carl Brumback, *What Meaneth This?: A Pentecostal Answer to A Pentecostal Question* (Springfield: Gospel Publishing, 1947), 89-96.

[22] Klaude Kendrick, *The Promise Fulfilled: A History of the Modern Pentecostal Movement* (Springfield: Gospel Publishing, 1961), 53.

were less than successful. After the tragic death of Parham's youngest child, Bethel College closed, and Parham entered another period of introspection. During this time, he wrote and published what became the first book of Pentecostal theology, **Kol Kare Bomidbar: A Voice Crying in the Wilderness.**[23]

Parham's first successful Pentecostal meetings were in Galena and Baxter Springs, Kansas, and in Joplin, Missouri, in 1903 and 1904. Hundreds were saved, healed, and baptized in the Holy Spirit as Parham preached to thousands in the booming mine towns.[24]

Following the fruitful meetings in Kansas and Missouri, Parham set his eyes on the Lone Star State. In the spring and summer of 1905, the evangelist conducted a highly successful crusade in Orchard, Texas, and then he moved his team to the Houston-Galveston area. After returning to Kansas for a few months, he moved his entire enterprise to Houston and opened another Bible college. "The Bible Training School," as it was called, provided ten weeks of intensive Pentecostal indoctrination.[25]

When he moved to Houston, Parham must have had no idea that in less than three years the Apostolic Faith message would literally spread around the world, yet he would become almost irrelevant to the movement that he had founded.

This chapter is a revision of an article which originally appeared in Dr. Martin's book, In the Beginning, published by Christian Life Books in 1994.

---

[23] Goff, *Fields*, 83-86.
[24] Goff, *Fields*, 87-94.
[25] Vinson Synan, *The Holiness-Pentecostal Movement in the United States* (Grand Rapids: Eerdmans Publishing, 1971), 103.

Charles Fox Parham
Photo used by permission
Apostolic Faith Report

The Charles F. Parham family
Top Row: Charles Parham and Lilian Thistlethwaite
Middle Row: Esther, Sarah and Baby Wilford
Bottom Row: Claude and Phillip
Photo used by permission
Apostolic Faith Report

Bethel College - Topeka, Kansas
Larry Martin Collection

Another view of Stone's mansion
Photo used by permission
Flower Pentecostal Heritage Center

2 The Background: Life in Southern Louisiana

The great American poet, Ralph Waldo Emerson once said, "An institution is the lengthened shadow of one man."[1] The same thing can be said about a revival or spiritual movement, and the Pentecostal/Charismatic renewal of the twentieth century is an extension of the shadow of an humble black pastor, William Joseph Seymour.

Seymour was born in Centerville, Louisiana, on May 2, 1870, only five years after Lee's surrender at Appomattox ended the Civil War.[2] Centerville was, and still is, a sleepy little town in southern Louisiana, situ-

---

[1] Quoted in John W.V. Smith, *Heralds of a Brighter Day: Biographical Sketches of Early Leaders in the Church of God Reformation Movement* (Anderson, IN: Gospel Trumpet Company, 1955), 11.

[2] William Joseph Seymour, *Standard Certificate of Death*: California State Board of Health, 2 October 1922.

ated about midway between Lafayette and Houma. Located in St. Mary Parish, Centerville is about five miles from Franklin, the center of parish government.[3]

The tiny town is located on the Bayou Teche, called "the most elegant of all the bayous." For those unfamiliar with the geographical phenomenon, a bayou has been defined as "a place that seems often unable to make up its mind whether it will be earth or water, and so it compromises." The Bayou Teche, sometimes 200 feet wide, meanders for nearly 100 miles through Louisiana. It is graced by the largest and most beautiful moss-draped live oak trees in the state. Some are 20 feet wide at the trunk.[4]

At the time of Seymour's birth, the principle industries of the area were cotton, corn, rice, sugar cane, and cattle. Before the Civil War, St. Mary Parish boasted the "most flourishing" plantations in the state.

In 1869, Colonel Samuel H. Lockett, a professor of engineering at Louisiana State Seminary, began traveling throughout Louisiana preparing an official survey. July found him in St. Mary Parish, where he reported, "As an agricultural district, it is difficult to conceive of its superior. And yet, a want of labor caused much of even this fine country to be lying untilled and idle." Further, he said, "Much of this excellent country is lying waste, the fields grown up in cocklebur and other weeds, roads reduced to narrow trails, plantation houses and fences in a dilapidated condition. A general

---

[3]The author visited Centerville and St. Mary Parish on November 1, 1998 and August 14-17, 1999. Louisiana is divided into parishes, not counties.
[4]Peter S. Feibleman, *The Bayous* (New York: Time-Life Books, 1973), 30, 56.

air of desertion and desolation pervades the scene." Lockett described Centerville as a "neat little village."[5] It was in this place and on this land that William J. Seymour was born.

Yet, to fully understand the circumstances that shaped young Seymour's life, it is important to look beyond the geography and topography and to see the cauldron of boiling racial hatred that characterized Antebellum and Reconstruction Louisiana. Few, if any, southern states were more repressive in the treatment of blacks.

Before the Civil War, two out of five white families in Louisiana owned slaves. Ownership of slaves, however, was not limited to private citizens. The state of Louisiana also owned slaves, utilizing them in road building and similar enterprises. Forty-seven percent of the state's total population were slaves. In St. Mary Parish, more than 400 people owned nearly 13,000 slaves. Some slave owners had only one or two slaves while others had as many as 400.[6]

The Planter's Banner, Franklin's weekly newspaper, carried regular notices of slave auctions at the town center. Slaves of all ages, including even an infant, were placed on the auction block. It was not uncommon for slaves to be listed with other property. One listing said, "31 likely Slaves of both sexes, 9 horses, 6 mules, 12 work oxen, 300 hogs, stock and sheep."

Slaves in St. Mary Parish were as expensive as they were plentiful. The Franklin newspaper announced that

[5]Samuel H. Lockett, *Louisiana As It Is: A Geographical and Topographical Description of the State* (Baton Rouge: Louisiana State University Press, 1969), 23,101.
[6]United States Census, St. Mary Parish, Louisiana, 1860.

one "Negro in no way remarkable" brought a price of $2300.[7]

Laws regulating slaves were inhuman at best and barbaric at worst. A black could be killed for hitting a white person hard enough to cause a bruise. Striking a white person the third time, regardless of the severity of the attack or the circumstances that precipitated it, was also cause for death.

A fleeing slave could be shot if he did not stop when a white person ordered him or her to do so. The Louisiana Supreme Court cautioned against trying to inflict a mortal wound, but made it clear that if the slave died there would be no charges since, "the homicide is a consequence of the permission to fire upon him."

Slave holders had little regard for black family life. Husbands and wives were often sold separately. In Louisiana, the only exception was that a child under ten years of age was required to be sold or imported with his or her mother.

One writer in St. Mary Parish described the treatment of slaves in the area: "I have known Negroes to remain weeks, with their bodies exposed to the severest of our cold weather, and in the warmest and sultriest, in the same clothing, until it became thick with filth exuded from their skins, and gathered from that with which they were surrounded."[8]

If, for some act of charity, a Louisiana slave was freed by his or her master, he or she had to leave the

---

[7]Miscellaneous newspaper articles and advertisements from the 1853 editions of the *Planter's Banner*, Franklin Public Library, Franklin, Louisiana.

[8]Bernard Brossard, *A History of St. Mary Parish* (n. p., 1977), 20.

state within thirty days. In 1852, the law was amended to require that the former slaves leave the United States. The law was changed again in 1857, totally banning private emancipation. The southern attitude toward blacks can be summed up in the words of the Chancellor of the South Carolina Court of Appeals: "A free African population is a curse to any country."[9]

It goes without saying that losing a bloody war, seeing their economy devastated, witnessing the emancipation of slaves, and being forced into a despised reconstruction did not improve the southern white man's attitude toward his black neighbors. Rich whites despised their former chattel for obvious reasons and poor whites hated them for taking the few menial jobs available to their class.

The Civil War and its aftermath were especially devastating to rice growers in Southern Louisiana where Seymour had been born. In 1860 the total southern sugar crop was more than 225 million pounds. By 1870, the number had fallen to less than 90 million pounds.[10] Without slave labor, the size of farms in Louisiana was radically reduced. In 1860, the average farm was 536 acres. One decade later, the size declined to only 247 acres.[11] Owners of large plantations were forced to sell. In St. Mary parish in 1860, there

---

[9]Kenneth M. Stampp, *The Peculiar Institution: Slavery in the Ante-Bellum South* (New York: Vantage, 1956), 30, 32, 62, 210, 211, 213, 214, 232, 233, 252.

[10]John A. Garraty, *The American Nation: A History of the United States Since 1865*, fifth ed. (New York: Harper and Row, 1983), 408.

[11]Harry J. Carman, Harold C. Syrett and Bernard W. Wishy, *A History of the American People, Volume 2: since 1865*, third ed. (New York: Alfred A. Knopf, 1967), 19.

were 90 land owners who held more than 50 slaves. By 1877, only 25 of these still held their farms.[12]

Another example of the high cost of the war is the value of farms and equipment. In 1860, Louisiana farms were valued at $248 million; thirty years later, their value was only slightly more than $110 million. Farm equipment valued at $18 million before the war was worth only $7 million in 1890.[13]

The southern infrastructure was all but destroyed. Roads were in terrible repair, and bridges were either burned or washed away. Riverboats had been captured by the Union or destroyed, and most railroads were in ruin. Further, mules, horses, wagons, and carriages were extremely scarce.[14]

The poor economy hit the freedman the hardest. In three years following the war, the United States government, through the Freedman's Bureau, distributed 15,000,000 rations to former slaves.[15] Even this did not keep many from starving. It is estimated that in 1865 alone, 100,000 blacks died from starvation or disease.[16]

Blacks who found field work in St. Mary Parish in 1866, were paid only $20 a month. Their meager salary

---

[12]Joe Gray Taylor, *Louisiana Reconstructed: 1863-1877* (Baton Rouge: Louisiana State University Press, 1974), 366, 367.
[13]Edwin Adams Davis, *Louisiana: The Pelican State* (Baton Rouge: Louisiana State University Press, 1975), 242.
[14]Carman, *History*, 14.
[15]Harry J. Carman, Harold C. Syrett and Bernard W. Wishy, *A History of the American People, Volume 1: to 1877,* second ed. (New York: Alfred A. Knopf, 1960), 724.
[16]Rebecca Brooks Gruver, *An American History, Volume 1:to 1877,* third ed. (Reading, MA: Addison-Wesley Publishing Co., 1981), 416.

was supplemented with a cabin (usually deplorable), rations, and fuel.[17]

Before and after the war, whites imposed legal restrictions on former slaves by using black codes. In Louisiana a black man was required to choose his employer for an entire year by the first ten days of January. If he did not fulfill the contract, for example by voluntarily leaving after several months, he would forfeit wages for the entire year.[18] Blacks who did not find work could be arrested for vagrancy and given fines that the courts knew they could not pay. They were then forced to work for the government or hired out to other employers for a period of up to twelve months.[19] This system was not much different from slavery.

During most of the war and during reconstruction, much of southern Louisiana, including St. Mary Parish, was under the supervision of federal troops, commanded by General Philip Sheridan. General Shepley, a subordinate to Sheridan, referred to Seymour's boyhood home "the obstinate proslavery parish of St. Mary."[20] Violence against blacks led another of Sheridan's officers to dispatch a detachment of soldiers to Franklin in 1876.[21]

---

[17]Taylor, 368.

[18]T. Harry Williams, Richard N. Current and Fred Freidel, *A History of the United States: to 1877,* second ed., revised (New York: Alfred A. Knopf, 1967), 701.

[19]Willie Malvin Caskey, *Secession and Restoration of Louisiana* (Baton Rouge: Louisiana State University Press, 1938), 189, 190.

[20]Peyton McCrary, *Abraham Lincoln and Reconstruction* (Princeton: Princeton University Press, 1978), 199.

[21]Joseph G. Dawson, III, *Army Generals and Reconstruction: Louisiana, 1862-1877* (Baton Rouge: Louisiana State University Press, 1982).

The federal government attempted to impose some justice for freedmen through its ill-fated reconstruction fiasco. Federal troops left Louisiana in 1877, when Seymour was only seven. All hopes for equality under the law were lost. By 1898, the whites had regained control of the state government and ordered a new constitutional convention. The theme of the convention can be summed up in the words of Thomas J. Semmes, former president of the American Bar Association, "We [meet] here to establish the supremacy of the white race..."[22]

Groups like the Ku Klux Klan terrorized Southern blacks, raping, beating and lynching them. The "most important, secret" organization in Louisiana was the Knights of the White Camellia, patterned after the Klan. The terrorist group was born in St. Mary parish in 1867.[23]

Another group that harassed blacks and their sympathizers in Franklin was paradoxically known as "Seymour's Knights." This group was formed to support the presidential candidacy of Horatio Seymour. Like the Klan, they wore uniforms and marched throughout the city streets.[24]

Whites who could no longer "own" blacks were determined to deprive and control them. In Franklin, laws were passed that prohibited blacks from entering

---

[22]Leon Freidman, ed., *Southern Justice* (Cleveland, OH: World Publishing Co., 1965), 62.
[23]Taylor, 162.
[24]Collin E. Delatte, "The St. Landry Riot: A Forgotten Incident of Reconstruction Violence," *Louisiana History* (Winter 1976), 45; Frank J. Wetta, "'Bulldozing the Scalawags': Some Examples of the Persecution of Southern White Republicans In Louisiana During Reconstruction," *Louisiana History* (Winter 1980), 49.

the town without permission of their employer. If they were on the streets after 10 p.m., they would be fined five dollars (which most could not pay) or be sentenced to five days in jail. Additionally, blacks could not sell goods, own firearms, or preach without a license.[25]

In 1867, Franklin's **Planter's Banner** reported, "We don't think the Negroes are fools enough to risk an open issue with the white people of this parish. There are too many among them who know what would be the terrible consequences to men of their race were such an issue brought about. But it will have a good effect for all white men to have their arms in working order in case the club meetings, the Diossys and other mean white men should directly or indirectly bring about a collision of the races in this parish." The paper further threatened, "Let the Negroes and mean white men beware!"[26]

Unfortunately, blacks found no better refuge in most churches than in society as a whole. In 1874, a Catholic publication wrote, "There is but one way now to manage the Negro. He is, as a class, amenable to neither reason nor gratitude. He must be starved into the common perceptions of decency."[27]

One engraving from 1870, the year of Seymour's birth, shows a black couple with an infant child cowering under a Klansman and a member of the white league. A burning school and lynched black man are in the background. The captions read, "This is a white man's government," "The lost cause" and "Worse than slavery."[28]

---

[25]Taylor, 98.
[26]"Disturbance in Franklin," *The Planter's Banner* (December 28, 1867), 2.
[27]Taylor, 281.
[28]Gruver, 423.

In one particularly calloused outbreak of hostilities in Grant Parish, between one hundred fifty and two hundred blacks were murdered. The atrocities committed against these unfortunate people are almost unspeakable. Nearly all were shot between three and twelve times, many in the back of the head, and the bodies of dozens were burned beyond recognition. A witness says the blacks "were shot down like dogs." **Harper's Weekly** reported, "A general feeling of insecurity prevails among the colored people of Louisiana, and hundreds are seeking safety in the swamps and forests."[29]

The Southern outrage against blacks continued with the enactment of "Jim Crow" laws that essentially denied the vote to blacks through grandfather clauses, poll taxes, and literacy tests. Public transportation and accommodations were segregated, with blacks almost always having far less than equal facilities.

An American historian describing the plight of Southern blacks said, "Forgotten in the North, manipulated and then callously rejected by the South, rebuffed by the Supreme Court, voiceless in national affairs, he and his descendants were condemned in the interests of sectional harmony to lives of poverty, indignity, and little hope."[30]

---

[29]"The Louisiana Murders," *Harper's Weekly* (10 May 1873), 396.

[30]John A. Garraty, *The American Nation To 1877: A History of the United States* (New York: Harper and Row, 1963), 447.

Centerville, Louisiana
Sugar cane, in the background, is still a major agricultural product.

Sugar cane harvest
Harpers Weekly - October 30, 1875
Used by permission
Library of Congress

The Bayou Teche Today
Larry Martin Collection

Bocage
An 1845 plantation house at Centerville
Larry Martin Collection

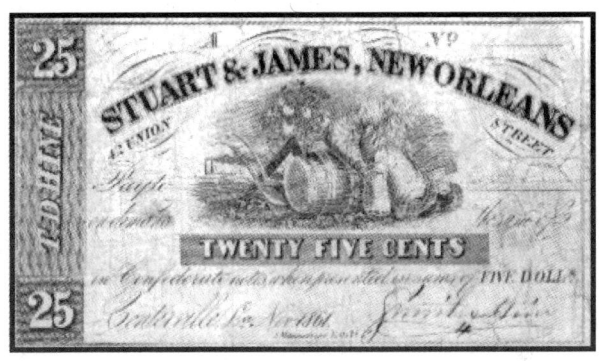

A Civil War Era
Confederate Twenty-five Cents Note
issued in Centerville, Louisiana in November 1861.

Larry Martin Collection

An 1881 Sketch of Centerville
(Notice that Federal Troops are still present).

Larry Martin Collection

Slave sale announcements
Planter's Banner, Franklin, Louisiana
1853

Black men hiding in Louisiana swamps to avoid violence
Harpers Weekly
May 10, 1873
Used by permission
Library of Congress

This engraving from 1870, the year of Seymour's birth, shows a black family much like his and demonstrates the difficult circumstances he inherited.
Used by permission
Library of Congress

3 The Roots:
The Seymour Family

William Seymour's parents were Simon Seymour, also known as Simon Simon (pronounced See-mone), and Phillis Salabar Seymour.[1] They were both former slaves, the children of slaves and at least second generation Louisianans.

---

[1] United States Census, St. Mary Parish, Louisiana, 1870, 1880, 1900; *Baptismal Record*, William Simon, Church of the Assumption, Franklin, LA, 4 September 1870. In the 1870 census and on most family baptismal records, the family's last name is listed as "Simon." In south Louisiana where French was often spoken in the 1870s (the Franklin newspaper was printed bilingual) the pronunciation would have been "See-mone." When the family name was permanently changed to Seymour is not know. Morris Bowens, a family friend testified "that Simon Simon and Simon Seymour are the one and same person, said Seymour being often called and named indifferently Simon Simon and Simon Seymour." See Morris Bowens, *General Affidavit*, 21 May 1897, Simon Seymour Pension File, National Archives and Records

Simon, a mixed race mulatto, was born in St. Mary Parish, Louisiana.[2] The exact date of his birth is not known but it was probably around 1841.[3] The identity of his white master is also unknown.[4] At age 21, Simon

---

Administration. Jefferson Ellis also swore that, "Simon Semon and Simon Seymour are one and the same person." See Jefferson Ellis, *General Affadivit*, Simon Seymour Pension File, National Archives and Records Administration. In 1870 Phillis is listed as Felicieta; in 1880 Phillis; and in 1900, Filiss. On the family baptismal records, her name is Felicie, Felicite, Felicity and Felicien. Her last name is spelled Salassas, Celabas and Salabas. It is likely that Simon who could read but not write and Phillis who could neither read nor write could not spell their own names, creating much of the confusion.

[2] United States Census, St. Mary Parish, Louisiana, 1870, 1880. Various places are given for Simon's birthplace, including Kentucky and New Iberia. This author has chosen St. Mary Parish because it is the place given by Simon when he enlisted in the military and where Phillis said he told her he was born. See Simon Seymour, *Compiled Military Service Record*, National Archives and Records Administration and Phillis Seymour to George S. King, 8 February 1896, Simon Seymour Pension File, National Archives and Records Administration.

[3] Not many dates for Simon's birth are the same. He may have been separated from his parents and would not have known when he was born. He said he was 21 when he joined the army in 1863. This would make his time of birth late in 1841 or in the first nine months of 1842. See Simon Seymour, *Compiled*. The 1870 and 1880 censuses would place his birth in 1837 or 1841, respectively. He was examined by a surgeon in July 1891 and the report says he was 55, placing his birth in 1836. See *Surgeon's Certificate*, Simon Seymour Pension File, National Archives and Records Administration. On another form, not dated, but probably 1891, he lists his age as 50. See *Declaration for Invalid Pension*, Simon Seymour Pension File, National Archives and Records Administration. This would confirm the years 1841 or 1842 for at least two times when he gave his own age.

[4] Phillis refers to "the lady that owned him." This could be a refernce to the wife of a slave master or his owner could have been a woman. See Seymour to King.

was 5'8" tall, had a dark complexion, black hair and black eyes.[5]

He was one of the first black Americans to serve in an all black regiment of the United States Army. Early in the Civil War, Lincoln had resisted the idea of enlisting blacks, especially slaves. Pressure, however, was building to use the "contrabands" in the military. This was particularly true in Louisiana where a regiment of free blacks had served in the Native Guard, supporting the Confederate forces.[6] One soldier wrote cynically, "What's the use to have men from Maine, Vermont, and Massachusetts dying down here in these swamps. You can't replace these men, but if a n----- dies, all you have to do is to send out and get another one."[7]

With the Emancipation Proclamation freeing all slaves held by the rebels on January 1, 1863, former slaves "of suitable condition" were actively recruited as volunteer soldiers.[8] This declaration forever changed not only the country, but also the Union army. Before the end of the conflict, more than 170,000 blacks served.[9]

General Benjamin F. Butler, who organized the first black regiment in Louisiana, reported, "Better soldiers

---

[5]Simon Seymour, *Compiled*. On another occasion, Seymour's complexion is listed as "light." See *Declaration for Pension*, Simon Seymour Pension File, National Archives and Records Administration.

[6]For a full account, see James G Hollandsworth, Jr., *The Louisiana Native Guards: The Black Military Experience During the Civil War* (Baton Rouge: Louisiana State University Press, 1995).

[7]Hollandsworth, 29.

[8]Budge Weidman, "Preserving the Legacy of the United States Colored Troops," *Prologue: Quarterly of the National Archives and Records Administration* (Summer 1997), 91.

[9]Rossiter Johnson, *Campfires and Battlefields: A Pictorial Narrative of the Civil War* (New York: Gallant Books, Inc., 1960), 237.

never shouldered a musket."[10] Not every white soldier, however, was so proud to serve with black troops, and prejudice continued throughout the war.

Simon enlisted as a private in the Union Army on October 10, 1863. His unit, 25th Regiment Infantry, was organized in New Iberia on November 21, 1863, and he was one of the original volunteers. Seymour, who enlisted for three years, was recruited by James Blanchard. The 25th was attached to the 1st Brigade, 2nd Division, Corps de Afrique, Department of the Gulf. The regiment saw duty at New Iberia, Franklin, and Brashear City.

In April 1864, the designation of the unit was changed to 93rd Regiment Infantry, United States Colored Troops. The new regiment was attached to the 2nd Brigade, the District of LaFourche and Department of the Gulf. The soldiers were involved in a skirmish with the confederates at Lake Fausse Point, on November 18, 1864. This was apparently the only battle in which Seymour's unit participated. Afterwards, the troops continued to see duty in south Louisiana until they were broken up on June 23, 1865.

When the 93rd was dissolved, Seymour was in the General Hospital in New Orleans, where he had been admitted on June 16, 1865. On July 14, he was transferred to the 82nd Regiment Infantry but was not released from the hospital until October 31.[11] On two occasions, Seymour suffered from fever; once he had

---

[10]Hollandsworth, 18.

[11]Simon Seymour, *Compiled*, 82nd Regiment Infantry; available at http://www.itd.nps.gov/unitzdocs/uus0082ri00c.html; Internet; accessed 31 August 1999, 1; *Record and Pension Office, War Department*, Simon Seymour Pension File, National Archives and Records Administration.

rheumatism and bronchitis. More important, he contracted chronic diarrhea, a problem that plagued him for the rest of his life.[12] It seems likely that he acquired a fever or parasite while marching in the swamps of Louisiana and Florida.

When Simon returned to duty, his unit was stationed at Apalachicola in the District of Florida. He served there until he was mustered out when the regiment disbanded in Barrancas, Florida, on September 7, 1866. Seymour never rose above the rank of private but was always present for duty and faithfully served his country.[13]

After his release from the military, Simon moved to Bayou Sale, where he met Phillis Salabar, his bride to be.[14] The couple became acquainted in January, about six months before their wedding.[15]

Phillis, a black woman, was born on November 23, 1844, on the Adilard Carlin (pronounced Car-line) plantation on Bayou Sale near Berwick City, St. Mary Parish.[16] More than likely, her parents were Michael and Lucy Sweet Selaba of Centerville. After emancipation, both parents were farm laborers.[17]

---

[12] *Surgeon's Certificate, Record and Pension.*

[13] Seymour, *Compiled*, 93rd Regiment Infantry; available at http://www.itd.nps.gov/unitzdocs/uus0093ri00c.html; Internet; accessed 31 August 1999.

[14] Jefferson Ellis, *General Affadivit*, Simon Seymour Pension File, National Archives and Records Administration.

[15] Seymour to King.

[16] Seymour to King; United States Census, St. Mary Parish, Louisiana, 1870, 1880, 1900; Bowens, *Affidavit*; Phillis Seymour, *Standard Certificate of Death*, 3 February 1940; *Declaration for Pension*.

[17] United States Census, St. Mary Parish, Louisiana, 1870.

Carlin, born in 1800, and his wife, Carmilite, were very affluent planters. They probably raised rice, the principle crop of the region. In 1860, his real estate was valued at $150,000 and his personal property, $160,000. He owned 112 slaves, including Phillis, accounting for much of his great wealth.[18] The latter reported, Carlin was "the only master I ever had."[19]

Phillis had several siblings, including Polly, Antirnette, Adaline and Michael.[20] Harriet Bedford, another slave on the Carlin plantation helped with Phillis' childhood care.[21] Like most slave children, Phillis could neither read nor write and "never had the advantages of an education."[22]

Phillis and Simon were married in Franklin on July 27, 1867. Simon needed Washington Mitchell to help him with the one hundred dollar bond the parish required for the license.[23] The ceremony was performed by R. K. Diossy, a Methodist minister.[24] Diossy performed ceremonies for dozens of freedmen

---

[18] United States Census, St. Mary Parish, Louisiana, 1860.
[19] Seymour to King.
[20] United States Census, St. Mary Parish, Louisiana, 1870. In 1870 Michael was 62 years of age; Lucy, 48; Polly, 20; Antirnette, 18; Adaline, 17; Michael, 15. All the family ages would fit within the ages of slaves owned by Carlin in 1860.
[21] Harriet Bedford, *General Affidavit*, 11 September 1893, Simon Seymour Pension File, National Archives and Records Administration.
[22] Phillis Seymour, *General Affidavit*, 23 February 1895, Simon Seymour Pension File, National Archives and Records Administration.
[23] *Bond Certificate*, St. Mary Parish, Marriage License Book 1867, 504.
[24] Ann C. Loveland, "The 'Southern Work' of the Rev. Joseph C. Hartzell, Pastor of Ames Church in New Orleans, 1870-1873," *Louisiana History* (Fall 1975), 401.

when marriage became legal for the former slaves.[25] His fraternizing with blacks earned him the scorn of his white brothers. The Franklin newspaper said he and his companions stir "up the worst spirit among the Negroes. What little talent they have is in the service of Satan."[26]

The legal witnesses to the wedding were Michael Salabar, Jefferson Ellis and Charles Brown.[27] Morris Bowens, another observer at the wedding, said that following the ceremony, they "repaired" to the Carlin plantation where a "dinner and supper were given to celebrate the said marriage."[28] For a short time, at least, the couple must have remained in Carlin's employ.

Because slaves had not been allowed the privilege of matrimony, Phillis was married before her parents. Michael and Lucy were united on September 19, 1868. Simon was a witness.[29]

On September 4, 1870, Simon and Phillis brought their infant son, William, to the Church of the Assumption, a Roman Catholic church in Franklin, Louisiana, for Christian baptism. He was christened

---

[25] *Marriage License*, Simon and Sellaba, St. Mary Parish, Marriage License Book 1867, 586; Recorded in St. Mary Parish, Marriage Record Book 1863-1879, 76.
[26] "Disturbance in Franklin," *Planter's Banner* (28 December 1867), 2.
[27] *Marriage License*, Simon and Sellaba.
[28] Bowens, *Affidavit.*
[29] *Marriage License*, Salabar and Sweet, St. Mary Parish, Book 1863-1879, 142. It is also possible that Lucy was a second wife and not Phillis' mother. On this occasion, Simon is listed as "Seymour" and Michael is "Salabar." On the same day, Jane Salabar, perhaps another sibling of Phillis was married to Nat Porter. See *Marriage License*, Porter and Salabar, St. Mary Parish, Book 1863-1879, 142.

"William Simon" by Father M. Harnais. Charles Morette and Azelie Peter were godparents.[30] William's middle name, Joseph, must have been added later perhaps at the time of his conversion.

Simon Seymour was employed as a brick maker or brick molder, the same vocation he had had before entering the army.[31] He could read but could not write. He could, however, scribble his own name.[32]

Almost nothing is known of Seymour's childhood or adolescence. His parents had a large family, but most of their children did not live to adulthood. Rosalie, an older sister born in 1869, died before 1880. Simon, Jr., was born May 29, 1872; John Emmuas, March 2, 1874; Benjamin, June 4 or 5, 1875; Amos, probably 1876; Andrew, February 11, 1879; Julia, May 11, 1880; Caleb, October 13, 1882; Jacob, June 7, 1885; and, Isaac, March 31, 1887.[33]

---

[30] *Baptismal Record*, William Simon.

[31] United States Census, St. Mary Parish, Louisiana, 1880; Simon Seymour, *Compiled*. On most records, Seymour only made "his mark." See his signature on Simon Seymour, *General Affidavit*, 23 April 1891, Simon Seymour Pension File, National Archives and Records Administration.

[32] Simon Seymour, *General Affidavit*, 23 April 1891, Simon Seymour Pension File, National Archives and Records Administration. On most records, Seymour only made "his mark."

[33] United States Census, St. Mary Parish, Louisiana, 1880; 1870; 1900; *Baptismal Record*, William Simon; *Baptismal Record,* Simon Simon, Church of the Assumption, Franklin, LA, 8 September 1872; and *Baptismal Record*, John Emmuas Simon, Church of the Assumption, Franklin, LA, 7 June 1874; *Baptismal Record,* Julia Simon Seymour, 31 July 1880, Simon Seymour Pension File, National Archives and Records Administration; *Baptismal Record,* Jacob Simon Seymour, Church of the Assumption, Franklin, LA, 19 August 1893; *Baptismal Record,* Isaac Seymour Simon, Church of the Assumption, Franklin, LA, 19 August 1893; Phillis Seymour,

John died before 1880. Benjamin died on June 10, 1875; Andrew, July 10, 1879; and, Caleb, September 1883. None of the latter three children reached their first birthday.[34] Apparently there was also another daughter, Emma, although nothing of her birth and death dates can be established.[35] Illness and bereavement were a constant presence in the Seymour home.

In 1880, William, ten years old, was attending school. He could read, but had not yet learned to write. In fact, his deprived surroundings afforded little opportunity for formal education. It is reported that even as an adult he had difficulty reading and this was confined primarily to the Bible.[36]

On August 8, 1883, when William was 13, his father purchased a four-acre farm bordering the beautiful Bayou Teche. Located just east of Centerville in the tiny village of Verdunville, the new home must have provided a wonderful place for an adolescent boy to

---

Affidavit, 23 February 1895; *Declaration for Widow's Pension*, Simon Seymour Pension File, National Archives and Records Administration; Interview, Lucille Seymour, 14 August 1999. Lucille is the widow of Van Seymour, son of Jacob, William's brother. Van spent time in California with "Uncle William and Aunt Jenny." See also St. Mary Parish, Louisiana, *Book "3H" of Conveyances*, 93, 24 October 1912.

[34] United States Census, St. Mary Parish, Louisiana, 1880; 1870; *Baptismal Record*, John Emmuas Simon, Church of the Assumption, Franklin, LA, 7 June 1874; Phillis Seymour, Affidavit, 23 February 1895.

[35] United States Census, St. Mary Parish, Louisiana, 1900. The date given on the census, October 1885, is obviously wrong, being too close to the known birth of Jacob. It seems this child could be Julia, since no other child is mentioned in any of the pension requests and this census is confirmably flawed in many ways.

[36] Charles William Shumway, "A Critical History of Glossolalia," Ph. D. dissertation, Boston University, 1919, 115.

fish, hunt, and reflect on the wonders of God's creation. The property cost Simon one hundred and twenty-five dollars.[37]

Near the end of the decade of the 1880s, Simon Seymour became very ill. His condition was described as "weak and feeble" and "hardly conscious."[38] In 1890, he requested a permanent disability or invalid pension from the military. He suffered from dysentery, chronic diarrhea, rheumatism, and affliction of the eyes.[39] On July 16, 1891, he was examined by a physician in New Orleans. The doctor recommended a limited pension because of piles, but said Seymour's general appearance was "healthy."[40] Without any evidence, one is left to guess about the fairness and willingness of a Southern doctor to assist an emancipated slave who had served the Union forces and helped put down the former's rebellion.

During the night of November 14, 1891, Simon Seymour died, suffering from severe chills. A doctor was called, but did not respond. The Reverend Valsin Hernandez was also called, but Seymour had passed away before he arrived.[41] Phillis lovingly nursed him to the end, closed his eyes in death and dressed him for burial.[42]

---

[37]St. Mary Parish, Louisiana, *Book "V" of Conveyances*, 581, 14 February 1884.

[38]Joanna Jenkins, *General Affidavit*, 14 June 1893, Simon Seymour Pension File, National Archives and Records Administration.

[39]*Invalid Pension*, Simon Seymour Pension File, National Archives and Records Administration.

[40]*Surgeon's Certificate*, Simon Seymour Pension File, National Archives and Records Administration.

[41]Valsin Hernandez, *General Affidavit*, 14 June 1893, Simon Seymour Pension File, National Archives and Records Administration.

[42]Jenkins, *Affidavit*.

The next day, Hernandez officiated at the obsequies which were held at the home. Seymour was buried in an unmarked grave in the New Providence Baptist Church cemetery.[43] His request for a disability pension was officially denied two weeks after his death.[44]

Three children under sixteen years of age were left in the Seymour home at the time of Simon's death. From all the evidence available it appears that William, Simon, Jr., and Amos had left home to find employment elsewhere.[45] Phillis reported she had "no means of income whatsoever" and she supported her family by her own "manual labor."[46] A neighbor reported that Phillis had no income from her land, but sustained herself and the children with a vegetable garden, corn and potatoes.[47]

Phillis was literally impoverished. She lived in a small cabin without a chimney. The family farm was assessed at only $100.[48] Her personal property consisted of "one old bedstead, one old chair and one old mattress." The total value of all her belongings was "about fifty-five cents."[49]

---

[43] Hernandez, *Affidavit*.

[44] *Invalid Pension*, Simon Seymour Pension File, National Archives and Records Administration.

[45] These young men are not mentioned in any of the pension requests. Admittedly, this could be an intentional omission to enhance the prospects of qualifing.

[46] Phillis Seymour, *General Affidavit*, 10 February 1896, Simon Seymour Pension File, National Archives and Records Administration.

[47] Clark Wilkerson, *General Affidavit*, 30 April 1895, Simon Seymour Pension File, National Archives and Records Administration.

[48] F. P. Perret, Abstractor of Titles, St. Mary Parish, Louisiana, 11 February 1896, Simon Seymour Pension File, National Archives and Records Administration.

[49] Phillis Seymour, *Affidavit*, 10 February 1896.

With hungry children to feed, in 1894 Phillis sold one half of the farm for only thirty dollars.[50] The struggling family continued to live on what was left of the farm in Verdunville.

For more than a year, Phillis tried to draw a widow's pension from the government. On June 6, 1893, she was finally able to qualify for eight dollars a month plus two dollars each for her three minor children.[51] With this meager sum, she was forced to continue rearing her family in abject poverty.

The family's limited resources were further strained in 1894, when Phillis spent four months in the charity hospital in New Orleans. She was suffering from a carbuncle.[52]

Although the church was called upon at times of transition such as weddings, births and deaths, the depths of the Seymour's faith is not known. Traditions say Seymour's early religious training was as a Baptist.[53] This seems highly unlikely, considering the

---

[50]St. Mary Parish, Louisiana, *Book "DD" of Conveyances*, 654, 13 November 1894. Phillis bought the property back for $30.00 in 1907. St. Mary Parish, Louisiana, *Book "UU" of Conveyances*, 296, 25 June 1907.

[51] *Widow's Pension*, 577, 804, Simon Seymour Pension File, National Archives and Records Administration; *Widow's Pension*, 472, 276, Simon Seymour Pension File, National Archives and Records Administration. The pension was raised to $20 in 1916 and eventually raised to $40 before Phillis's death in 1940.

[52]Phillis Seymour, *Affadivit*, 10 February 1896.

[53]Vinson Synan, *The Holiness-Pentecostal Tradition: Charismatic Movements in the Twentieth Century* (Grand Rapids: Eerdmans, 1997), 93. Although Seymour's affiliation with the Baptist has not been documented, it is asserted by Synan and in many biographies. Lucille Seymour said Phillis was a member of New Providence Baptist Church in Centerville when she died, but there are no records available from the church.

family's long Roman Catholic tradition.[54] If this w the case, he was yet unconverted. From his you however, he was reported to have had "visions" anu held a strong premillennialist view of unfulfilled prophecy.[55]

---

[54] Most of the Seymour children were baptized at the Church of the Assumption in Franklin. See *Baptismal Record*, William Simon; *Baptismal Record*, Simon Simon, *Baptismal Record*; Jacob Simon; *Baptismal Record*, Isaac Seymour Simon; *Baptismal Record*, Julia Simon Seymour; and *Baptismal Record*, John Emmuas Simon.

[55] Charles William Shumway, "A Critical Study of 'The Gift of Tongues,'" A. B. dissertation, University of Southern California, 1914, 173; Shumway, "A Critical . . .," 115.

United States Colored Troops in Louisiana
Larry Martin Collection

Simon Seymour's military service record

Members of the
Corps de Afrique
Port Hudson, Louisiana
Photo used by permission
The National Archives

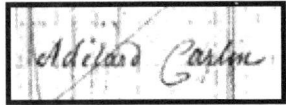

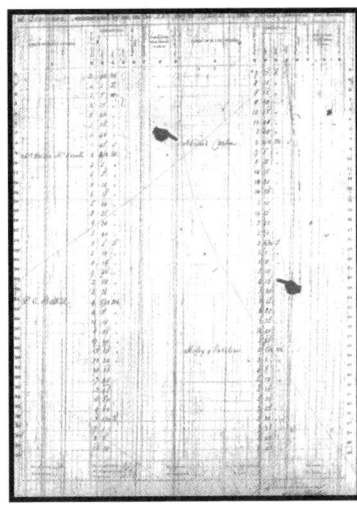

A page from the 1860 United States Census listing the slave property of Adilard Carlin. Phillis Seymour would be one of the 15-year-old females. Slaves, considered less than human, were not counted by name.

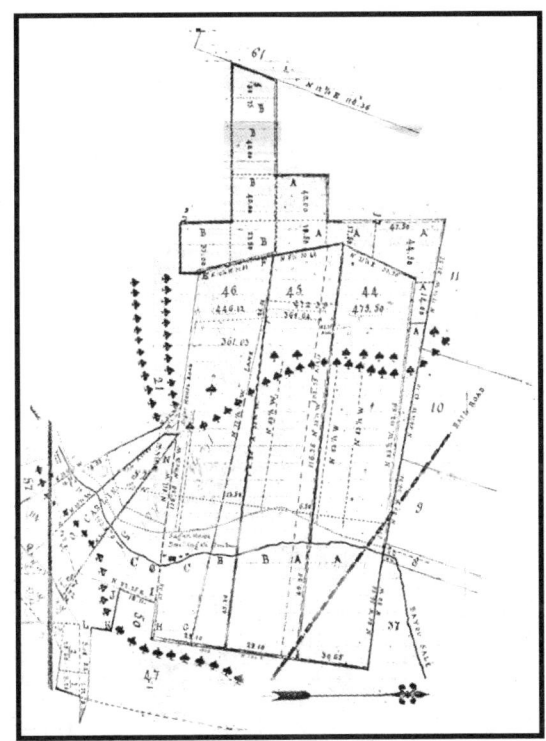

The Adilard Carlin Plantation
William J. Seymour's Birthplace
Larry Martin Collection

Marriage license
Simon Simon and Phillis Salabar

**Family Register Page from Seymour Relative's Bible
List of Phillis Salabar's sibling--
Pauley, Michell, Jane, and Antonet**
Larry Martin Collection

Baptismal record
William Simon (Seymour)

Catholic Church
Franklin, St Mary's Parish, Louisiana
Larry Martin Collection

An old bar in Verdunville, owned by W. J. Seymour's nephew, Van Seymour. Van spent some time living at the mission in Los Angeles.
Larry Martin Collection

Overtaken by vegetation, this is the Verdunville home of Seymour's brother Jacob. His mother died here.
Larry Martin Collection

Although this is not the Seymour family, this 1902 postcard is typical of the way they lived.

Larry Martin Collection

4 The Sojourn: Seymour in the North

With these crises at home, it is no wonder that Seymour would leave southern Louisiana at an early age. He was seeking to escape the poverty and oppression of the uncomfortable and poverty-laden parish of his birth and childhood. It was very common for blacks of the time to flee the South for better opportunities. One writer stated "the Negroes are 'wild to come Norf.'"

Desiring to migrate to the North and actually getting there were two different matters. Some blacks were able to pay their own ways after a good year's work, but this was very difficult for anyone in Seymour's economic class. Those relying on assistance from others often received the help from their families and friends, Northern employers, or employment agencies that brought blacks north with the promise of work.[1] Seymour, it seems, worked his way from city to city, trying to find the northern "promised land."

Facing the challenge of these difficult circumstances, it appears that Seymour left his family and headed for Memphis, Tennessee, in 1891.[2] For centuries, Memphis, on a cliff 80 feet above the Mississippi River, had been the site of forts for the French, Spanish and Americans. The city itself, however, was designed and named in 1819. The fledgling city prospered during the Civil War but faced numerous challenges in the decades that followed. So much cholera and yellow fever were in Memphis, that non-residents were suggesting the entire city should be burned. By the time Seymour arrived, residents had begun a revitalization that included the digging of hundreds of miles of ditches to drain mosquito breeding areas.[3]

How Seymour traveled from Southern Louisiana to Memphis is still unknown. It is possible he traveled on the railroad. The tracks through Centerville had been laid when Seymour was eight.[4] It is also possible, perhaps probable, that Seymour traveled the

---

[1]Lillian Brandt, "The Make-Up of Negro City Groups," *The Survey: The Negro in the Cities of the North* (New York: Charity Organization Society, 1905), 11, 16.

[2]It is impossible, with the evidence now available, to definitively say that the William Seymour in Memphis was W. J. Seymour. It does, however, seem likely that he is the man since he appears and disappears in the city directories at the appropriate times. See footnotes six and nine.

[3]Lori Erickson, *Mighty Mississippi: Traveler's Guide* (Aldsaybrook, CT: The Globe Pequot Press, 1995), 132, 133.

[4]Douglas J. Nelson, "For Such a Time As This: The Story of Bishop William J. Seymour and the Azusa Street Revival: A Search for Pentecostal/Charismatic Roots," Ph. D. dissertation, University of Birmingham, England, 1981, 159.

Mississippi River from New Orleans or Baton Rouge on a river steamboat. This would have been an attractive option for a person of Seymour's economic condition.

Travelers who could not afford a cabin could obtain deck passage at a discount of up to 80 percent. Working with the boat's crew could bring a further reduction in the fare. Although the "deckers" were often exposed to the elements, had to supply their own meager rations, and were subjected to a very dangerous journey, thousands chose this method of transportation. Unfortunately, a lack of accommodation and sanitation often forced deckers to travel in "filth," while diseases (especially cholera) were prevalent.[5]

In Memphis, Seymour boarded with Henry S. and Lydia Seymour who were residents at 94 Pontotoc. Perhaps the couple were relatives of the traveler. Not only do they share the same name, but Simon Seymour, was a brick maker and Henry was a brick layer. On July 19, 1891, during the two years that William was in Memphis, Henry died prematurely at the age of 43.[6]

Seymour had two jobs in Memphis. First, he worked as a porter for Joseph Celle who had a barber shop and

[5] Wayman Norbury, *Life on the River: A Pictorial History of the Mississippi, the Missouri, and the Western River System* (New York: Crown Publishers Inc., 1971), 232, 233.

[6] *Polk City Directories,* Memphis, TN, 1890, 649; *Polk City Directories,* Memphis, TN, 1891, 980; *Polk City Directories,* Memphis, TN, 1892, 883, 1192; *Polk City Directories,* Memphis, TN, 1893. It is important to note that William was a boarder and the other Seymours were listed as residents, eliminating the possiblity that he was part of the imediate family. According to his death certificate, Henry was born in Tennessee and lived his life in Memphis. With forced family separations common during slavery a relationship between William and Henry is still possible. See Henry Seymour, *Pre-1902 Death Records,* Memphis/Shelby Co. Archives, Memphis, Tennessee.

grocery store at 32 Jefferson.[7] In 1892, he worked as a driver for the Tennessee Paper Co.[8]

Apparently the migrant left Memphis in 1893 and headed on up the Mississippi to St. Louis. For the next several years he would visit a number of cities, like Memphis and St. Louis, that were famous to blacks who had fled slavery during the days of the "underground railroad."[9]

From 1880 to 1900, the black population in St. Louis exploded. The large cities in Missouri had a 78 percent increase in black residents in this period.[10] Many of the newcomers were forced to live in conditions described as "grimy and foul beyond our powers of description," "wretched" and "sinks of iniquity." Four out of five St. Louis residents lived in tenement houses, where "black and white people are mixed up promiscuously."[11]

---

[7] *Polk City Directories*, Memphis, TN, 1892, 232, 883.
[8] *Polk City Directories*, Memphis, TN, 1892, 883.
[9] Gruver, 282. To the best of this author's knowledge, it has never been reported that Seymour lived in Memphis, St. Louis or Chicago. The information was found after studying Seymour's pattern of moving north and east (Indianapolis to Cincinnati) along former routes of the underground railroad and then looking at Gruver's map of the former slave's northern exodus. Seymour was found by reading census records and contacting libraries in many cities along the route. Since William Seymour appears and then disappears in these cities at the appropriate times, it seems more than reasonable that he made the journey and lived in each of the cities. The author must admit, however, that the Memphis and St. Louis connection have not and cannot be proven beyond doubt with the evidence now available.
[10] Brandt, 2.
[11] J. A. Dacus and James W. Buel, *A Tour of St. Louis or the Inside Life of a Great City* (St. Louis: Western Publishing Co., 1878), 413, 416, 417.

Seymour lived near the downtown area, boarding at 205 N. 12th and 820 Market. Still unconverted, he worked as a bartender in one of St. Louis' almost 1500 saloons. On Twelfth Street alone, there were four saloons within two blocks of Seymour's home.[12] Just over a mile from Seymour's Market Street home was the Rosebud Bar, a nationally known center for ragtime music. It was advertised as a "headquarters for colored professionals."[13]

Seymour moved to Indianapolis, Indiana, at the age of 25.[14] Indianapolis at the time had a number of very successful black business and professional men. One gentleman, Mr. Puryear, was also a member of the city council.[15] By 1900 the city had a black community of 16,000, about nine percent of the entire population.[16]

Seymour's homes in Indianapolis were 127 1/2 Indiana Avenue and later 309 Bird Street.[17] He found employment as a waiter in some of the city's finest hotels.[18] The enterprising young man worked at the

---

[12] *Gould City Directory*, St. Louis, MO, 1893-4, 1288; 1895-6, 1895.

[13] John A. Wright, *Discovering African-American St. Louis: A Guide to Historic Sites* (St. Louis: Missouri Historical Society, 1994), 27.

[14] Glenn A. Cook, *The Azusa Meeting: Some Highlights of this Outpouring* (n.p., n.d.), 2; Shumway, "Study," 173.

[15] G. F. Richings, *Evidence of Progress among Colored People* (Philadelphia: George S. Ferguson, Co., 1903), 276-277.

[16] Emma Lou Thornbrough, *The Negro in Indiana before 1900: A Study of a Minority* (Indianapolis: Indiana Historical Bureau, 1957), 15.

[17] Indianapolis-Marion County Public Library, letter to the author, 15 December 1998; *Polk City Directory*, Indianapolis, IN, 1896, 782; 1898, 810; 1899, 835.

[18] Cook, *Azusa*, 2; Shumway, "Study," 173.

Bates Hotel at the corners of Illinois and Washington, the Denison at Pennsylvania and Ohio, and the Grand at Illinois and Maryland.[19] The Grand Hotel Cafe, where Seymour served, was called "Indianapolis' best cafe."[20]

More than likely, Seymour would have joined a secret black trade union, the Knights of Industry of the Hotel Brotherhood. The organization was founded in 1885 by H. J. Poe.[21] A person working as a waiter could earn two to five times as much in a northern city than similar employment would pay in the South.[22]

Conditions in the North, however, were not always as good as Southern myth had portrayed them. One contemporary wrote "difficulty in obtaining a suitable place to live meets the Negro who comes to a large northern city." Many houses and apartments were simply not available to blacks at any price. When they found quarters, blacks could be expected to pay more than people of any other race.[23]

While in Indianapolis, Seymour was converted and joined the all-black Simpson Chapel Methodist Episcopal Church.[24] This life-changing encounter with Jesus Christ

---

[19] "Negro Bluk Kissed," *Indianapolis Morning Star* (3 June 1907), 3; *Polk City Directory*, Indianapolis, IN, 1896, 1001.

[20] "Indianapolis' Best Cafe," *Indianapolis Morning Star* (30 June 1907), 26.

[21] Nelson, 159; Thornbrough, 354.

[22] A waiter in Atlanta was paid from $1.00 to $2.50 a week, while a hotel waiter in Cambridge, MA was paid $5.00 a week. See Carol D. Wright and Oren W. Weaver, eds., *Condition of the Negro in Various Cities: Bulletin of the Department of Labor* (Washington, D. C.: Government Printing Office, 1897), 305, 307, 320.

[23] Brandt, 2.

[24] Shumway, "Study," 173. Nelson says Seymour joined Simpson Chapel Methodist Episcopal Church, 160. Simpson Chapel

marked the beginning of a new pilgrimage for Seymour. Like Nicodemus in the New Testament, he was born again. The old things of his life were passed away, and all things became new. It was the most important event in Seymour's already eventful life. He traded sin for salvation; disgrace for God's grace; the bottle for the Bible; and doubts for shouts.

Seymour's life had a new purpose. He was no longer traveling from place to place just to escape the poverty and oppression of the South. Now he was a spiritual pilgrim heading for the celestial city on high.

During the time Seymour was in Indianapolis, Simpson Chapel had two pastors: Louis M. Hagood and George A. Sissle. The church was also located in two different facilities: first, at Howard and Second Streets; then, in July 1899 at Missouri and Eleventh.[25]

Church membership in the life of blacks of this period was more than just a religious experience. According to a contemporaneous survey, the black church was "the center of the social life and efforts of the people. What the church sanctions and supports is of the first importance and what it fails to support and sanction is more than apt to fail. The Negro church historically, as to numbers and reach of influence and dominion, is the strongest factor in the community life of the colored people. Aside from the ordinary functions of preaching, prayer, class meetings and Sunday

---

is often misidentified as an African Methodist Episcopal congregation. For an example, see Thornbrough, 370.

[25] *Polk City Directory*, Indianapolis, IN, 1897, 118; 1898, 116; *History of Simpson Church* (n.p., 1924), 6,7. In 1966, Simpson, Christ and Gorman churches merged to form University United Methodist Church. See "Our Church History," typescript, Depauw University.

school, the church is regarded by the masses as a sort of tribune of all of their civic and social interests. Thousands of Negroes know and care for no other entertainment than that furnished by the church."[26]

Still, there was another element to religion in the life of black Americans. It can be illustrated in an anecdote from the life of abolitionist Frederick Douglass. On one occasion, Douglass was so depressed by the cruelties of slavery that he told an audience, "Oh, God surely must be dead; He does not answer our prayers."

In the audience, Sojourner Truth stood to her feet and replied, "Fred Douglass, God is not dead! To your knees, oh ye benighted sons of Africa; to your knees; and remain there. There, if nowhere else, the colored man can meet the white man as an equal and be heard."[27] Seymour, oppressed and abused because of his race, found his equality in the courtroom of God.

As the Methodists drifted toward the left, many conservative members left their ranks, starting a national Holiness movement. Seymour felt especially alienated since the Methodists did not endorse his premillennialist views or his fascination with "special revelations."[28] In only a few years, he found a new church home among the stricter Holiness sects. In fact, a number of prominent leaders in the early Pentecostal movement moved first from Methodism to Holiness and then to the Apostolic Faith.

---

[26]Fannie Barrier Williams, "Social Bonds in the 'Black Belt' of Chicago," *The Survey: The Negro in the Cities of the North* (New York: Charity Organization Society, 1905), 41.

[27]Delilah L. Beasley, *The Negro Trail Blazers of California* (New York: Negro Universities Press, 1919), 46.

[28]Shumway, "Study," 173.

Indianapolis was the "gateway" to many blacks on their way to Chicago and other large cities.[29] Seymour was no exception. Chicago, Illinois, became Seymour's home in 1900. With a population of two million, he had never lived in a larger city.[30] Of all the cities of the north, it is reported that Chicago offered "the largest liberty to citizens of all colors . . ." When Seymour arrived in Chicago, the black population of the city was slightly more than 30,000. With the influx of Seymour's fellow Southerners, this population had grown by 1,000 percent in thirty years; in another five years, it had swollen to over 50,000.[31]

Finding employment in Chicago at the turn of the century was particularly challenging for a black man. In 1905, Fannie Williams wrote, "the colored people of Chicago have lost in the last ten years nearly every occupation of which they once had almost a monopoly." Williams continued, "White men and women have supplanted colored men in nearly all the first-class hotels and restaurants."[32] Despite the hardship, Seymour once again found work as a waiter.[33]

Housing was also a problem in Chicago. African-Americans were not welcome in white residential areas and most were crowded into the "Black Belt," a

---

[29] Ida Webb Bryant, *Glimpses of the Negro in Indianapolis, 1863-1963* (n. p.: n. d.).

[30] *Leaves of Healing* (6 January 1900), 336.

[31] Williams, 40; Bessie Louise Pierce, *A History of Chicago: Volume III, The Rise of a Modern City, 1871-1893* (Chicago: University of Chicago Press, 1957), 48.

[32] Williams, 43.

[33] United States Census, Cook County, Illinois, 1900. This census gives Seymour's place of birth and the place of birth for his parents as Tennessee. This is obviously incorrect since all were born in Louisiana. However, in 1910, the Los Angeles census said his

"forbidding and demoralizing" place in the south division along Clark and Dearborn Streets.³⁴ Seymour boarded with seven other people in a boarding house at 2329 Dearborn. His fellow boarders were laborers, porters, and cooks.³⁵

Apparently Seymour stayed in Chicago for a very short time.³⁶ Still it is unlikely that Seymour could have lived in Chicago without encountering the ministry of John Alexander Dowie, faith healer and founder of the Christian Catholic Church. Most converts to Dowie's church came from Methodism.³⁷ His churches across Chicago seated almost 10,000. Dowie also had a dozen or more institutions throughout the city, including Zion Divine Healing Home, Home of Hope, a junior school

---

parents were born in Virginia. In 1870 his father's birthplace was Kentucky. This William Seymour is a black male, born in May, 1870 and working as a waiter. Furthermore, Seymour disappeared from the Indianapolis City Directories after 1899. There is a possible contradiction to these theories of Seymour's travels. In 1900 he is listed with his family in the census in Louisiana. There are several explanations for this. First, Seymour's family may not have understood the enumerator and listed all family members. It is also possible, but less likely, that Seymour was visiting in Louisiana and still would have been listed in Chicago if his rent was paid at the boarding house. It is notable that Seymour's birth date and age are incorrect (by almost five years) as is his brother's. Seymour was probably not present and his mother admitted she did not know the birthdates of her children, but a sister kept the "correct" records. Phillis Seymour, *General Affidavit*, 23 February 1895, Simon Seymour Pension File, National Archives and Records Administration.
³⁴Williams, 40; Pierce, 48.
³⁵United States Census, Cook County, Illinois, 1900.
³⁶Unless Seymour had a different job and address, his name does not appear in any city directories available to the author. See Chicago City Directory, Chicago, Illinois, 1897, 1534; 1898, 1994; 1900, 1720; 1901, 1786; 1902, 1842; 1903, 1927. 1899 was not available.
³⁷*Leaves of Healing* (10 February 1900), 525.

and a college. In early 1900, the church pledged, "Zion will reach every home in Chicago."[38]

Dowie's position on racial integration was radical for his time. He insisted on integrated seating in his facilities and promised that at least one black man would serve on his board of twelve apostles.[39] In his periodical, *The Leaves of Healing*, Dowie argued the "the whiter you are, the less strong you are." He wrote, "The time has come for this horrible so-called 'race prejudice' to be wiped out" and "There is only one race—the children of Adam and Eve."[40]

In some ways, Charles F. Parham emulated the ministry of Dowie and hoped to be his successor. The latter's racial tolerance was a notable exception. Parham was especially interested in Dowie's emphasis on prayer for the sick. Later, Seymour, too, adopted a strong theology of divine healing.

Continuing to move east, Seymour located in Cincinnati, Ohio in 1901. He worked as a waiter and roomed at 23 Longworth and 437 Carlisle Avenue.[41]

Like every northern city he visited, Cincinnati was a major stop in the underground railroad. In fact, the leading organizer of the "railroad," Levi Coffin, was from Cincinnati. In this southern Ohio city, Seymour must have encountered many of the prejudices he had known

---

[38] *Leaves of Healing* (20 January 1900), 395, 400.

[39] Grant Wacker, "Marching to Zion: The Story of John Alexander Dowie's 20th Century Utopian City–Zion, Illinois" *Assemblies of God Heritage* (Fall 1996), 8;

[40] John Alexander Dowie, *Leaves of Healing* (11 June 1904), 228; John Alexander Dowie, *Leaves of Healing* (24 September 1904), 803.

[41] *Cincinnati City Directory*, Cincinnati, Ohio, 1901, 1576; 1902, 1637.

in the South. Most blacks lived in two slum areas known as "Bucktown" and "Little Africa."⁴² Late in the nineteenth century, a New York newspaper carried the story of a public school principal and teacher in Cincinnati who were thrown out of a city restaurant, reporting, "The sole trouble was the fact that they were coloured."⁴³

The motto of the city of Cincinnati is from Matthew 19:26, "With God all things are possible."⁴⁴ A few years later, in Los Angeles, Seymour would learn just how true this passage really could be.

While in Cincinnati, Seymour was "sanctified," a spiritual experience claimed by Holiness people.⁴⁵ Sanctification was considered "an instantaneous work of God wrought in the soul of a regenerated man or woman in answer to perfect consecration, unswerving faith and importunate prayer... That work, which cleanses the heart from all sin, no matter how preceded by mortification of spirit and crucifying of the flesh, is done in a moment, in the twinkling of an eye, by the mighty power of God."⁴⁶ It is reported that Seymour made a "second" trip to the altar and "prayed until he testified to being wholly sanctified."⁴⁷

---

⁴²Henry Louis Taylor, Jr., ed., *Race and the City: Work, Community, and Protest in Cincinnati, 1820-1970* (Urbana: University of Illinois Press, 1993), 115.

⁴³W. Laird Clowes, *Black America: A Study of the Ex-Slave and His Late Master* (London: Cassell and Co., Ltd., 1891), 98, 99.

⁴⁴Walter Haulghurst, *Ohio: A Bicentennial History* (New York: W. W. Norton and Co., 1976), 8, 9, 92.

⁴⁵Shumway, "Study," 173.

⁴⁶B. Carradine, *The Sanctified Life* (Cincinnati: M. W. Knapp, Pentecostal Publisher, 1897), 17.

⁴⁷James S. Tinney, "William J. Seymour: Father of Modern-Day Pentecostalism," in Randall K. Burkett and Richard Newman,

At the time of his sanctification, Seymour joined the Church of God reformation movement with headquarters in Anderson, Indiana.[48] The group was known at the time as the Evening Light Saints or Evening Light Church of God Holiness. The Saints believed that God would send an unprecedented outpouring of the Holy Spirit before Jesus returned for the church. Their scriptural theme was Zechariah 14:7, ". . . but it shall come to pass, that at evening it shall be light."

Seymour would have received a hand of fellowship from the Saints, a group that welcomed blacks and the poor from its birth. By 1900, there were 30 black leaders in the movement where whites and blacks "worked hand in hand." The Saints' teaching on Christian unity not only included breaking down sectarian barriers, but also class, gender, and racial barriers. But to the earliest Saints, unity was much more than just a teaching; it was a reality.[49]

The Church of God prefers to claim that God, not any man, was the founder of the group. However, the origins of the movement can be traced to Daniel S. Warner. Warner, who began his ministry in 1867, was part of a group known as the Northern Indiana Eldership of the Church of God, a split from the

---

eds., *Black Apostles: Afro-American Clergy Confront the Twentieth Century* (Boston: G. K. Hall and Co., 1978), 216.

[48] Cotton, Emma "The Inside Story of the Azusa Street Outpouring," *Message of the Apostolic Faith* (April 1939), 1. This author and Glenn Gohr visited Anderson, Indiana, but a search of the Church of God Archives at Anderson University provided no information on Seymour. Ministerial lists from the time are no longer available, if they ever existed.

[49] John W. V. Smith, *A Brief History of the Church of God Reformation Movement* (Anderson, IN: Warner Press, 1976), 107, 121-124.

Winebrennerian Church of God. He was also the editor of **The Gospel Trumpet**. In 1881, Warner urged the small denomination to separate from the National Holiness Association. When they refused, he was joined by five couples who established the first congregation in the Church of God reformation movement, a strictly nonsectarian group.

Warner proposed that all true Christians should abandon denominations and join his group. This gave the Saints the nickname "come-outers." Even before the split with the Indiana Holiness group, Warner said, "The Lord . . . gave me a new commission to join holiness and all truth together and build up the apostolic church of the living God." Another early leader, A. J. Kilpatrick said that any Christian who was a member of a denominational church was a member of "two" churches and Jesus "built only one church."[50]

Several items in the policies and polity of the reformation movement influenced Seymour and his future ministry. First and foremost was the church's views of Christian unity, followed by the doctrine of sanctification.

Although the Church of God has never adopted a statement of faith, they have always been strong champions of sanctification as a second work. Warner's first book was **Bible Proofs of a Second Work of Grace**. The church's doctrinal position on sanctification can be identified in this statement from Anderson College School of Theology, "Persons are sanctified by the cleansing and empowering work of the Holy Spirit who establishes the lives of believers in perfect love

---

[50]Smith, 12-15, 30, 33.

and enables those lives to be lifted above the domination of sin."⁵¹

The Church of God's strict standards of holy living impacted not only Seymour, but the Pentecostal movement in general. Early Saints would not drink tea or coffee. Women could not wear lace and ruffles; men could not wear neckties, and neither gender could wear gold. All professional entertainments were also considered too worldly for the Saints.⁵²

The pattern of ministry established by the Evening Light Saints ministers also had a profound effect on Seymour. Long before the invention of airplanes, reformation pioneers traveled so quickly from place to place they referred to their work as a "flying ministry." Warner would go for weeks without missing a single day of preaching, sometimes up to four times. It was not unusual for him to spend up to eight hours in the pulpit in a single day and then take time for seekers at the altar. Seymour would later follow a similar schedule at the Azusa mission.⁵³

It is also likely that Seymour encountered the teaching of Martin Wells Knapp while in Cincinnati. Knapp was a Methodist minister who accepted the Holiness experience of sanctification in the early 1880s. He published a Holiness paper, *The Revivalist*, founded the International Holiness Union and Prayer League, and God's Bible School. Knapp was a strong proponent of holiness, divine healing and premillenarianism.

---

⁵¹J. Gordon Melton, *The Encyclopedia of American Religions: Religious Creeds*, volume two (Detroit: Gale Research, Inc., 1994), 150.
⁵²Smith, 32, 33.
⁵³Smith, 41, 69.

Knapp completely severed his ties with the Methodist church in 1900 after he was censured in 1898 for holding an unauthorized revival meeting. This created an interesting paradox, since one reason why Wesley started the Methodist movement was his resentment of orders by the Church of England telling him where he could and could not preach. The "revivalist" died in 1901, perhaps before Seymour was in Cincinnati, but his ministry lived on through the institutions he had established.[54]

A severe case of smallpox left Seymour blind in his left eye. His face was so scarred by the disease that he wore a beard through the remainder of his life. Contemplating on the ravages of the disease, Seymour yielded to what he felt was a divine call to the ministry. A call that he had resisted until afflicted and near death.[55]

Seymour began his formal ministry when he was credentialed by the Saints. By today's standards it may seem strange that he would receive ministerial credentials without receiving formal education, but this was common in the reformation movement. One leader

---

[54]Nelson, 163,164; Elmer T. Clark, *The Small Sects in America* (New York: Abingdon-Cokesbury Press, 1937), 76; J. Gordon Melton, *Religious Leaders of America: A Biographical Guide to Founders and Leaders of Religious Bodies, Churches, and Spiritual Groups in North America* (Detroit: Gale Research, Inc., 1991), 255. Through a series of mergers Knapp's group became part of the Pilgrim Holiness Church and finally the Wesleyan Church.

[55]Shumway, "Study," 173; "Weird Babel of Tongues" *Los Angeles Daily Times* (18 April 1906), II, 1. It is often reported that Seymour had a glass eye. Apparently this is not true. He could not see out of one eye and it was obviously afflicted. More than likely, there was a milky film or scale over the pupil of the eye. Shumway says the smallpox incident was in Ohio; some others say Indianapolis.

wrote, "All theological institutes and missionary training schools are run too much on the theoretical plan, which is detrimental to spirituality and tends to fill the head and empty the heart."[56]

Seymour left Cincinnati after 1902. His whereabouts from that time until he arrived in Houston in 1905 cannot be definitively confirmed. It is possible, if not likely, that he lived in Columbus, Ohio. Columbus, the capital city of the "Buckeye State," was described as "a neighborly place," with "quiet streets under arching trees" and "people sitting on front porches." Unlike some of the busy metropolitan areas where Seymour had lived previously, in Columbus "well before midnight the downtown streets were silent and empty."[57]

In 1904 and 1905, a "William J. Seymour" lived at 439 King and 315 West Eighth. His occupations were listed as "salesman" and "commercial traveler."[58] Working as a traveling salesman would have allowed Seymour to make several trips to the South, including Jackson, Mississippi, and Houston, Texas. What he encountered on these journeys, like his experiences of salvation and sanctification, would dramatically change his life and spiritual pilgrimage.

---

[56] Smith, 96.
[57] Havighurst, 138.
[58] *Polk City Directories, Columbus, OH, 1904-5*, 892; *Polk City Directories, Columbus, OH, 1905-6*, 978; The listing is for William J. Seymour. Although the directory does not identify people by race, a research librarian confirmed that both addresses would be consistent with African American communities at the time of Seymour's residency; Sam Roshon, letter to Larry Martin, 15 April 1999. The odds that another black man named William J. Seymour would appear in Columbus, Ohio, and then disappear from the directories in the years that Seymour's residence is unknown seem staggering. This is especially true since Seymour's pattern was to travel eastward.

Purported to be an early image of W. J. Seymour
Larry Martin Collection
Courtesy of Bishop Oree Keyes

The Belle of Memphis
Photo used by permission
NationsBank, St. Louis, Missouri

Life in the slums of St. Louis near the turn of the century
Larry Martin Collection

Downtown Chicago at Madison Street in the '90s
Larry Martin Collection

Three hotels where Seymour worked in Indianapolis
From the left, Grand, Bates, Dennison
Photos used by permission
Bass Photo Company Collection
Indiana State Historical Society

The Grand Hotel Cafe where Seymour waited on tables
Larry Martin Collection
From **The Indianapolis Star**

This 1901 syndicated cartoon depicts a black waiter in caricature.
Larry Martin Collection
From the **Joplin Daily Globe**

5 The Divine Appointment: Parham and Seymour

In the winter of 1904-1905, Seymour traveled by "special revelation" to Jackson, Mississippi. He received spiritual advice and training from Charles P. Jones.[1]

Jones had been raised as a Baptist, graduated from Arkansas Baptist College and pastored several Baptist churches in Arkansas, Alabama, and Mississippi. He was introduced to the Holiness doctrine of sanctification as a second work of God's grace, which he defined as "that act of Divine grace whereby we are made holy. In justification, the guilt of sin is removed; in sanctification, the inclination to sin is removed. Sanctification must be definitely experienced to fit us to see the Lord."[2] In 1894 he claimed the experience. Jones was

---

[1] E. Myron Noble, *Like as of Fire: Newspapers from the Azusa Street World Wide Revival* (Washington, DC: Middle Atlantic Press, 1994), vii; Shumway, "Study," 173.

[2] Melton, *Encyclopedia* (Detroit: Gale Research, Inc., 1994), 321.

forced out of the Baptist church for embracing and preaching the doctrine.[3]

After a period of fasting and prayer, in 1894, Jones hosted the first of a series of annual Holiness conventions in Jackson. These were attended by Charles H. Mason, J. A. Jeter, and other black leaders. A nondenominational fellowship, Christ's Association of Mississippi of Baptized Believers, resulted from the conventions. Later the Church of God in Christ, an important player in the early Pentecostal revival, was born from this association.[4]  Jones parted with Mason over the tongues issue in 1907 and founded the Church of Christ Holiness.[5] From the beginning, Jones wanted to establish a new faith that would make him "one of wisdom's true sons, and like Abraham, 'a friend of God.'"[6]

According to Shumway, after the visit with Jones, Seymour was more firmly grounded in his already strongly held premillennialist views.[7] One of the tenets of Jones' church was, "We believe that the Lord Jesus Christ will return to judge the quick and the dead; and that we who are alive at His coming shall not precede them that are asleep in Christ Jesus."[8]

William J. Seymour journeyed from Ohio to Texas to search for family members who had been lost to

---

[3]J. Gordon Melton, *Religious Leaders of America* (Detroit: Gale Research, Inc., 1991), 232.

[4]C.E. Jones, "Church of God in Christ," in Burgess, *Dictionary*, 204.

[5]Elmer T. Clark, *The Small Sects in America* (New York: Abingdon-Cokesbury Press, 1937), 120; Melton, *Religious*, 232.

[6]Frank S. Mead, *Handbook of Denominations in the United States, ninth edition* (Nashville: Abingdon, 1990), 77.

[7]Shumway, "Study," 173.

[8]Melton, *Encyclopedia*, 321.

him because of slavery and the reconstruction.[9] He found relatives in or around Houston and made a temporary home there.[10] While in the city, he attended a black Holiness church pastored by Lucy Farrow.

Lucy Farrow was born a slave in Virginia, in August, 1851. As a young girl she was sold, perhaps with other family members, and sent further south.[11] Farrow was the niece of the famous abolitionist and leader of the underground railroad, Frederick Douglass.[12]

In 1871 she lived in Mississippi, but she migrated to Texas before 1900. Farrow, a widow, was the mother of seven children, but only two of her offspring survived until 1900. In Houston, she lived in the home of her twenty-nine year old son, James Pointer and his wife, Florence. Pointer was a switchman for the railroad, employed by the H.& T. C. Yards.[13] The family

---

[9]Shumway, "Critical," 113. Shumway says Seymour was searching for his parents. There is a definite error here. Seymour was born after slavery ended and his mother was still in Centerville. He could have been searching for other family members.

[10]Seymour is not listed in any Houston city directory, suggesting that he never established permanent residency in the city. This author believes the amount of time he spent in Houston has been greatly exaggerated. As stated in a previous chapter, he was listed as a resident of Columbus, Ohio in the 1905-6 city directory.

[11]"Mrs. Lucy F. . .," *The Apostolic Faith* [Los Angeles] September 1906; United States Census, Harris County, Texas, 1900.

[12]Cecil M. Robeck, "The Impact of the Azusa Street Revival:The Impact on Pentecostal Missionary Vision," AGTS Spring Lectureship Audio Cassette (16 March 1989).

[13]United States Census, Harris County, Texas, 1900; Houston City Directories, 1899; 1900-1901; 1902-03; 1903-04; 1905-06. In the directories, Farrow's name is misspelled Farrell and Farrar. Special thanks to Rev. Calvin Durham for providing Houston directories.

was very mobile, living at 1806 Clay, 1626 Winter, 1717 Edwards, and 1606 Dart.

Seymour became the interim pastor of Farrow's church when she left the "Lone Star State" to serve as governess and cook for another Holiness preacher in Kansas City. Her new employer was the Apostolic Faith evangelist, Charles F. Parham.[14] The Parhams, either with affection or patronage, referred to Farrow as "Auntie."[15]

Apparently the church was either not large enough or affluent enough to support a pastor, and Farrow was forced to rely on secular employment. Seymour also supported himself, once again working as a waiter.[16]

Late in the fall of 1905, Farrow returned to Houston with the news that while in Kansas she had been baptized in the Holy Ghost, evidenced by speaking in tongues. Farrow shared the message with Seymour who had some initial resistance to the teaching, believing like most Holiness people that he had received the Holy Ghost when he was sanctified.

The Evening Light Saints taught that speaking in other tongues could be restored to the church in the last days, but they labeled the experience of Parham's group a "counterfeit" and a "pretension." An article in **The Gospel Trumpet**, official organ for the Saints, ridiculed the group's tongues speaking, saying the

---

[14]Cotton, 1; Shumway, "Study," 173; B. F. Lawrence, *The Apostolic Faith Restored* (St. Louis: Gospel Publishing House, 1916), 64.

[15]Parham, *Life*, 118.

[16]*John G. Lake: His Life, His Sermons, His Boldness of Faith* (Fort Worth: Kenneth Copeland Publications, 1994), 87.

students at Topeka "chattered an incomprehensible jargon."[17]

After a period of prayer and honest searching of the word of God, Seymour asked God to "empty him of his false ideas." The Lord revealed to him that he had been mistaken in his doctrinal position and, as a result, he accepted the idea that the Holy Spirit baptism was a third work of grace.[18]

Later that year, Parham moved his ministry headquarters to Houston and held services in Bryan Hall. He also established a short-term Bible college similar to the one where the Holy Spirit fell in Topeka. Apparently, the school, which opened in late December, was first conducted at Caledonia Hall on Texas Avenue near Main Street, and then moved to a three-story home at 503 Rusk Avenue on the corner of Brazos Street. Classes were offered in a number of theological subjects, including "conviction, repentance, conversion, consecration, sanctification, healing, the Holy Spirit in His different operations, prophecies, the book of Revelation and other practical subjects."[19]

Farrow and Seymour both attended Parham's services. A worker in Houston recalled that they "seldom missed a service. They were hungry for all of God's blessings."[20]

Seymour also enrolled in Parham's daily Bible school classes. Mrs. Parham said he "faithfully" attended the

---

[17]Jennie C. Rutty, "The Gift of Tongues," *The Gospel Trumpet* (18 September 1902), 3.

[18]Cotton, 1.

[19]Parham, *Life*, 140; Goff, 105; Ethel E. Goss, *The Winds of God: the Story of the Early Pentecostal Movement (1901-1914) in the Life of Howard A. Goss* (Hazelwood, MO: World Aflame Press, 1958), 65, 66.

[20]Parham, *Life*, 161.

classes. [21] Howard A. Goss, a Parham associate, vividly remembered Seymour attending the 9 A. M. meetings.[22] Goss also recalled the daily activities of the students, "We were given a thorough workout and a rigid training in prayer, fastings, consecration, Bible study and evangelistic work. Our week day schedule consisted of Bible Study in the morning, shop and jail meetings at noon, house to house visitations in the afternoon, and a six o'clock street meeting followed by an evening evangelistic service at 7:30 or 8:00 o'clock."[23]

Warren Faye Carothers and Parham taught Seymour the "doctrines held by the movement." Apparently the humble servant of God did not protest the insult of listening to the lectures from the hallway, since he was not allowed in Parham's racially segregated classroom.[24] Later, in what sounds more like an excuse

---

[21]Parham, *Life*, 142.
[22]Goss, 73; Lawrence, 64.
[23]Goss, 65.
[24]Shumway, 173; Lawrence, 55, 64. Carothers was an extremely colorful character, worthy of further study. His life crossed Seymour's in several places. He taught him in the Bible school, issued his Apostolic Faith credentials and ministered in Los Angeles when Charles Parham split the Azusa Mission. Carothers not only was an early participant in the Apostolic Faith Movement, but was an early General Presbyter of the Assemblies of God. He was an attorney, a federal judge, an amateur astronomer, the head of Houston Abstract Company and an organizer of the city's Board of Realtors. He wrote a number of articles and several books including *Church Government* in 1909. See also W. F. Carothers, "History of the Movement," *The Apostolic Faith* [Houston] (October 1908), 1; "Brother Carothers Now in Work," *Word and Witness* (July 1915), 7; "Half Century in Houston Observed by Carothers," *Houston Post*, (14 December 1943); "Judge W. F. Carothers," *Houston Post*, (12 February 1953), D7; "W. F. Carothers, Realty Board Founder Dies," *Houston Chronicle*, (12 February 1953); "W.F. Carothers," Texas *State Bar Journal* (April 1953), 261.

than an apology, Mrs. Parham explained, "In Texas, you know, the colored people are not allowed to mix with white people as they do in some other states."[25]

Also because of his race, Seymour was not allowed to tarry at the altar with whites and, therefore, did not have liberty to seek the Holy Spirit baptism. Although these circumstances prevented him from immediately receiving the experience, he accepted without further reservations the Pentecostal doctrine that speaking in tongues was the evidence of the Holy Ghost baptism. He and Parham preached side-by-side but only to segregated crowds in black neighborhoods.[26]

Despite the limitations imposed upon him due to his race and his lack of formal education, Seymour's deep hunger for the things of God and keen intellect allowed him to excel in the Bible school studies. Later, he would be able to recite Parham's teachings "word for word."[27] Seymour, already trained in sound Holiness doctrines, rejected Parham's more extreme teachings such as the annihilation of the wicked and an eighth day creation.[28]

Parham originally hoped to send Seymour to minister to his "own color" elsewhere in Texas.[29] But God

---

[25] Parham, *Life*, 137.

[26] Shumway, "Study," 173; Lawrence, 64.

[27] Parham, *Life*, 161.

[28] "Pentecost with Signs Following," *The Apostolic Faith* [Los Angeles] (December 1906), 1; "Annihilation of the Wicked," *The Apostolic Faith* [Los Angeles] (January 1907), 2. The eighth day creation was a strange idea that the seven days in which the Bible says God created the universe were not literal days, allowing for a much longer time span. But man was created on the eighth day, separate and apart from the other days of creation.

[29] Lawrence, 55; Parham, *Life*, 142.

willed something better for His humble servant, and He was soon to set those grand plans in motion.

The Houston church that Seymour pastored was visited by Neely Terry from Los Angeles. Terry received her Pentecostal baptism while in Houston.[30] Returning to her home state of California, she summoned the zealous Seymour to come to the West Coast and share the Apostolic Faith message at the Holiness church she and her family attended. The church was pastored by Julia Hutchins.[31] No doubt, Seymour was anxious to go west, not only to share the faith, but also to find the "promised land" of racial equality he had not found in his northern sojourns and certainly did not find in Texas.

In addition to his own plans for Seymour, Parham did not want him to leave for California until he had received his own Holy Spirit baptism.[32] Carothers admitted that when Seymour "suddenly announced that he was called of God to go to California," that the Texas workers were "disappointed somewhat." However, with high hopes that the Apostolic Faith message would spread to a new region of the country, and Seymour, feeling "it was the leading of the Lord," Parham and his students helped him raise the rest of his expenses for the trip west and wished him "Godspeed." They hoped that he would soon return to help with the "important work" in Texas.[33]

---

[30] James L. Tyson, *The Early Pentecostal Revival: History of Twentieth-Century Pentecostals and the Pentecostal Assemblies of the World, 1901-1930* (Hazelwood: Word Aflame, 1992), 95, 96; A.C. Valdez, *Fire on Azusa Street* (Costa Mesa, CA: Gift Publications, 1980), 18.

[31] Cotton, 1, 2.

[32] Lawrence, 64.

[33] W. F. Carothers, "History of Movement," *The Apostolic Faith* [Houston, Texas](October 1908), 1; "Bro. Seymour's Call," *The*

One of the students who had been baptized in the Holy Spirit in Topeka was Opal Stauffer Wiley. Wiley, originally from Joplin, Missouri, had traveled with the Apostolic band to Houston. According to Wiley family members, she prayed with Seymour on more than one occasion to receive the Holy Spirit baptism. She laid her hands on him and prayed for his success as he left to preach in Los Angeles.[34]

On his way to the coast, Seymour visited some well-known Holiness missions, including Alma White's Pillar of Fire Church in Denver. White, who became one of the bitterest opponents of Pentecost, criticized Seymour's appearance and demeanor, setting a pattern of biased stereotypes against the preacher that continue even until today.[35]

Apostolic Faith [Los Angeles] (September 1906), 1; Goss, 73; Parham, *Life*, 142. Although Mrs. Goss is wrong on many of the facts and Mrs. Parham is very biased, their works are important.

[34] Stanley Wayne, "Early Revivals," in *Perpetuating Pentecost: A Look at the Formation and Development of the Southern Missouri District Council of the Assemblies of God* (Springfield, MO: Southern Missouri District, 1989), 5-13; Kathleen Joan Foster Stafford, *Pentecostal Pioneer—Opal Stauffer Wiley*, typescript, Flower Pentecostal Heritage Center; Glenn Gohr interview of Mrs. Raye Wiley Batson, Fall 1989; Mrs. Raye Wiley Batson, personal interview, 13 November 1998; Glenn and Kathleen Stafford, personal interview, 13 November 1998.

[35] Alma White, *Demons and Tongues* (Zarephath, NJ: Pillar of Fire Publishers, 1936), 67, 68. White had several reasons to be prejudiced against Seymour and the Pentecostal movement. First, after years of a troubled relationship her husband left her when he became a Pentecostal. For more information, see Alma White, *My Heart and My Husband* (Zarephath, NJ: Pillar of Fire Publishers, 1923). White was also a racist and Ku Klux Klan sympathizer. For more information on this subject, see Susie Cunningham Stanley, *Feminist Pillar of Fire: The Life of Alma White* (Cleveland, OH: The Pilgrim Press, 1993). Nelson's dissertation gives an excellent

Charles P. Jones
Founder of the Church of Christ Holiness
Larry Martin Collection

defense of Seymour's appearance, which White called "untidy." If Seymour was less than proper in his dress, it should be considered in light of both the Holiness tradition of plain dress and the fact that he had traveled from Houston to Denver on a train. As a black man, he would not be permitted comfortable, or in many cases even clean, accommodations while in transit.

The residences of Lucy Farrow in Houston no longer exist. These houses on the blocks near the railroad tracks where she lived are typical of the home where she lived with her son.
Larry Martin Collection

Charles F. Parham
with a group of his early followers in Holy Land costumes.
Larry Martin Collection

Charles F. Parham's band of Apostolic workers at Bryan Hall in Houston.
(Parham is in the center, Opal Wiley is second from left in row two)

Photos used by permission Apostolic Faith Report

The Bible Training School - Houston, Texas
Parham's family is on the porch. Notice the "Apostolic Faith Movement" and "Headquarters" Banners.
Larry Martin Collection

Howard A. Goss
Photo used by permission
Flower Pentecostal Heritage Center

Warren F. Carothers
Larry Martin Collection

Alma White
Pastor of Denver's Pillar of Fire Church
Larry Martin Collection

6 The City: Los Angeles, California

Two hundred and twenty-five years ago, the area now known as Los Angeles was inhabited by the Gabrielino, a tribe of Native Americans. These generally peaceful and affable people had held the land virtually undisturbed for centuries.[1]

The Spaniards first visited the area in 1542. More than two centuries later, on August 6, 1771, a group of soldiers, sailors, and missionaries established San Gabriel, the first European mission near present-day Los Angeles.

When the company arrived at the site, they were immediately surrounded by a party of armed Indians who they assumed to be hostile. Fearing the loss of life, a priest unveiled a canvas with a painting of Mary, the mother of Jesus. The natives were "subdued" by

---

[1] John and Laree Caughey, *Los Angeles: Biography of a City* (Berkeley: University of California Press, 1976), 3.

the image, threw down their bows and arrows, and laid their beads and other trinkets at the feet of the painting. The incident changed the attitude of the Native Americans who then welcomed the European guests to their area.[2]

By decree of California's Spanish Governor Don Felipe de Neve on September 4, 1781, the first settlement was established in the area. The founding name was *el pueblo de Nuestra Senora la Reina de los Angeles,* or, in English, The Town of our Lady the Queen of the Angels. The original party of colonists was composed of eleven men—three Spaniards, two blacks, two mulattos and four Indians—and their families.[3] It is not often reported that twenty-six of the original founders were black.[4]

Heads of households were required to be "a man of the soil, healthy, robust and without known vice or defect." Three families left within six months, leaving the town with a starting population of only 32.[5]

By 1790 the city had grown considerably with a total population of 141, eighty of whom were under sixteen years of age. Although no blacks were listed, the group included 22 mulattos, 1 European, 72 Spaniards, 7 Indians and 30 mestizos.[6]

The area provided a pleasant climate, adequate water and good soil. The colony grew beyond all expectations. In the 1830s, a decade after Mexico declared its independence from Spain, the population

---

[2]Caughey, 41, 42, 55.

[3]Caughley, 66-71.

[4]Charlotta A. Bass, *Forty Years: Memoirs from the Pages of a Newspaper* (Los Angeles, n.p., 1960), 2.

[5]Caughey, 66-71.

[6]Caughey, 75. A mulatto is a person of mixed white and black ancestry. A mestizo is mixed white and Native American ancestry.

reached 1,000, making Los Angeles the largest settlement in California.[7]

In 1846, the United States gained control of California through the Treaty of Guadalupe Hidalgo. On September 9, 1850, the territory became the thirty-first state to join the union.[8] At statehood, Los Angeles was an humble agricultural village with only 1,610 people. The town had no railroads, no natural harbor and very few streets.[9]

This, however, was changing when the gold rush in 1848 started a great migration to northern California and an increased demand for the cattle raised on the rancheros around Los Angeles. One observer noted, "Everybody in Los Angeles seemed rich, everybody *was* rich, and money was more plentiful at that time, than in any other place of like size, I venture to say, in the whole world."[10]

From 1850 to 1860, the population of Los Angeles grew by 172 percent to 4,385. In the next decade they had a 27 percent growth to 5,728.[11]

The result of this growth was a great deal of social unrest. Under Spanish rule, law and order were easily maintained by the church and the strong Catholic family. One traveling preacher observed, "The name of this city is in Spanish the city of Angels, but with much more truth might it be called at present the city of demons." Taking note that there was not a Protestant church or minister in the city in 1856, the **Star** reported

---

[7] Robert Fogelson, *The Fragmented Metropolis* (Cambridge, MA: Harvard University Press, 1967), 7.

[8] Rockwell D. Hunt, *California in the Making: Essays and Papers in California History* (Westport, CT: Greenwood Press, 1953), 53.

[9] Fogelson, 1.

[10] Fogelson, 15.

[11] Fogelson, 21.

the situation "presents a case of destitution, we are certain, without precedent in the state."[12]

Spanish/Mexican California was almost totally Catholic, but Protestant Christianity made some early inroads into the state. In 1826, the first person to arrive in California by traveling overland was Jedediah Strong Smith, known as the "Bible toter."[13] His guide was Jim Beckworth, a black trapper and trader.[14]

The president of Harvard, Edward Evertt, exhorted miners to go to the West Coast "with the Bible in one hand and your New England civilization in the other and make your mark on the people and the country."[15] The Los Angeles press also appealed for missionary assistance.[16]

The California Conference of the African Methodist Episcopal church organized on April 6, 1865. California had over 4,000 "free people of color" at the time. The first African Methodist Episcopal church in the state had been dedicated in San Francisco more than a decade earlier, on February 22, 1852. The Episcopal Church and African Methodist Episcopal Zion church were also involved in early missionary work among California's black population.[17]

It can be argued that, even though it went through many changes, Los Angeles essentially remained a Mexican pueblo until the 1880s. Beginning in 1887, competition between railroads led to a rate war, causing the city to grow dramatically. Los Angeles

---

[12] Fogelson, 26, 27.
[13] Hunt, 119.
[14] Bass, 7.
[15] Hunt, 119.
[16] Fogelson, 27.
[17] Beasley, 158-160.

experienced a real estate boom and completed the transition from pueblo to American city.

In 1880, the census showed 11,183 inhabitants. Because Los Angeles had a population of less than 10,000 previous to this time, governance of the city had been controlled by acts of the state legislature. By 1889 the city had drawn up its own charter and began self government. A mayor, nine councilmen and a board of education were elected.[18] By 1885, the population grew to about 20,000.[19] This, however, was just the beginning of Los Angeles' phenomenal growth.

The city had grown to 50,000 by 1890. A small percentage of the city, 1,250 people, was black, many of whom had fled the oppression of the southern states.[20] In another ten years, the city's population exceeded 100,000. By 1910 the number was 319,000 and 7,599 were black.[21]

When the revival started on Azusa Street in April 1906, there were approximately 228,298 residents in Los Angeles. This was more than double the figures from federal census taken only six years previously. Los Angeles was the seventeenth largest city in the United States.[22]

The population of the city tells only one part of the multifaceted story of a growing metropolis. Ralph Bunche, a black native of Los Angeles, who later worked for the Department of State and United Nations illustrated the social and economic condition of blacks

---

[18]Lynn Bowman, *Los Angeles: Epic of a City* (Berkeley: Howell-North, 1974), 203.

[19]Fogelson, 21.

[20]Fogelson, 76, 77.

[21]Fogelson, 76, 78.

[22]"228,298 Is Population of this City," *The Los Angeles Express* (14 April 1906), 1.

in his city with a story of a black man from Texas who visited California. In Texas, the man had been in quasi-slavery, subservient to his white "boss."

After his trip west, he refused to go back to his old job. The master approached him, saying, "Sam, you'd better come on back on the job. We've just killed a new batch of hogs, and I've got some mighty fine hog-jowls for you."

Sam shook his head and replied, "Uh uh boss. You ain't talkin' to me, no suh. I've been to Los Angeles and I don' want yo' old hog-jowls, cuz I'm eatin' high on up on de hog now!"[23]

A contrasting anecdote was created when a white man from Texas applied for a job at **The Eagle**, a Los Angeles newspaper serving the black community. The man told the black editor, "I am from Texas and down there whites never address Negroes as 'Mr.' and 'Mrs.' So, if you please, I would like to know your first name." The editor informed the stranger that he did not allow employees to become so familiar. The Texan had traveled more than a thousand miles to receive his first lesson in "racial tolerance."[24]

Unfortunately, this perception of Los Angeles as a promised land for blacks, was part reality and part myth. It is true that the city offered more opportunities and equality for blacks than anywhere in the deep south. Nevertheless, blacks in Los Angeles did not have the privileges for advancement available to whites. For example, in 1930 blacks made up less than four percent of the total population but more than 72 percent of the city's porters were black, as were 31 percent of janitors. Less than one half of one percent of doctors were black and less than two percent of Los Angeles

---

[23]Caughey, 284.
[24]Bass, 15, 16.

lawyers were black. A *de facto* segregation pervaded the city and blacks and other non-whites were often refused "food in restaurants, rooms in hotels, tickets at theaters, rides in jitneys, and other services in public accommodation. They were also denied communion by religious congregations, brotherhood by fraternal orders, affiliations by commercial organizations, and membership in the metropolis' other voluntary associations."[25]

Charlotta Bass described the situation of her black kinsmen with eloquence, "The Negro people understood clearly why they had come to what they considered the Promised Land. They came believing that their economic status would change from poverty in ghettoes to a better standard of living in better homes and communities. They came hoping also that they were leaving behind that peculiar American brand of discrimination practiced against them in their old home, that humiliated them and reduced their status to second class citizenship. When the first breath of race hate poison was blown in their faces, they became aware that although they had left Texas, Jim Crow had followed close on their heels to their new home."[26]

Los Angeles' newspapers were filled with advertisements and cartoons that were insulting and demeaning to blacks. There was a definite tension between the races. On April 6, 1906, just days before Holy Ghost revival began in Los Angeles, John Davis, a black man was taken into custody for a "statutory offense." The authorities had chased him for nearly a mile. Fearing that Davis would be lynched, "a mob of nearly a

---

[25]Fogelson, 199, 201.
[26]Bass, 21.

hundred Negroes" tried to prevent him from being arrested by a police detective.[27]

To this city of mixed signals, God would send William J. Seymour, an humble servant who in so many ways proved that he was ahead of his times and bigger than his environment.

---

[27]"Negro Is Captured after Long Chase," *The Los Angeles Express* (7 April 1906), 5.

An early Twentieth Century photo of Los Angeles
The city that was "congenial" to "fanaticisms and humbugs."

The Larry Martin Collection

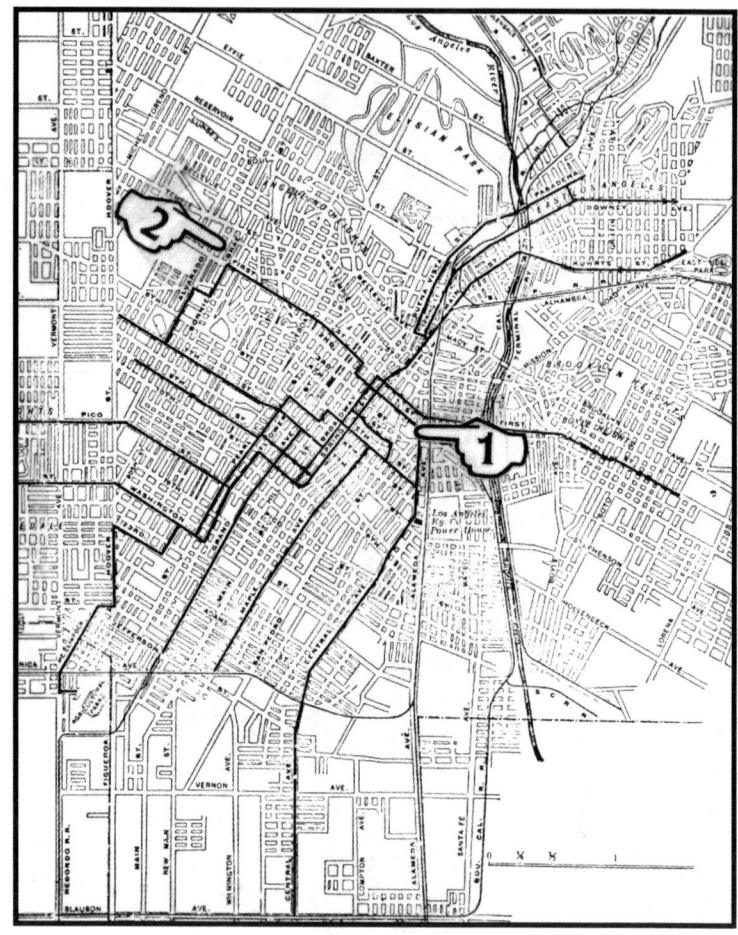

This is a map of the Los Angeles railway system in 1898, just eight years before the revival began.
(1) 312 Azusa Street
(2) 214 North Bonnie Brae Street

Clippings from the July and August 1906 issues of the
Los Angeles Express
give glimpses of life in the city as the revival began.

Property in LA County for $1.00 per acre?

This mower wasn't needed at the mission. In dry weather the board walk was surrounded by dust from the streets. In rainy weather, the faithful walked in mud.

People came to the revival by every available means of transportaion, including horse-drawn carriages adn automobiles. In 1906, $79.50 would buy a bike buggy but a Jackson automobile would cost $1,350.00.

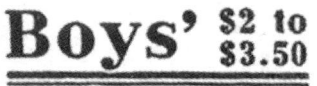

These clothes are typical of those worn during the revival. A boy visiting the mission could purchase a suit for $1.19 but if his dad wanted to dress up for the meeting he would have to pay $6.95 for a wool suit.

"SOMETHING NEW EVERY DAY"

Jacoby Bros.

361-333-335 SOUTH BROADWAY
BOTH PHONES 133

Art Dept. Specials for Wednesday

100 dozen spachtel scarfs, shams, etc.; beautiful open-work designs; large squares and long scarfs with linen centers; very handsome. The assortment includes values up to $2.75 each. Extra Special for Wednesday's selling, 95c.

75 Linen Suits...... $3.95

Values Up to $10.00

THIS WILL BE OUR SPECIAL FOR WEDNESDAY

There are pretty Etons, some embroidered, some with insertion, and some plain tailored effects. The skirts of any of the suits are worth more than we ask, but to make a final cleanup we sell them Wednesday for $3.95.

Up to $2.00 Wash Skirts $1.00

Not many left, but they come in fine quality Indian Head and Linene, trimmed straps and folds. Choice, $1.00.

Up to $4.00 Wash Skirts .. $1.95

This lot comprises some of the finest Linens and Mercerized Poplins so popular this season. A very choice assortment for $1.95 each.

Skirts Made Free Balance of This Week
You Pay For Material Alone

Wednesday morning we reopen our skirt tailoring department, and as a special introductory offer, we will make a skirt, to your measure, of any $1.25 material in the store, for $4.95. Remember, this offer is for this week only. Choose your material—any style or color.

$1.50, $2.00, $2.50 and $3.00
Gowns 98c

98c

$1.75
Drawers
And Corset Covers
At 98c

A fine ladies linen suit could be bought for $3.95, while gowns and "drawers" were only $.98.

In 1906 **The Los Angeles Express** ran this unbecoming caricature of a black police officer, Patrolman Glenn.
It further illustrates the racial prejudice and animosity toward African-Americans in the "City of Angels."

This blatantly racist advertisement from the **Los Angeles Express** would not be tolerated any where in America today. Yet at the turn of the century this kind of stereotyping and buffoonery was prevalent even in more tolerant California.
The caption reads, "Say, Missus, dis yar coon's too tired to beat dat carpet..."

These blocks from the comic pages of the **Los Angeles Express**, further demonstrate the disgraceful caricature of black Americans.

As these articles from the **Los Angeles Express** in the summer of 1906 illustrate, the lynching of black men was very common place in America during the Azusa Street revival.

7 The Preparation: Hunger for God

The Azusa Street revival, like every great move of God, was not born in a vacuum. In 1916, Frank Bartleman, a Los Angeles participant, wrote, "It would be a great mistake to attempt to attribute the Pentecostal beginning in Los Angeles to any one man, either in prayer or in preaching . . .'Pentecost' did not drop suddenly out of heaven. God was with us in large measure for a long time before the final outpouring. It was not a mushroom of a night by any means."[1]

As 1906 drew near, Los Angeles was ripe for a spiritual awakening. Several churches in the area had been praying for a revisiting of the first century Pentecost. Bartleman, a Holiness evangelist, was busy stirring the city with tracts and calls for revival. He

---

[1] Lawrence, 72, 73.

said, "Day and night the Spirit was heavy upon me. . . until it seemed I must die."[2]

Bartleman, born in Carversville, Pennsylvania on December 14, 1871, was the son of immigrants. After a difficult childhood, Bartleman found Christ on October 15, 1893. He testified, "He entered powerfully into my soul." Soon, Bartleman accepted a call to the ministry. In his lifetime, he preached, first as a Baptist, then as a Methodist, next as a cadet in the Salvation Army, and afterwards with the Free Methodists, Wesleyans, and Holiness. Finally, he closed his ministry as a non-aligned independent. While living in Chicago, Bartleman was privileged to meet the great evangelist D. L. Moody, one of the many men that influenced his life.

Evangelizing in the South, Bartleman witnessed the ill treatment of blacks. He said, "There seemed little justice for the man whom God had made with the black skin." He developed a love for blacks and other down-and-out people, commenting, "They needed our help the most."

Bartleman lived by "faith," which often meant living on the verge of poverty and starvation. His family endured tremendous hardships as they traveled across the country, arriving in Los Angeles on December 20, 1901. He said, "The Spirit had led us to Los Angeles for the 'Latter Rain' outpouring."[3]

Joseph Smale was also making an important spiritual contribution in Los Angeles. Smale was born in England on July 7, 1867. He was educated in Spurgeon's

---

[2]Frank Bartleman, *My Story: The Latter Rain* (Columbia, SC: John M. Pike, 1909), 26.

[3]Frank Bartleman, *From Plow to Pulpit: From Maine to California* (Los Angeles: n.p., 1924), 5-132.

College in London. He started his public ministry as a street preacher in England's capital city. Afterwards he pastored a church in Great Britain for three years. Resigning his church, Smale immigrated to the United States and assumed the pastorate of the Baptist Church in Prescott, Arizona.[4]

Smale left Arizona and moved to southern California where he became the pastor of the prestigious First Baptist Church in Los Angeles on January 22, 1898. From the beginning, Smale had problems at the church with ten percent voting against his election. These comments from the new pastor were an indicator of his hunger for God and a predictor of his stormy relationship with the more traditional First Baptist, "Reformation is not the first need of humanity, but regeneration. If you would have pure politics, clean government, a moral society with peace and contentment reigning, men must have new hearts, and they must let God work through them as they seek to do his will."[5]

Smale led the church through a successful building program, but he was always "an evangelist at heart." Evening services at First Baptist were always directed toward the lost. Famed evangelist D. L. Moody was a guest in the church's pulpit.

A group of lay leaders within the church asked for Smale's resignation in 1902. During three business meetings, one of which lasted eleven hours, the

---

[4]Joseph Smale, *Standard Certificate of Death*: California State Board of Health, 16 September 1926; "Rites for Churchman Tomorrow," *Los Angeles Daily Times* (18 September 1926), II, 1.

[5]Herbert L. Sutton, *Our Heritage and Our Hope* (Los Angeles: Continental Graphics, 1974), 24.

disgruntled members called Smale, "unfriendly," "injudicious," "arbitrary," "arrogant," "dictatorial" and more. The church minutes reported, "While our pastor was speaking the weight of the complaints had been almost perceptibly vanishing and the turning of sympathy toward him could well nigh be felt."[6]

In 1905, Smale preached a series on "Is There Eternal Punishment for those Who Die Christless?" Apparently the gravity of the message and the problems at First Baptist had taken a toll on Smale's health. He requested a sabbatical and visited Greece, Egypt, the Holy Land and Great Britain. While in Wales he visited Evan Roberts, leader of a mighty outpouring of the Holy Spirit. When he returned to the United States, Smale hoped for an identical outpouring in Los Angeles. His first Sunday sermon was "The Great Welsh Revival." The service lasted from 11:00 A. M. until 2:15 that afternoon.[7]

On Monday and Tuesday, he continued sermons on the subject and would have presented the same topic on Wednesday, "but the Spirit led the meeting" and there was no chance to preach. It was reported that "The Spirit has come upon some of the members in a remarkable way."

On the following Sunday morning, the clerk reported, "At the close of the first hymn . . . one member remained standing and witnessed that she had been filled with the Spirit. Then followed testimony, prayer and praise until about 1:30. The Pastor had no opportunity to preach." That evening Evangelist A. P. Graves asked Smale to forgive him for an offense the evangelist had caused. This,

---

[6]Sutton, 27, 28.
[7]Sutton, 29.

too, was interpreted as a sign of revival as the Holy Spirit was "making clean the House of God."

For fifteen weeks revival services continued at First Baptist. Hungry people from all over the city gathered twice each day at 2:30 P. M. and 7:45 P.M. to believe God for revival. The slogan for the meetings was "Pentecost has not yet come, but it is coming."

Members of First Baptist began to complain that church activities were neglected. The usual method of receiving finaces through pledges was replaced by free-will offerings. Church finances declined and the choir director was released.

The "church dignitaries" could not tolerate this new emphasis on revival and some called on the pastor to desist or "get out." Professor Melville Dozier, a deacon, and his wife, Barton, who served as church collector, took the side of the dismissed choir director and complained that there was too much noise and confusion in the meetings. Dozier also suggested that visitors should be asked to stay away from First Baptist on Wednesday night so the church could be left to its own members for at least one night each week.

Following the Sunday morning service, the church voted to give Dozier a dismissal letter. He refused to accept the letter unless it was voted on by all the members at a called meeting. That night, Smale tendered his resignation and a majority of the church voted to accept. The clerk closed the minutes of the meeting by writing, "May God have mercy on this church for rejecting His anointed."

Bartleman, who had been attending the revival meetings, lamented, "What an awful position for a church to take, to throw God out."

Within two weeks, 190 members had requested transfers of membership. Smale started the First New Testament Church which was located in Burbank Hall, next to the Burbank Theater on Main Street.[8] Bartleman was one of the charter members, as were many of the former leaders and members of First Baptist Church. The prayer for revival continued.[9]

While Smale's group was in a spiritual battle for Los Angeles, Elmer K. Fisher, pastor of First Baptist Church in nearby Glendale was waging a similar assault on his city. Often, the spiritually hungry pastor would go to his church and pray all through the night. After preaching a series of sermons on the need for revival and the Holy Spirit, his deacons also informed him they did not want that kind of preaching in their

---

[8]"Curb Preacher Scores Theater," *The Los Angeles Express* (1 May 1906), 7. Smale's congregation left the hall in the summer of 1906 and worshipped in a tent. A controversy with their landlord arose following an outdoor service in May. The services were held outside the theater and hall every evening before the services began inside. Theater attendees would stop and listen to the preaching on their way to watch the theatrical performances. A problem arose, however, when one of the participants gave a testimony and said, "He who goes to the theater is on the road to hell." Needless to say, the owner of the theater and hall was not thrilled with his tenants and the church moved when their lease was fulfilled.

[9]Sutton, 30; Frank Bartleman, *Azusa Street* (South Plainfield, NJ: Bridge Publishing, Inc., 1980), 13-27. This is a reprint of Bartleman's 1925 work *How Pentecost Came to Los Angeles: How It Was in the Beginning*. Although it is definitely one man's view of the events, it is a valuable source; Lawrence, 70, 71; Stanley M. Horton, "Pentecostal Explosion," *The Pentecostal Evangel* (7 October 1962), 8. According to Sutton, so many leaders left First Baptist, that when elections were held that week, only three officers had previously held a position in the church.

church. Fisher was quick to offer his resignation and joined Smale at the First New Testament Church.[10]

It is also significant that the English preacher F. B. Meyer conducted meetings in Los Angeles in the spring of 1905. Meyer was a "deeper life" evangelist, pastor and author associated with the "Keswick" movement. He spoke warmly of the revival in Wales, which he had recently visited. Robert Anderson says that Meyer spoke to "large" crowds.[11] Meyer's preaching made a deep impact on Bartleman who wrote, "My soul was stirred to its depths."

Bartleman continued to work hard for revival, praying, preaching, writing and distributing G. Campbell Morgan's tract, "Revival in Wales" and S. B. Shaw's book, **The Great Revival in Wales.** He had also begun written correspondence with Evan Roberts in Wales. The Welsh revivalist responded, "Congregate the people who are willing to make a total surrender. Pray and wait. Believe God's promises. Hold daily meetings. May God bless you is my earnest prayer."[12]

The Methodist churches in Los Angeles were also eager for a spiritual awakening. From March 11 to 21, 1906 a "'ten days' Pentecostal convention" was held at the First Methodist Church located at Sixth and Hill Streets. The meetings sponsored by a group called the Pacific Pentecostal Association, were held each day at 10:30 A. M. and 7:00 P. M. Joseph Smith, a Methodist,

---

[10]Horton, "Pentecostal," 8, 9; Ruth Fisher Steelberg Carter, "I Remember or What Pentecost Means to Me," typescript, *Pentecostal Evangel* Files, Flower Pentecostal Heritage Center.

[11]Bartleman, *Azusa,* 7; Anderson, 64.

[12]Bartleman, *Azusa,* 7, 10, 11, 15.

and E. F. Walker, a Presbyterian were the featured speakers.[13]

At 919 Boston Street a group of Armenian immigrants met for services in the home of Demos and Goolisar Shakarian, grandparents of Full Gospel Business Men's Fellowship International founder, Demos Shakarian. The family had recently moved from their homeland to escape Turkish persecution. The problems in Armenia had been anticipated by a prophecy that warned the Shakarians and others to flee.

Six years earlier Grandfather Demos and other family members had spoken in tongues after receiving prayer from Russian missionaries. They were seeking a similar experience in Los Angeles.[14]

Certainly the Shakarians were not the only ones in the city who had experienced glossolalia. Early testimonies tell of one lady in Los Angeles who spoke in tongues several months before the Azusa Street revival and another person who had had the experience thirty-five years earlier.[15] Mrs. Elmer Fisher also had a "wonderful" experience with the Holy Spirit, when she spoke in tongues and prophesied, several years before the Azusa Street revival. As we shall see, what happened to these individuals, although very real to them, was quite different from the Pentecostal outpouring on Azusa Street. None of these realized that

---

[13] "Will Preach in Elk's Hall," *The Los Angeles Express* (10 March 1906).

[14] Demos Shakarian, *The Happiest People on Earth* (Old Tappan, NJ: Revell, 1975), 15-24.

[15] Thomas G. Atteberry, "Tongues," *Apostolic Truth* (December 1906), 1, 2.

tongues were the unique initial, physical evidence of a New Testament Holy Spirit baptism.

Hundreds more, no doubt, were seeking for a revival in their city. Among them were Louis and Cena Osterberg and their son A. G. Osterberg, the young pastor of the Full Gospel Assembly at 68th and Denver. The senior Osterbergs were also newcomers to the "city of angels," arriving from Michigan, having previously lived in Chicago where they had met William H. Durham, pastor of the North Avenue Mission.[16]

Other pastors who had a deep hunger for more of God and would eventually be receptive to a new Pentecost included A. G. Garr at the Burning Bush Mission; Thomas G. Atteberry, pastor of People's Church; William Manley of the Household of Faith; William Pendleton, a Holiness preacher; and Ansel H. Post, another Baptist. One young observer said, "For a long time people had been crying out for a deeper walk with God."[17]

A small Holiness sect with a couple dozen churches located mostly in the Los Angeles area held a camp meeting near Downey, California, in August of every year. In 1905, the theme of the meeting was God's desire to send an outpouring of His Holy Spirit. The message was straight forward, if the Holiness people

---

[16]A.G. Osterberg, "I Was There," *Full Gospel Business Men's Voice* (May 1966),11-13, 18-21; A.G. Osterberg, "Tears–The Secret of the Azusa Street Revival," *The Voice of Healing* (July 1954), 5, 24; Dean Osterberg, letter to the author, 22 August 1998; Dan L. Thrapp, "Pentecostal Sects Convene Here," *The Los Angeles Times* (9 September 1956), III,11.

[17]Clara Davis, *Azusa Street Till Now* (Tulsa: Harrison House, 1989), 18.

did not "dig in" and get the blessing, God was going to pass them by and "raise up a people who would."[18]

At about the same time as these prophetic words were being preached at the camp meeting, God was at work, gathering the group that would receive Pentecost when it came to Los Angeles. The series of events that brought them together began at the Second Baptist Church. Founded in 1885, Second was Los Angeles' first black Baptist church and the second black congregation in the city.[19] C. H. Anderson served as pastor of the church from 1888 until December 1907.[20] Mrs. Julia Hutchins, a member of the church, had been teaching sanctification as a second work of God's grace. This caused quite a disturbance in the Baptist church and Pastor Anderson and his congregation could not tolerate this deviation from traditional Baptist doctrine. Mrs. Hutchins and eight families were expelled from Second Baptist.[21]

Looking for a church home, the estranged group of black believers temporarily joined William Manley, the white pastor of the Household of Faith mission meeting in a tent near 1st and Bonnie Brae Streets. The groups soon divided along color lines, with Hutchins' group moving into another tent near 7th and Broadway.[22]

---

[18]Davis, 16.

[19]"Historical African American Churches in L.A.;" available from http://www.ussc.edu/dept/Info/Ref/BHM/exhibit/churches.html; Internet; accessed August 1998, 1.

[20]Sutton, 26; Beasley, 161.

[21]Thomas R. Nickel, *Azusa Street Outpouring: As Told to Me By Those Who Were There* (Hanford, CA: Great Commission International, 1956), 4; Osterberg, "I Was," 6; Shumway, "Study," 173.

[22]Shumway, "Study," 172; Bartleman, *Azusa*, 14.

As winter approached and with it, the threat of rains, the saints moved their services into the 214 Bonnie Brae Street home of Richard and Ruth Asbery, one of the participating families. The Asberys lived in a middle class black neighborhood which had comfortable, but not wealthy homes.[23]

Richard was a janitor in an office building. In 1905, Richard was 40 years of age and was a native of Louisiana. Ruth, born in Virginia, was 47. The couple had been married for 20 years, had lived in Texas and had nine children. Only six of the children survived until 1910. Four children, Willie Ella (also Willella), Robert, Morton, and Richard, were living in the home.[24]

On Monday nights, the group would hold a gospel concert in front of the house, attracting curious families from the neighborhood. As the crowd grew, they would be invited inside for an evangelistic service. Among those won to Christ through these efforts was Jennie Evans Moore who lived with other family members across the street from the Asberys at 217 Bonnie Brae.[25] Miss Moore was employed as a cook by an influential white family.[26]

Jennie Moore was born in Austin, Texas on March 10, 1874. Her parents were Jackson and Eliza Moore.[27] Before moving to Bonnie Brae, Miss Moore had lived

---

[23]Davis, 17.

[24]United States Census, Los Angeles County, California, 1910.

[25]Shumway, "Study," 172; Moore's address is added by Nelson, 217.

[26]Shumway, "Study," 172; Alexander A. Boddy, "At Los Angeles, California," *Confidence* (October 1912), 233.

[27]Jennie Evans Seymour, *Standard Certificate of Death*: California State Board of Health, 2 July 1936.

on Grand Avenue where she was a servant in the home of Walter B. Cline.[28]

Another of the faithful at Bonnie Brae was Edward S. Lee, 45, a janitor at a bank located at Seventh and Spring Streets. Lee, "a much esteemed saint" and his young wife Mattie, 22, lived on South Union Avenue near First Street. He was a member of Peniel Mission. Two years earlier, Lee had met Charles F. Parham and learned about the Holy Spirit baptism evidenced by speaking in tongues. He had been seeking the experience since that time.[29]

Although the home at 214 Bonnie Brae was not small and had a double parlor, by February, it was too crowded for the meetings to continue there. A small building at 9th and Santa Fe was leased for the services.[30]

Hutchins continued to be in charge of the congregation, with different members sharing leadership duties. The lay ministry model did not work as well as was originally hoped. Bad doctrines were preached and some inappropriately tried to gain ascendancy over the others by harsh means. All seemed to sense the need for a man of God to teach them the Word. They prayed that God would send them a "Holiness" man.[31]

---

[28]United States Census, Los Angeles County, California, 1900.

[29]Cotton, 1; Shumway, "Study," 174; Shumway, "Critical," 115; Ewart, 72; United States Census, Los Angeles County, California, 1910.

[29]Cotton, 1; Shumway, "Study," 174; Shumway, "Critical," 115; Ewart, 72; United States Census, Los Angeles County, California, 1910.

[30]Shumway, "Study," 172; Shumway, "Critical," 115.

[31]Shumway, "Study," 172.

Neely Terry, a cousin of the Asberys, had just returned from Houston, Texas, where she had met Parham, had received the Holy Spirit baptism, and had spoken in tongues.[32] She had also met a black Holiness pastor, William Joseph Seymour. Since he had impressed her as a "very Godly man," she recommended Seymour to the fledgling congregation. After prayer, the church agreed to send Seymour an invitation with his train fare. He agreed to come and "give them some Bible teaching." The Los Angeles group believed Seymour had already received the Holy Spirit baptism, but he, too, was only a seeker.[33]

For more than a year these humble saints had been praying for "more power with God for the salvation of lost and suffering humanity."[34] In God's perfect timing, He was about ready to answer their prayers.

---

[32]Valdez, 18; Nickel, 4; Osterberg, "I Was," 7; Tenney, 218. Osterberg says Terry "had been in a Pentecostal revival down there where they spoke in tongues according to Acts 2:4." Tenney says Terry was also a student at Parham's school. Nelson doubts that Terry received or even heard about speaking in tongues while in Houston. He also ignores Shumway's claim that Lee had learned about Pentecost from Charles F. Parham. It is this author's opinion that Nelson demonstrates a bias toward Seymour's role.

[33]Lawrence, 55, 73; Nickel, 4; Tyson, 95, 96; Cotton, 1; W.J. Seymour, *The Doctrines and Discipline of the Azusa Street Apostolic Faith Mission of Los Angeles, CA (n.p., 1915)*, 12. It is often reported that Seymour came to Los Angeles to assume the pastorate of the church. This does not seem to be true. Seymour himself said he only came to give Bible teaching and he also said the saints in Texas were expecting him to return from Los Angeles in one month, See "Azusa Mission," *The Apostolic Faith* [Los Angeles] (April 1907), 2.

[34]"Pentecost with," 1.

Frank Bartleman
Photo used by permission
Flower Pentecostal Heritage Center

Joseph Smale
Larry Martin Collection
Courtesy of Sandy Rogers of First Baptist Church, Los Angeles

The First Baptist Church Board of Deacons
(Joseph Smale is in the center,
Prof. and Mrs. Melville Dozier are on Smale's right in the front row)
Larry Martin Collection
Courtesy of Sandy Rogers of First Baptist Church, Los Angeles

Elmer K. Fisher
Larry Martin Collection
Courtesy of Lloyd Colbaugh

A. G. Garr
Larry Martin Collection

The Shakarian family

The Boston Street home
Photos used by permission
Flower Pentecostal Heritage Center

Rev. and Mrs. A. H. Post

Photo used by permission.
Flower Pentecostal Heritage Center
(Assemblies of God Archives)

C. H. Anderson
Larry Martin Collection
Courtesy of Sandy Rogers of First Baptist Church, Los Angeles

Louis and Cena Osterberg
Larry Martin Collection
Courtesy of Dean Osterberg

The Richard Asbery Home
214 Bonnie Brae

Jennie Evans Moore
Photos used by permission
Flower Pentecostal Heritage
Center

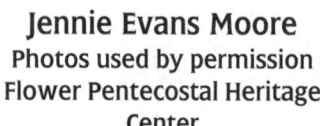

Jennie Moore's Home in 2000
217 Bonnie Brae
Larry Martin
Collection

8 The Result: Holy Ghost Outpouring

The Holiness church on Santa Fe in Los Angeles was eager to see the "man of God" they had heard so much about. When Seymour arrived in Los Angeles on February 22, 1906, all the saints were "happy to see him."[1] They believed it was as "truly a call from God as when He sent His holy angels to tell Cornelius to send for Peter."[2] Seymour started services in the Holiness church on February 24.[3] Seymour preached on regeneration, sanctification and faith healing. As expected, he also preached on the necessity of being baptized in the Holy Spirit and speaking in tongues.[4] Although Seymour admitted that he, himself, had not had the experience of speaking in tongues, he taught

---

[1] Cotton, 2.
[2] "Pentecost with," 1.
[3] Seymour, *Doctrines,* 12.
[4] Shumway, "Study," 173.

it was a necessary sign of the Holy Spirit baptism and asked the church to meet him that afternoon at three o'clock to pray with him until "all received their Pentecost."⁵

Some of the group believed that since they were sanctified, they already had the Holy Spirit baptism. Others, probably those familiar with Parham's teaching, did not believe they had received because the New Testament signs were not following them.⁶ Pastor Hutchins herself was less than receptive to Seymour's message because of the emphasis on tongues and his strong premillennialist views. After several meetings, she locked Seymour and his supporters out of the building!⁷

President J. M. Roberts, the director of the Southern California Holiness Association and several Holiness ministers were brought into the church, perhaps partially at least due to the insistence of W. H. McGowan, who, with his family, had been attending the meetings. Seymour was given a chance to defend himself and his doctrine. According to one witness, Roberts was glad Seymour was seeking the baptism and he hoped the visitor from Texas would soon receive. However, the Holiness brethren believed they had received the Holy Spirit when they were sanctified

---

⁵"Pentecost with," 1.

⁶"Pentecost with," 1.

⁷Shumway, "Critical," 115; Shumway, "Study," 173. It is often stated that Seymour was locked out of the building after his first sermon. This is not true. Shumway says it was the fifth meeting and Seymour himself says, "one night they locked the door against me." See "Bro. Seymour's Call," 1. Hutchins later embraced Pentecost, was baptized in the Holy Spirit, and took the message to Liberia, West Africa.

and did not need another experience. Roberts did, however, ask Seymour to contact him and let him know when he had received the Spirit baptism.[8]

Nevertheless, Seymour was asked not to preach the Pentecostal message in the Holiness church. Seymour found himself hundreds of miles from home with no place to preach, no way to fulfill his mission and more than likely without enough money to return to Houston.

The unfortunate turn of events not only left the pilgrim unemployed and with very little or no money, but also without room and board. The displaced preacher found harborage in the home of Edward S. Lee, a member of the Peniel Mission, who had merely invited Seymour home for lunch. Fortunately for Seymour and Lee, the hospitable host would not allow the guest from Texas to be turned out into the street.[9]

With no one to look to but the Lord, Seymour entered into a time of prayer and fasting. Even before he had heard the Pentecostal message, he had an intense hunger for more of God. John G. Lake, who later became a personal friend of Seymour, recalled Seymour's testimony, "Prior to my meeting with Parham, the Lord had sanctified me from sin, and had led me into a deep life of prayer, assigning five hours out of the twenty-four every day for prayer. This prayer life I continued for three and a half years, when one day as I prayed the Holy Ghost said to me, 'There are better things to be had in the spiritual life, but they must be sought out with faith and prayer.' This so quickened my soul

---

[8]"Bro. Seymour's Call," 1; Bartleman, *Azusa*, 71. Bartleman reports that Roberts was a seeker for the Holy Spirit at his mission.

[9]Cotton, 2.

that I increased my hours of prayer to seven out of twenty-four and continued to pray on for two years longer, until the baptism fell on us."[10]

Lee and Seymour began to pray together each day when the former returned home from work.[11] Soon, cottage prayer meetings began as other spiritually-hungry members of the church visited Seymour in the Lee home. This little group of seekers became determined to receive their Pentecost "at all costs," sometimes praying all night long.[12] Men would also leave their jobs just to spend time in prayer.[13]

Seymour tried to explain what happened when people received the Holy Spirit baptism. At times, he told them, people would shake under the power and anointing of the Holy Spirit. This seemed foolish to some of the people, and Seymour could not explain it adequately to satisfy their curiosity.[14]

In the mean time, the spirit of prayer consumed Lee. At times he would go into the basement of the bank where he was employed and "hide away," spending hours in prayer.[15] One day while seeking the Lord, Lee had a vision. He knew he was awake, because he was praying, but he saw two men come toward him. He knew them to be Peter and John. Both men lifted their hands to heaven, began to shake under the power

---

[10]John G. Lake, "Origin of the Apostolic Faith Movement," *(The Pentecostal Outlook* September 1932), 3. This article was originally written in 1911; Also see *John G. Lake: His Life*, 87, 88.
[11]Cotton, 2.
[12]Shumway, "Critical," 115.
[13]Shumway, "Study," 174.
[14]Cotton, 2.
[15]Cotton, 2.

of God, and spoke in other tongues. The Holy Spirit came upon Lee and he, too, began to shake. The entire experience frightened Lee, as it might almost anyone, and he jumped up wondering what was happening.[16]

That night, Lee came home and told Seymour, "I know now how people act when they get the Holy Ghost." Lee's hunger was intensified, and he sought even more earnestly.[17]

Jennie Moore, who had never had such an experience in her life, was also given a vision. Moore saw three cards, and each one had two languages written on it. In total, they were French, Spanish, Latin, Greek, Hebrew and Hindustani.[18] Although blessed by the experience, at the time she had no idea what the vision meant.

One evening when his faith was high, Lee told Seymour, "If you will lay your hands on me, I will receive the baptism." Seymour hesitated, remembering the Bible said to lay hands "suddenly" on no one. Later in the night, feeling it was time, the minister placed his holy hands on the seeker and said, "Brother, I lay my hands on you in Jesus' name."

Lee fell to the floor like a dead man. Mrs. Lee was so scared, she cried, "What did you do to my husband?" Seymour realized that they were so frightened that the Lord could not finish his work at that time, so he prayed that Lee would get up. In a "few minutes" Lee got up and sat in a chair, but he had had a touch from

---

[16]Cotton, 2.

[17]Cotton, 2.

[18]"Music from Heaven," *The Apostolic Faith* [Los Angeles] (May 1907), 3.

heaven and would never be the same. From that day forward, he sought God day and night.¹⁹

Before long, the meetings were moved to the Richard Asbery residence at 214 North Bonnie Brae Avenue.²⁰ The small group of black believers waited on God, occasionally joined by a few white visitors, such as the McGowans. Frank Bartleman visited for the first time on March 26.²¹ Despite much opposition, services and serious seeking continued for several weeks.

Concerned that no one had received the baptism, Seymour sent to Houston for two helpers, Joseph A. Warren and Lucy F. Farrow.²² Farrow, the Houston pastor, was especially gifted to lay hands on people who would then receive the baptism in the Holy Ghost with evidentiary tongues. Howard Goss once saw a line of twenty-five people stand before her for prayer. As she prayed for them, "many began to speak in tongues at once."²³

Warren was a 45-year-old grandfather who had received a miraculous healing from persistent "chills."²⁴ In Houston, Warren had worked as a drayman or driver for Hugh Waddell, Henke and Pillot, Houston Trunk Factory, and Joseph F. Meyer Company. He had lived at several addresses, including 613 Taylor, 812 Robin and

---

¹⁹Cotton, 2.

²⁰Shumway, "Critical," 115.

²¹Bartleman, *Azusa*, 41.

²²Lawrence, 56, 64; "Pentecost with," 1; "Mrs. Lucy F. Farrow . . .," *The Apostolic Faith* [Los Angeles] (September 1906), 1; Cotton, 2.

²³Lawrence, 66; Goss, 98. See also Cotton, 2.

²⁴"Divinely Healed," *The Apostolic Faith* [Los Angeles] (September 1906), 4; United States Census, Los Angeles County, California, 1910.

509 Henderson.²⁵ Apparently, he, like Seymour, was an earnest seeker for Pentecost but had not yet received his baptism.²⁶

Services on Friday, April 6 lasted far into the night. Seymour encouraged the small group to begin a ten day fast, trusting God for His blessing. Remarkable services were also held on Saturday and Sunday at Bonnie Brae.²⁷ Two different, but not especially contradictory accounts of what took place on Monday, April 9, the third day of the fast, exist. Emma Cotton, an early participant, remembered Lee asking Farrow to pray for him. Like Seymour, she hesitated at first, but while at dinner, she rose from her chair, went to Lee, and prayed for him. Lee fell from his chair and spoke in tongues for a "few minutes." Lee's wife and brother-in-law thought it strange that God did not do "much" through him.²⁸

According to Charles Shumway, who interviewed the participants, Lee became ill after fasting three days and asked Seymour to pray with him for his healing. At about 6:00 P. M., while Seymour was there, Lee asked the preacher to pray for him that he might receive the Holy Spirit. As Seymour laid hands on him, Lee was baptized in the Spirit and began speaking in tongues.²⁹ It is not implausible that both accounts are true, taking place the same evening in the Lee home. The latter

---

²⁵Houston City Directories, 1899; 1900-1901; 1902-03; 1903-04; 1905-06. Special thanks to Rev. Calvin Durham for providing copies from the Houston directories.

²⁶"Pentecost with," 1.

²⁷Lawrence, 74; Shumway, "Study," 174.

²⁸Cotton, 2.

²⁹Cotton, 2; Shumway, "Critical," 116. Douglas Nelson questions Cotton's account, accusing her of "gender" bias.

experience following Seymour's prayer, being more satisfying to Lee.

The weather was fair and warm that evening as Seymour and Lee made their way to the prayer meeting on Bonnie Brae Street.[30] The service began as usual. Only blacks were present. They had a song, three prayers, and some personal testimonies. Seymour preached on the Holy Spirit using Acts 2:4 as his text. When he finished, Lee lifted his hands to heaven and began speaking in tongues. Jennie Moore, resting on an organ stool, fell quickly to the floor. Immediately, she began speaking in tongues, the first woman in Los Angeles to receive. As she spoke, she was reminded of her vision. She said it seemed like "a vessel broke within me and water surged up through my being." When this rush reached her mouth, she spoke in all six languages she had seen on the cards in her vision and after each message in tongues, there was an interpretation in English. After this, Moore, who had never played the piano before that time, went to the keyboard and played the instrument while singing in tongues.[31]

The outpouring that followed must have been wonderful. When Moore fell to the floor a number of others were also struck down "as by a bolt of lightning from Heaven." Some were in trances for up to five hours. Several, including a Brother Hughes, a Sister Traynor and her two children, Bud and Sis, were

---

[30] "Fair Weather the Forecast," *The Los Angeles Express* (9 April 1906), 1.

[31] Shumway, "Study," 175; Nickel, 5; "Music from Heaven," 3; Nelson, 190-1. The piano that Moore played is still in the Asbery home, which is now maintained as a museum by the Church of God in Christ.

baptized in the Holy Ghost in a few minutes. The Asbery's daughter, Willie Ella, ran from the kitchen to see what was happening.

The exuberant congregation ran into the front yard, still speaking in tongues and magnifying God. Bud Traynor stood on the front porch preaching and prophesying. Jennie Moore prophesied in the Hebrew language. The meeting lasted until 10:00 in the evening.[32] Pentecostal revival had arrived in California.

The outpouring of the Spirit on Bonnie Brae did not catch the attention of Los Angeles' newspaper reporters. Instead, on April 10, **The Los Angeles Express** carried the story of the previous evening's service at a revival in Newman Methodist Church. The evangelist, R. S. Marshall, and his work in Los Angeles, although notable, have been long since forgotten. But, what happened that night on Bonnie Brae will be remembered as long as church history is recorded and revival fires continue to burn.[33]

Despite the silence from the secular press, by the next morning, there was such a crowd of observers, visitors could not get near the house. Among those who persisted and did get inside, many fell under the power of God when they entered the Asbery home.[34]

Over the next three days, services continued almost day and night. Crowds of both blacks and whites filled the house and the yard. A writer described it like this, "The porch became the pulpit and the street became

---

[32]Shumway, "Study," 174; Nickel, 5; Shumway, "Critical," 116; Nelson, 190-1.

[33]"Big Crowds Attend Revival Services," *The Los Angeles Express* (10 April 1906), 7.

[34]Cotton, 2

the pews."[35] Hundreds were saved and many healed or baptized in the Holy Spirit. Several "sanctified wash women" were baptized in the Holy Ghost and May (Mrs. G. V.) Evans was the first white person to receive the Pentecostal blessing.[36] F. W. Williams, another black brother who had been attending the meetings, soon received his baptism.[37]

Witnesses said the house literally shook as in the days of the Acts of the Apostles.[38] On one occasion, the porch gave way under the weight of the crowd, but no one was injured and the porch was quickly repaired.[39]

On the third day after the initial outpouring, Thursday, April 12, Seymour received his Pentecostal baptism.[40] Seymour and a white brother had tarried late, seeking the Holy Spirit. Seymour's companion, weary and discouraged said, "It is not the time." Seymour, refusing to quit, replied, "Yes, it is, I'm not going to give up." In a short time, he came through to the baptism and spoke in tongues. He testified that it was like a "sphere of fiery, white-hot radiance falling upon him."[41] The Asbery's son, Morton, said Seymour "fell under the power of the Holy Ghost like he was dead, and spoke in unknown tongues."[42] Describing the

---

[35]Nickel, 5, 6.

[36]"The Same Old Way," *The Apostolic Faith* [Los Angeles] (September 1906), 3.

[37]C. L. Witherspoon, Houston Ward, Suzie Matthews and Lola Robinson, typescript, Apostolic Faith Mission Church of God, 1.

[38]Ewart, 77; Shumway, "Study," 175.

[39]Nelson, 57, 70.

[40]"Pentecost with," 1.

[41]Nelson, 58.

[42]Russell Chandler, "Pentecostals: Old Faith, New Impact," *The Los Angeles Times* (11 January 1976), I 22.

event later, Seymour said, "We had prayed all night, when at four o'clock in the morning, God came through the window."[43]

During the day on Good Friday, Jennie Moore was assisting her employers and a guest attorney with a dinner party. As the event concluded and her mistress was addressing her, Moore started speaking in tongues. As one can imagine, the mistress was "scared" and all present were concerned. Thinking that something was seriously wrong with Moore and that she might be "losing her reason," the employers insisted, against her protestations, that she take a week off to "rest."[44]

Cena Osterberg was at the Crocker Street Hospital praying for someone with a broken leg when she heard about the meetings. A black lady from the Bonnie Brae meetings heard her pray and entered into the intercession. After the joint prayer, she told Cena about the meetings and invited her to attend. When she arrived at her home, she asked Louis, her husband, to go with her to the meeting.

At first, Louis was hesitant, for as a hard-working carpenter, he was weary from the day's work. Cena, determined not to miss a blessing, went to the meeting alone and was greatly impressed. The following night, she shared her testimony at the Full Gospel Assembly, where her son, A. G., pastored.[45]

Soon A. G. Osterberg and three of his men, Brothers Holler, Dodge and Weaver, attended the meeting.

---

[43]Lake, 3. Lake is attempting to describe the April 9 meeting, but the facts of his account seem to fit better with April 12.

[44]A. A. Boddy, "At Los Angeles, California," *Confidence* (October 1912), 233.

[45]A. G. Osterberg, "From the Personal Writings of A. G. Osterberg," typescript.

Before they got to the house, they heard the singing; with some sense of relief they said, "They are singing just like we do." His mother had failed to mention the racial composition of the meeting, and the pastor, having never worshiped with blacks, was not prepared for the interracial mix. Commenting to himself, he said, "What kind of a mess are we getting into here?" All walls were broken down, however, when he heard the black brothers and sisters testify and then pray "with such earnestness that tears were running down their faces." The people would also tremble and shake under God's power. Osterberg noted that the whole trend of the meeting was, "we are hungry for more of God."

A lady from the congregation spoke in tongues and Osterberg remembered Paul's writing to the Corinthians. Soon another lady went to the piano and began to play as she sang in tongues. To the curious observer, "It was harmonious and beautiful." Others on their knees began to speak in tongues. When they arose their faces looked like angels. "There was nobody praying for them; nobody laying hands on them; nobody trying to urge them on to something; it was just simply God opening the window of heaven and throwing down upon them, the blessings that they themselves could not contain."

Osterberg did not get into a mess, but something got into him. Remembering the meeting, he recalled, "We got humble pretty quick or we didn't get very far."[46]

It was evident that the news of Pentecostal revival was rapidly spreading through all quarters of the city.

---

[46]Jensen and Perkins. For many years, Osterberg served the Assemblies of God as a District Superintendent in Southern California.

William Joseph Seymour (ca. 1909),
pastor of the Apostolic Faith Gospel Mission

Larry Martin Collection
Courtesy of Gary Garrett

The Asbery porch
Photos used by permission
Flower Pentecostal Heritage Center

The Asbery home today and the Bonnie Brae Street Sign
Larry Martin Collection

The piano played by Jennie E. Moore
Larry Martin Collection

F. W. Williams and Mrs. Williams
Larry Martin Collection
Courtesy of Sarah A. Ward

9 The Place: "Old Azusa"

Seymour and his followers searched for any facility large enough to accommodate a growing revival. They found a vacated African Methodist Episcopal (A. M. E.) church building at 312 Azusa Street. The 40 by 60 feet structure was just off San Pedro near downtown Los Angeles. Azusa Street was a two-block long dirt lane. The mission was located on a block that reached a dead end near a freight terminal for the railroad. The Los Angeles River flowed on the other side of the terminal. Across the river, the street recommenced for the second block.

The legal description of the property was "lots seven and eight of Orange Tract, City of Los Angeles, County of Los Angeles, State of California."[1]

---

[1]Mortgage Deed, 31 December 1930, Book 10511, pp. 277, 278, Los Angeles County, California.

Before the church obtained the property, it had been owned by Bridget "Biddy" Mason. Mason was born a slave in Georgia. She never knew the names of her parents. She was brought to California from Hancock County Mississippi, via Salt Lake. Her master decided to leave California and move to Texas. When they stopped in Los Angeles County, the news spread that Mason and others were being taken to Texas and back into slavery. The county sheriff issued a writ preventing the owner from taking the slaves out of California.

After a long and sometimes disappointing attempt to flee slavery, Mason won her freedom in the California courts on January 19, 1854. Trained as a nurse on a Southern plantation, she became a successful midwife, made some money, and invested it very well. Becoming one of the wealthiest and most respected women in the city, by the 1870s, she owned a large acreage in what became downtown Los Angeles, including 312 Azusa Street. The A. M. E. church was started in the bedroom of Mason's home on Spring Street between Third and Fourth.[2]

The church was originally established as Stevens A. M. E. Some of the Bonnie Brae attendees had been members of the church when it was first built.[3]

Founded in 1872, Stevens A. M. E. (now First A. M. E.) was the oldest black church in Los Angeles. It was started with a "small membership and labored under many disadvantages to pay for the old church property

---

[2]Takeshi Nakayama, "African American Roots of Little Tokyo," *The Rafu Shimpo* (13 February 1998), 1; Bass, 23, 24; Beasley, 90, 109.

[3]Shumway, "Study," 175.

on Azusa Street." Under the capable leadership of Pastor J. E. Edwards the debt was paid in 1902.[4]

In the years following 1888, Azusa Street began to change as large warehouses were built near the church. Disturbed by the decline of the area, in 1903 the congregation moved into more comfortable facilities and a better neighborhood at Eighth Street and Towne Avenue. The name of the church was also changed to First A. M. E. Church.[5]

After the congregation moved out, the function of the building was changed. The former upstairs sanctuary was partitioned and converted into living quarters for renters. A fire in one of the apartments partially destroyed the building and the pitched church roof was replaced by a flat asphalt roof.[6] In 1906, the deteriorating two-story structure was being used by a contractor as a warehouse for construction materials and a stable for hay and stock.[7]

The windows were broken out of the old building and the exterior stairs were removed. The only reminder that the building had once served as a house of worship was the former upstairs entrance that retained the shape of a gothic window.[8]

---

[4]Beasley, 160.

[5]"Historical African American Churches in L. A," available from http://www.ussc.edu/dept/Info/Ref/BHM/exhibit/churches.html; Internet; accessed 8 August 1998, 1.

[6]G. F. Taylor, *The Spirit and the Bride: A Scriptural Presentation of the Operations, Manifestation, Gifts and Fruit of the Holy Spirit in His Relation to the Bride with Special Reference to The "Latter Rain" Revival*, (N.P., 107), 94.

[7]Bartleman, *Azusa*, 47; Davis, *Azusa*, 16; Osterberg, "I Was," 12; Rachel A. Sizelove, "A Sparkling Fountain for the Whole Earth," *Word and Work* (June 1934), 1.

[8]Russell Chandler, "Pasadena Cleric Recalls Mission," *The Los Angeles Times* (11 January 1976), II, 5; Nickel, 6; Florence Crawford,

The structure, as dilapidated as it must have appeared, fit well into the neighborhood. Azusa Street itself was said to be similar to "a back alley" in an Eastern city.[9] One writer described the surrounding area as a "slum."[10] Stables, wholesale houses, lumber yards and a tombstone shop surrounded the old church building. Saloons in the locale and other unwholesome activities gave the district a "skid row flavor."[11]

Seymour was able to rent the building, still marked with a large "for sale" sign, for only eight dollars each month.[12] Sawdust was scattered on the dirt floor of the large, barn-like room downstairs. Straw matting was placed around the altars. The ceiling was low and the joists were exposed. The walls were unfinished, but had been whitewashed. Fire damage was still visible on the walls and ceiling, and cobwebs were in the joists and windows. The building had no indoor plumbing, and a smelly outhouse behind the building was the only available restroom.[13]

Skeptical visitors on a wet night in December 1906 were not impressed with the edifice. They gave this unflattering appraisal, "The building was a humble one, and the so-called 'saints' were meeting in the basement. It had been raining considerably. There were no side walks to step upon and we had to wade through

---

The Light of Life Brought Triumph, (Portland: Apostolic Faith, 1936), 7.

[9]"It Is a Counterfeit Pentecost," *The Burning Bush* (27 December 1906), 4.

[10]"Bible Pentecost," *The Apostolic Faith* [Los Angeles] (November 1906), 1; Sizelove, "Sparkling," 1.

[11]Nelson, 192; "Bible Pentecost," 1; Sizelove, "Sparkling," 1.

[12]Nickel, 6; Shumway, "Study," 176.

[13]Nelson, 193; Taylor, *Spirit*, 94,95; Sizelove, "Sparkling," 1; Chandler, II, 5.

the mud at the danger of slipping constantly, and this would give a little idea of what we saw inside.

"On entering the building we found the surroundings unfit for public gatherings . . . The hall is a very plain, unplastered room that would be far more suitable as a place for 'assembling' horses, than people."[14]

Even an avid follower, Clara Lum, wrote, "It was the most humble place I was ever in for a meeting."[15] Other sympathetic visitors compared the rough quarters to Bethlehem's manger.[16]

A crude pulpit was fashioned from two wooden shoe crates stacked one on top of the other and covered with a cotton cloth. According to one attendee, a junk man would value the lectern at about "fifteen cents." There was no raised platform and seating was arranged in a square around the makeshift pulpit.[17]

Arthur G. Osterberg, who also worked as a "straw boss" for a major construction company was working on the gas building next to the Huntington Building at Sixth and Main Streets. He asked three of the men on his crew if they wanted some overtime and hired the men to help clean and renovate the building. They worked for almost a week on the rundown building.[18]

---

[14]"It Is a Counterfeit," 4.
[15]Clara Lum, "Miss Clara Lum Writes Wonders," *The Missionary World* (August 1906), 2.
[16]Sizelove, "Sparkling," 11.
[17]Valdez, 5; Taylor, *Spirit*, 94; Bartleman, *Azusa*, 47; Ernest S. Williams, "Memories of Azusa Street," *Pentecostal Evangel* (24 April 1966), 7. Many have not understood the "shoe box" pulpit because they visualize contemporary individual cardboard shoe boxes. At the turn of the century, multiple pairs of shoes were shipped in larger wooden crates.
[18]Osterberg, "I Was," 12, 13; Jerry Jensen and Jonathan Ellsworth Perkins interview of A. G. Osterberg, May 1966.

The men brought in nail kegs and rough wooden planks for benches and added some odds and ends chairs.[19]

J. A. Warren and some other worshipers built an altar but Osterberg said it was too flimsy. He approached his employer, J. B. McNeil, a very successful builder, and asked for some 2 x 16's, saying he would replace them if they were needed. A friend of the pastor/builder with a long "express" truck carried the planks to the mission and Osterberg built the altar. When Osterberg went to pay McNeil, once a student for the priesthood, he replied, "Well, I would be a poor former Roman Catholic priest that couldn't do that much for some colored religious folks."[20] Most worshipers never knew they were kneeling at a "Roman Catholic" altar.

The second floor of the building provided an apartment for Seymour and other church workers. Another long narrow room upstairs that stretched the length of the building would become the Pentecostal upper room. A sign would be placed in the room, "No talking above a whisper."[21]

Almost a year before the revival began, Frank Bartleman had prophesied, "Los Angeles is a veritable Jerusalem. Just the place for a mighty work to begin. I have been expecting just such a display of divine power for some time. Have felt it might break out any hour. Also that it was liable to come where least expected, that God might get the glory." God found that "least expected" place at 312 Azusa Street.[22]

---

[19]Bartleman, *Azusa*, 47; Taylor, 94; Jensen and Perkins.
[20]Taylor, 94; Valdez, 20; Jensen and Perkins.
[21]Bartleman, *Azusa*, 55.
[22]Bartleman, *Azusa*, 16.

161

The earliest photo of the building as the
Stephens A. M. E. Church
312 Azusa Street
Photo used by permission
Miriam Matthews Collection

Biddy Mason
Larry Martin Collection

A muddy day in the Azusa Street neighborhood.
An 1870's photo of Second and San Pedro, one block from the mission.
Photo used by permission
Security Pacific Collection/Los Angeles Public Library

The Apostolic Faith Gospel Mission (Ca. 1906)
312 Azusa Street
Los Angeles, California
One of the earliest photos of the mission

Photo used by permission.
United Pentecostal Church Archives

A. G. Osterberg
Larry Martin Collection
Courtesy of Dean Osterberg

10 The Beginning: The First Weeks

The first service in the mission was probably held on Saturday, April 14, 1906, the day before Easter. According to one early participant, the building could provide seating for no more than a few dozen seekers.[1] Perhaps no more than ten to twenty saints gathered for daily services as evening services continued for a few nights at Bonnie Brae.[2]

On Easter Sunday, Jennie Moore attended Pastor Smale's First New Testament Church which was still worshipping at Burbank Hall. At the close of the service time was given for people to share personal testimonies. Moore told about the prayer meetings at Bonnie Brae and her experience with tongues speaking.

---

[1] Lawrence, 74.

[2] "Pentecost Has Come," *The Apostolic Faith* [Los Angeles] (September 1906), 1. With all the publicity surrounding the cottage meetings and only word of mouth to advertise the move to a new location, it seems this would be a necessity.

She said that Baptists were receiving the Pentecostal baptism. Following the testimony, she gave a long utterance in tongues. Ruth Asbery followed with the interpretation in English, "This is that prophesied by Joel." The effect on the congregation was varied. Some shouted, others spoke in tongues and some ran into the street in fear. After the benediction, many from the congregation stood on the sidewalk discussing the significance of what had occurred.[3]

That Sunday afternoon, services were held at Bonnie Brae where God was "working mightily."[4] Mack E. Jonas attended the Azusa Street Mission for the first time that evening. He said, "I had never been in a meeting like that before."[5] The news continued to spread.

On Tuesday, April 17, the **Los Angeles Daily Times** sent a reporter to the mission. His article, although very critical, could not have been more timely. The piece appeared on page one of section two on Wednesday, April 18, under the title, "Weird Babel of Tongues." He described the congregation as "colored people and a sprinkling of whites." Seymour was caricatured as an "old exhorter" who cried, "Let tongues come forth." The reporter's assessment of the meeting can be summed up in one word, "pandemonium."[6]

---

[3]Shumway, "Study," 176; Boddy, "At Los Angeles," 233; Nickel, *Azusa*, 4, 8; Bartleman, *Azusa*, 43; Carter, "Notes." Boddy says it was a Methodist Church; Nickel says Peniel Hall. Bartleman, who was present, and Ruth Carter join Shumway in saying, "The New Testament Church."
[4]Bartleman, *Azusa*, 43.
[5]Leonard Lovett, "Black Origins of the Pentecostal Movement," in Vinson Synan, *Aspects of Pentecostal-Charismatic Origins* (Plainfield, NJ: Logos, 1975), 132.
[6]This article will be reprinted in its entirety in another volume of this series, Larry Martin, ed., *Holy Ghost Revival on Azusa Street: Skeptics and Scoffers* (Joplin, MO: Christian Life Books).

At 5:12 A. M. the same morning, most of California was shaken by a deadly, magnitude 7.8 earthquake that all but destroyed San Francisco. At least 700 people were killed and property losses exceeded $400 million (1906 dollars).[7] Author Jack London described the devastation: "Not in history has a modern imperial city been so completely destroyed. San Francisco is gone."[8]

Shortly before noon on the 18th, two earthquakes shook Los Angeles within ten minutes of each other. People had gathered to read telegraphic dispatches of the disaster in San Francisco when the ground trembled beneath their feet. "Thousands ran in panic when the earthquake struck."[9]

The impact of this seismic activity on the Azusa revival should not be underestimated. Frank Bartleman wrote concerning the earthquake, "It had a very close connection with the Pentecostal outpouring . . . Men began to fear God . . . This paved the way for the revival."[10]

On April 20, the **Los Angeles Express** published a cartoon depicting the Grim Reaper with his sickle of death poised over the city of San Francisco. The caption

---

[7]Wayne R. Thatcher, Peter L. Ward, David J. Wald, James W. Hendley II and Peter H. Stauffer, "When Will the Next Great Quake Strike Northern California?" (April 1996); available from http://quake.wr.usgs.gov/QUAKES/FactSheets/When/; Internet; accessed October 1998, 1.

[8]Jack London, "The Story of an Eyewitness," reprinted from *Colliers* (5 May 1906); available from http://www.sfmuseum.org/hist5/jlondon.html; Internet; accessed October 1998, 3.

[9]"Earthquake and Graft Prosecution Timeline 1906," available from http://www.sfmuseum.org/hist/timeline.html; Internet; accessed October 1998, 5.

[10]Lawrence, 74.

read, "Ye Know Not What a Moment May Bring Forth."[11] This poignant message in a secular medium was a shocking reminder of the brevity of life.

Bartleman immediately published a tract about the earthquake which was widely read. In a matter of weeks, 40,000 were distributed in Los Angeles alone.[12]

A. G. Garr wrote his Burning Bush colleagues and reported, "How much this makes me think of the coming of Jesus! No one was looking for this awful disaster, but today on our streets you can hear nothing but the 'renewed horrors' coming on the cities around San Francisco as well as Frisco itself. It seems the fires of Hell were fanned by the festivities of sin until the iniquity of this great city reached the throne of God, and now they have reaped the reckless wrath of eternal justice."[13]

On the night after the earthquake, only "about a dozen" black and white worshipers were at the mission, but very quickly, more seating was provided and more seekers began to gather. Although Rachel Sizelove says there were only about a dozen present for an afternoon meeting in June, there must have been much larger crowds at night.[14] A. G. Osterberg said there were 100 present at his first visit to the mission. This was probably in the evening since he was empoyed by the McNeil construction company during the day.

Despite these small beginnings in a humble barn, Osterberg's report continued that within thirty days,

---

[11] "Ye Know Now What a Moment May Bring Forth," *The Los Angeles Express* (20 April 1906), 9.
[12] Bartleman, *My Story*, 42.
[13] A. G. Garr, "From Los Angeles," *The Burning Bush* (17 May 1906), 3.
[14] Sizelove, "Sparkling," 11.

"The meetings were attended by people of every group on the face of the earth."[15]

---

[15]Dan L. Thrapp, "Pentecostal Sects to Convene Here," *The Los Angeles Times* (9 September 1956), III, 11. Sizelove says it was July when large crowds were beginning to gather.

The Azusa Street Mission
Photo used by permission
Flower Pentecostal Heritage Center

The mission and W. J. Seymour
Photo used by permission
Flower Pentecostal Heritage Center

William J. Seymour
Photo used by permission
Flower Pentecostal Heritage Center

The first newspaper story about the revival
Los Angeles Daily Times
Wednesday, April 18, 1906
"Weird Babel of Tongues"

173

THE EARTHQUAKE ! ! !

"Come, and let us return unto the Lord: for He hath torn, and He will heal us; He hath smitten, and He will bind us up."—Hosea 6:1.

But what has God to do with EARTHQUAKES?

"And THERE SHALL BE EARTHQUAKES in divers places. But all these things are (but) the beginning of sorrows."—Matt. 24:7-8. Judgment for sin.

"Arise, go to——, that great city, and cry out against it; for their wickedness is come up before Me."—Jonah 1:2.

Her sins have reached unto heaven, and GOD HATH REMEMBERED HER INIQUITIES."—Rev. 18:5.

"When Thy judgments are in the earth, the inhabitants of the world learn righteousness." Isa. 26:9.

"God is angry with the wicked every day." —Psalm 7:11.

For IT IS GOD that "removeth the mountains and overturneth them in His anger; THAT SHAKETH THE EARTH out of her place, and the pillars thereof tremble."—Job 9: 5-6.

Therefore, "stand in awe, and sin not." (Psalm 4:4), LEST HE RETURN, and "wring out A FULL CUP."—Psalm 73:10.

"The mountains quake at Him, and THE EARTH IS UPHEAVED at His presence.

"His fury is poured out like fire, and the rocks are broken asunder by Him."—Nahum 1:5-6.

"I WILL PUNISH the world for their evil, and the wicked for th

"THE EARTH SH place, in the day 13:11-13.

And how else s subjection? and w

God must needs times. And who deserved? God d

"The fear of th wisdom."—Prov.

"THE EARTH SH

Frank Bartleman's Earthquake Tract
Written April 21-28, 1906

Buildings crumble in San Francisco
Photo used by permission
National Information Service for Earthquake
Engineering
University of California, Berkeley

San Francisco burning after earthquake
Photo used by permission
National Information Service for Earthquake Engineering
University of California, Berkeley

Crack in a San Francisco street, about 18th Street looking east

Looking North on Kearney Street from Post Street
Photos used by permission
National Information Service for Earthquake Engineering
University of California, Berkeley

This solemn warning from the secular press would strike fear in anyone's heart

From the **Los Angeles Express**

11 The Revival: Heaven on Earth

Only months after the mission was opened, Osterberg reported that as many as 1300 attended the services; up to 800 crowded into the building and the rest standing on the boardwalk outside observing through the low windows and open doors. Every inch big enough for a chair was "jammed full."[1]

The Los Angeles Daily Times reported, "The room was crowded almost to suffocation. Many were seated in the windows and scores who could not enter crowded around the lobby and struggled for a view. . ."[2]

Many were surprised, if not perplexed, by God's choice of instruments and locations, but no serious

---

[1] Osterberg, "I Was," 18; Jensen and Perkins.
[2] "Women with Men Embrace," *The Los Angeles Daily Times* (3 September 1906), 11.

seeker could doubt that God was sending revival. When Dr. J. G. Speicher left Zion, Illinois, for Los Angeles, he was a skeptic and a critic. He described himself as "bitter and opposing all these things." He "abominated" the Pentecostal movement. Arriving at Azusa, he testified, "I soon lost sight of the human in the more marvelous manifestations of the divine." Speicher said, "I saw and heard things that broke down my prejudice completely for I became convinced that it was none other than the wonderful power of the Holy Spirit that was working through this people."[3]

William Manley, pastor of an "un-denominational" mission in Oakland and editor of the **Household of God**, visited Azusa Street for the first time in August 1906. He said, "God had full control from first to last." The Holiness editor was so touched by the Holy Spirit, he told his readers, "This is the most heavenly place I ever was in. My soul is charmed and filled, and is dancing for joy."[4]

When Pastor William Durham of Chicago arrived in February 1907, he said, "As soon as I entered the place, I saw that God was there."[5] Clara Lum who had reported that Azusa "was the most humble place I was ever in for a meeting" added "but have never seen the power of God manifest in so many people, nor have I ever seen such manifestations of his power."[6]

For three years, services at the Apostolic Faith Mission were held three times each day-morning,

---

[3] J. G. Speicher, "As Dr. Speicher Sees It," *Zion City News* (28 June 1907), 1, 2.

[4] William F. Manley, "True Pentecostal Power with Signs Following," *The Household of God* (September 1906), 7.

[5] William H. Durham, "Personal Testimony of Brother Durham," *Pentecostal Testimony* (n.d., Vol III, Number 2), 3.

[6] Lum, "Miss Clara. . ," 2.

afternoon and night-seven days a week.[7] More often than not, there was no break in the services, with people staying all day and sometimes until dawn. Lawrence Catley, an early attender, said the services lasted from "can to can't."[8] Another observer said, "The place was never empty. The people came to meet God. He was always there."[9]

The atmosphere was so charged with God's Holy Spirit that people would worship all day without thoughts of food. The Osterberg family had the habit of gathering around their table for coffee and Sunday lunch at 2 o'clock in the morning after a full day and night at Azusa. The spiritual bread served at God's table was better than anything waiting at home.[10]

The services were dynamic. Everything was spontaneous. There was lots of prayer, singing hymns, singing in tongues, testimonies, scripture reading and then preaching. People shouted, shook, prophesied and spoke in tongues. At times men would fall all over the house, like an army slain on the battle field or they might "rush for the altar enmasse."[11] Jennie Moore led the singing, and favorite hymns included "Under the Blood," but the most popular was "The Comforter Has Come."[12]

---

[7]Cotton, 4. Apparently there were some short breaks in the schedule to allow the leaders to "meet alone, daily, with the Father, Son and Holy Spirit for instruction." See Manley, 7.
[8]Society for Pentecostal Studies Interview of Lawrence F. Catley, 1974.
[9]Bartleman, *Azusa*, 58.
[10]Jensen and Perkins.
[11]Bartleman, *Azusa*, 60.
[12]Nickel, 9; Bartleman, *Azusa*, 57; Manley, 7. "The Comforter Has Come" was written by Frank Bottome and William J. Kirkpatrick furnished the tune. It was first published in 1890 and is based on John 14:16, 26. See Donald P. Hustad, *Dictionary-*

It was not uncommon for worshipers to see bands of angels. Sarah H. Payne received the Holy Spirit baptism at the mission when she heard "the real message of His soon coming." A few nights later, she heard a legion of angels singing, "Behold, I come quickly." The heavenly visitors sang unbroken verses from the final chapter of Revelation and a few lines from other parts of the Bible.[13] Others reported seeing the "glory over the building."[14]

Prayer was a central part of the meeting. During a normal service, the congregation would be down on their knees six or eight times, praying for special requests.[15]

Seymour and others would often prophesy as was the case on March 2, 1907, when William Durham received the Holy Spirit baptism. Seymour had retired to his apartment to rest, but the Lord spoke to him saying, "Brother Durham will get the baptism tonight." He came back down to the altar in time to hear Durham speaking in tongues. Seymour raised his hand and prophesied that wherever Durham preached, the Holy Spirit would fall on the people.[16]

Testimonies often lasted for hours "as so many had so much to tell of God's blessings." On one night, little Ruth Fisher stood for a "long time" waiting her turn to testify. When the leader, presumably Brother Seymour,

---

Handbook to Hymns for the Living Church (Carol Stream, IL: Hope Publishing Co., 1978), 77.

[13] Sarah Haggard Payne, "The Fulfillment of a Life Dream," *The Weekly Evangel* (13 January 1917), 4.
[14] Bartleman, *Azusa*, 60.
[15] Jensen and Perkins.
[16] Durham, "Personal," 4.

said, "All right little girl," her courage failed her. She "became frightened and sat down."[17]

When proud men would come into the building, the Spirit would arrest them and humble them before the congregation. Bartleman said, "The breath would be taken from them. Their minds would wander, their brains reel. Things would turn black before their eyes. They could not go on." The church would simply pray, and God would do the rest.[18]

Los Angeles was a very cosmopolitan city at the time of the revival. One resident said, "I suppose there is not a tongue or people on earth not represented here, more or less."[19] Many times foreign residents or visitors in Los Angeles would come to the mission and hear people speaking in their native language. This phenomenon convinced and converted many skeptics that had visited mission because of curiosity or criticism.

Sister Prince, one of the early leaders of the mission, once spoke in perfect German, a language she did not know. Two visitors, both German born, in different parts of the building interpreted the message in tongues to the people close to them. Later they compared notes and found their interpretations were the same.

---

[17]Carter, "I Remember," unpublished manuscript, (1964), 1. Ruth Fisher, the daughter of Elmer Fisher was four years old when the revival began at Azusa. She later married Wesley Steelberg, an Assemblies of God General Superintendent. After his death, she wed Howard Carter, General Superintendent of the Assemblies of God in Great Britain and Ireland.

[18]Bartleman, *Azusa*, 60.

[19]Etta Auringer Huff, "A Scriptural Pentecost," *The Herald of Light* (14 July 1906), 10.

On another occasion a missionary from the Philippines came to the meeting to "expose the tongue deception." Anger rose up within him as he reached the mission. To his dismay, the believers recognized his poor spiritual condition and began praying for him. He was so furious he wanted to whip that evening's preacher. Soon, however, a woman approached him and began to speak in the dialect of a hostile island tribe where he had been serving. He knew that no one present would have knowledge of the language.

He was now struck by the authenticity of the experience and retreated to the upper room where the Holy Spirit laid him on the floor. He repented of his rebellion and the next day came to the "old plank" to seek his own baptism in the Holy Spirit. While in prayer, another woman came to him and spoke in a different language, also known in the Philippine islands. This time she said, "This is that," quoting the second chapter of Acts. This is all it took; the missionary went through to the Holy Spirit baptism and returned to his field of labor with a band of Pentecostal workers.

One lady was healed by the power of God and then fell into a trance for three days. She saw both heaven and earth and was given the gift of the Hebrew language. Her minister was fluent in biblical Hebrew so the "Lord sent her" to him. Although she had no knowledge of the language, she recited the twenty-third Psalm in "pure" Hebrew.[20]

Bartleman wrote that such instances were "too numerous to take space to mention."[21] Witnessing these

---

[20]Lum, "Miss Clara. . .," 2.
[21]Frank Bartleman, "Letter from Los Angeles," *Triumphs of Faith* (December 1906), 248-250.

miracles not only convinced many of the authenticity of the gift, but led multitudes to salvation.[22]

In fact, it is impossible to know how many were saved at the mission. The first person saved was a Hispanic worker who A. G. Osterberg hired to help with cleaning and getting the building in order for the first services to begin. Some black women from the Bonnie Brae prayer group were already at work in the mission, but when the new crew of workers arrived they immediately announced a prayer meeting. One of the ladies began witnessing to one of the workers, a Roman Catholic. Initially he resisted her witness, even trying to insult her with "smart" talk. She replied, "Don't you start to give me that kind of language. I want you to listen to me because you are going to have to give an account of yourself to Almighty God on the day of judgment." Soon he was off in a corner on his knees, weeping, praying and being born again.[23]

The first black man saved in the mission was Mack E. Jonas, converted on April 20, 1906, less than a week after the mission opened for the first service.[24]

If each individual testimony of the converted could be known and recorded, they would fill volumes. Bridget Welch, a drug addict who had been in and out of prisons for twenty years, was among the converts. Another morphine addict was saved and "has no more desire for the stuff." An infidel, who was twice committed to an insane asylum and who went from place to place denying Christ, was saved and was working to win others.

---

[22]Huff, "Scriptural," 10; Lawrence, 79.
[23]Osterberg, "I was," 13; Osterberg, "From the," 2.
[24]Lovett, 132, 135.

One man testified, "Last week I came in a backslider and half drunk and the Lord forgave my backsliding right in my seat and in a few days afterward, He sanctified me and baptized me with the Holy Ghost." A burglar who had been plotting to rob a house came to the altar at Azusa. He left his skeleton keys under the altar, was saved and baptized in the Spirit. [25]

Late in the summer of 1906, the mission sponsored a water baptismal service to immerse many of the new converts. About 500 "singing, shouting, joyful" pilgrims made the trip to Terminal Island, a beach near Los Angeles. The group spent all day worshiping the Lord and baptizing new converts. On this one day alone, Seymour personally baptized 106 in the Pacific Ocean.[26]

Seymour would lead the service from a chair behind the makeshift shoe box pulpit. Often he would bow low with his head inside the crates or leaning against their side, praying as the services progressed.[27] Witnesses remembered him as "very prayerful, a very quiet man."[28] The Azusa leader believed, "Our highest place is low at His feet."[29]

Like Evan Roberts in Wales, Seymour did not preach long or often, allowing things to go their own way, or

---

[25]"Sister Bridget Welch . . ." and "A young man saved . . .," *The Apostolic Faith* [Los Angeles] (November 1906), 1; "A man who . . .," *The Apostolic Faith* [Los Angeles] (October 1906), 1; "A brother testified . . .," *The Apostolic Faith* [Los Angeles] (December 1906), 3; "A burglar . . .," *The Apostolic Faith* [Los Angeles] (May 1908), 1.

[26]"A baptismal service . . .," *The Apostolic Faith* [Los Angeles] (September 1906), 4.

[27]Chandler, II, 1; Valdez, 5; Bartleman, *Azusa*, 58.

[28]Lovett, "Black," 132.

[29]"It is a blessed place. . .," *The Apostolic Faith* [Los Angeles] (December 1906), 3.

more appropriately "the Lord's way."[30] E. S. Williams, a regular participant said, "His preaching was very limited."[31] Yet, when he spoke, he ministered under such an anointing that his words changed the world.

What kind of a preacher was Seymour? A. G. Osterberg described him "as a slow speaking, humble, unpretentious, Bible loving, God fearing minister."[32] In another interview, Osterberg described Seymour and his preaching: "He was meek and plain spoken and no orator. He spoke the common language of the uneducated class. He might preach for three-quarters of an hour with no more emotionalism than that post. He was no arm-waving thunderer, by any stretch of the imagination. The only way to explain the results is this: that his teachings were so simple that people who were opposed to organized religion fell for it. It was the simplicity that attracted them."[33]

When William Manley attended, he described Seymour's message as "short" and "fiery." He said, "They speak with the most intense earnestness I have ever seen, and what they say is in the tenderest love. Not a harsh word is spoken. No denunciation of any one, except in tender love."[34]

Another witness recalled the response to Seymour's exhorting, "As soon as it is announced that the altar is open for seekers for pardon, sanctification, the baptism with the Holy Ghost, and healing of the body, the

---

[30] Donald Gee, *The Pentecostal Movement* (London: Elim Publishing Co., Ltd., 1949), 12.
[31] James Tinney interview of E. S. Williams, 8 November 1978.
[32] Jensen and Perkins.
[33] Thrapp, III, 11.
[34] Manley, 6.

people rise and flock to the altar. There is no urging. What kind of preaching is it that brings them? Why, the simple declaring of the Word of God. There is such power in the preaching of the Word in the Spirit that people are shaken on the benches."[35]

It was not the preaching, but one "Hallelujah" that captured Florence Crawford's heart. She said "It just went through my soul as she thought, 'God, I have heard the voice from Heaven.'"[36]

A holy awe filled the mission. When worshipers arrived, they wanted to meet God "first." Attendees did not salute each other or even shake hands with each other. Instead, they knelt by their chairs, which would be wet with tears, or they put their head under a bench or in a corner. They met men in the Spirit, not the flesh.

Neither songs nor singers were announced. Performances were never applauded. All of that was the "flesh." No one would stand to sing or testify unless they knew God had moved on them. Seymour said, "Dear loved ones, these meetings are different from any you ever saw in all your born days. These are Holy Ghost meetings and no flesh can glory in the presence of our God."[37]

Whoever was anointed with the message would stand and deliver it. It might be a man, woman, or child. The message could come from the back row or front row. A participant said, "It made no difference," and the official newspaper reported, "No instrument that

---

[35] "Bible Pentecost," 1.
[36] Crawford, *Light*, 9,10.
[37] Rachel Sizelove, "The Temple," *Word and Work* (May 1936), 2, 12; Bartleman, *Azusa*, 59.

God can use is rejected on account of color or dress or lack of education."[38]

It was wonderful when God moved on someone in the audience. One such time a little black girl rose to her feet and sang unto the Lord while tears coursed down her cheeks. Another leader in the mission announced to the participants, "God can use any member of the body, and He often gives the more abundant honor to the weaker members."[39]

One of the most remarkable features of the meetings was the "heavenly choir." As few as one or two or as many as twenty men and women would spontaneously join in an anthem, all in harmony and in different pitches, each singing in a language that was unknown to them. An observer described the manifestation by saying, "This singing service was literally inspired by the Holy Ghost. It was mostly in known tunes, but the words were chosen by the Holy Ghost."[40] "It was not a something that could be repeated at will, but supernaturally given for each special occasion and was one of the most indisputable evidences of the presence of the power of God."[41] Bartleman said it was "beyond description . . . the very foretaste of the rapture."[42] Williams reported, "It would sweep over the congregation, no words, just worshiping, intoning in the Spirit."[43] Many skeptics

---

[38]Bartleman, *Azusa*, 59; "Bible Pentecost," 1.
[39]Sizelove, "Temple," 12; Stanley Horton, "Twentieth-Century Acts of the Holy Ghost," *The Pentecostal Evangel* (21 October 1962), 18.
[40]Bartleman, "Letter," 251; Ewart, 78.
[41]Lawrence, 79, 80.
[42]Bartleman, "Letter," 251, 252.
[43]Tinney interview of Williams.

were convinced of the authenticity of Pentecost when they saw and heard this demonstration.

At times the meetings would become so boisterous that the police were called. On at least one occasion they were sent by the ministerial association. When the police interviewed neighbors and received no objections to the endless noise, they withdrew without hindering the meeting.[44]

With all the demonstrations of the Holy Spirit, some argued that the Azusa group was out of order. Nothing is further from the truth. Brother Seymour kept a constant rein, even if it was a loose rein, on the services. **The Apostolic Faith** reported, "This gospel cost us too much to run off into fanaticism..."[45]

In West Africa, there is a parable comparing discernment and holding an egg. If you hold it too loosely, it can fall and break. If it is squeezed too tightly it will be crushed and break. It must be held very carefully. Del Tarr noted that this same careful balance is needed while handling a move of God.[46] This is the kind of pastoral supervision Seymour gave to the Azusa revival.

Seymour himself described the decorum of the service: "Often when God sends a blessed wave upon us, we all may speak in tongues for awhile, but we will not keep it up while preaching service is going on, for we want to be obedient to the Word, that everything may be done decently and in order and without

---

[44]Nickel, 14; Valdez, 11; Bartleman, *Azusa*, 63.

[45]"This gospel cost . . .," *The Apostolic Faith* [Los Angeles] (Feb-March 1907), 1.

[46]Del Tarr, "Hold It Gently," *The Pentecostal Evangel* (8 November 1998), 20.

confusion."⁴⁷ He also told the congregation, "Now don't go from this meeting and talk about tongues, but try to get people saved."⁴⁸

The wise pastor counseled the church against "unbecoming and fleshly demonstrations." If someone would get too loud, pounding his or her seat, Seymour would tap that person on the shoulder and say, "Brother that is the flesh." While services were conducted downstairs, Bible study and prayer often continued upstairs. If the pastor was in the upper room and things got too boisterous while someone else was leading the services in the modest sanctuary, he would stomp on the floor or call out, "Hey!. . ., Hah!. . .,Hey!. . .Hah!" signaling a call to order.⁴⁹ Azusa Mission was not a place to blow off steam. Men did not "fly to their lungs," they flew to the mercy seat.⁵⁰

John G. Lake recalled a service when one man insisted on "getting up and talking every little while." Seymour endured the long-winded fellow for a long time, but finally ran out of patience with his disorderly conduct. Pointing his finger at the man he said, "In the name of Jesus Christ, sit down." Lake said the man did not sit down, he fell down and was carried out of the service.⁵¹

Clara Lum, who later left the mission, said Seymour had "true wisdom and gentleness in conducting the

---

⁴⁷William J. Seymour, "Gifts of the Spirit," *The Apostolic Faith* [Los Angeles] (January 1907), 2.
⁴⁸Lawrence, 86.
⁴⁹Sizelove, "Temple," 2; Lawrence, 86; Chandler, II, 5; Nelson, 235.
⁵⁰Bartleman, *Azusa*, 55.
⁵¹*John G. Lake: His Life . . .*, 252.

meetings. All realize that he is called of God and anointed for the work."⁵²

Elmer Fisher, another minister who led the services one night in 1908, announced to the congregation, "We have no planned program, nor are we afraid of anarchy or crooked spirits. God, the Holy Spirit, is able to control and protect His own work. If strange manifestations come, trust the Holy Spirit, keep in prayer, and you will see the word of wisdom go forth, a rebuke, an exhortation that will close the door on the enemy and show the victory won."⁵³

When asked about the physical demonstrations and manifestations, E. S. Williams recalled, "I think there was perfect liberty, far as I seen, never pressure put on anybody for or against."⁵⁴

As many as 100 at a time would be in the upper room seeking the Holy Spirit baptism or divine healing.⁵⁵ They would pray at three California redwood planks laid end to end on backless chairs.⁵⁶ Crutches, canes, pipes and other trophies of divine deliverance hung on the walls of the upper room.⁵⁷ One report said, "People were healed there every day."⁵⁸

---

⁵²Lum, "Miss Clara. . .," 2. This is a very significant quote, especially since some have tried to discount the importance of Seymour's role and define Azusa Street as a lay revival without ministerial leadership.

⁵³Stanley M. Horton, "A Night at Azusa Street," *The Pentecostal Evangel* (14 October 1962), 6.

⁵⁴Central Bible College Student interview of E. S. Williams, n.d.

⁵⁵Valdez, 9.

⁵⁶Taylor, 94; Ewart, 80.

⁵⁷Chandler, II, 1; Valdez, 9.

⁵⁸"In Azusa Mission. . .," *The Apostolic Faith* [Los Angeles] (May 1907), 2.

Emma Cotton described herself as a "walking drugstore." She suffered from weak lungs and cancer. After prayer at Azusa Street, she was instantly healed. For decades she never returned to a doctor. She said, "In those days . . . when they said God would heal you, you were healed."[59]

A. G. Osterberg saw his first miracle the first week the mission was opened. He said when people had a request for prayer, Seymour would say, "Let us stand and ask the Lord's help in this matter." Osterberg noticed a Catholic man in the congregation. He would cross himself and then watch the others to see how they prayed. As he came down the aisle with his wife, his face uplifted and clapping his hands, Osterberg noticed that the man had a club foot. After a few minutes of walking back and forth, Osterberg noticed he was no longer stumbling as he walked. The man was so deep in the Spirit he had not noticed the difference in his physical condition. When he realized he had been miraculously healed, he walked to the altar shouting, "Hallelujah."[60]

"I was a wreck in my body," was Florence Crawford's self-diagnosis. She was thin, diseased, and broken down after suffering from spinal meningitis. An early accident had left her with a spinal injury that required her to wear a harness with straps and a metal plate for eleven years. After visiting Azusa, she was completely healed. She testified, "Once diseased from the crown of my head to the soles of my feet, I was made sound and well through the blood of Jesus."[61]

---

[59] Cotton, 4.
[60] Osterberg, "From the," 3.
[61] Florence Crawford, *A Witness of the Power of God* (Portland: Apostolic Faith Church, n.d.), 5, 6.

One baby that accidentally swallowed medicine it had found in a closet was miraculously healed. The baby's body was already cold, but the mother cried out to God, "Lord, save my baby."[62]

When Maggie Bowdan first visited the mission, her husband, William, threatened to leave her if she got "mixed up" in the new sect. When Maggie came home baptized in the Holy Ghost, William changed his mind and became a seeker himself. He received a few nights later when they heard " a sound as a high wind" sweep the building. The Bowdans longed for another child and promised if God would hear their prayer they would give the baby back to him to preach the gospel. Once again, God came through and, Frank, their miracle baby, was given to God for the ministry.[63]

Rachel Sizelove's daughter, Maud, was afflicted with a kidney stone and had suffered miserably for almost twenty-four hours. According to her sister, Snowdie, she was "writhing in agony." Matt, another of the Sizelove children was sent to the mission to summon Seymour.

Seymour came to the home and approached the suffering child's bed. He opened a bottle of anointing oil, anointed the girl's head and said, "Little girl, do you believe God can heal you?" Seymour did not get "excited," he prayed "calmly" and believed God for healing. Instantly, the girl turned over in the bed and fell

---

[62]"A baby that...," *The Apostolic Faith* [Los Angeles] (January 1907), 1.
[63]Deborah Sims LeBlanc, *Like a Rose: Life, Times and Messages of the Late Bishop Frank R. Bowdan, D.D., 1910-1976* (Los Angeles: DLB Associates), 2,3).

into a "peaceful sleep." She slept through the entire night, healed by God's mighty power.[64]

A next-door neighbor was talking over a three strand barb wire fence when Lawrence Catley heard about God's power to heal. The lady said, "They pray and people get well." Catley was suffering from "consumption" and sorely needed a miracle. He asked his mother to take him to the mission. When she did, "God delivered him."[65]

These miracles of healing were not the only ways that God demonstrated His mighty power at Azusa Street. Demonic spirits were powerless when confronted with God's awesome presence. One young man fell before the altar at the front of the church. He groaned and foamed at the mouth as his body and limbs went through various contortions. Seymour courageously met the challenge and demanded, "Come out of him thou unclean spirit."

After almost three hours of spiritual warfare the man "turned and writhed on the floor, barking and snarling like a dog when finally the unclean spirit departed." The penitent was immediately baptized in the Holy Ghost and began speaking in tongues.[66]

Financial miracles were common place at Azusa Street. At the beginning of the meetings, offerings were never taken. A mailbox was placed in the meeting

---

[64]Fred T. Corum and Hazel E. Bakewell, *The Sparkling Fountain* (Windsor, OH: Corum and Associates, Inc., 1983), 39.

[65]Society for Pentecostal Studies interview of Lawrence Catley, 1974.

[66]"Tongues of Fire—Gift of Languages and Holiness Union," *Daily Oregon Statesman* [Salem] (4 October 1906), 6.

room with a sign above it, "Settle with the Lord." Members and visitors filled the box with their freewill offerings.[67] As God would speak, people would give. One witness says that Seymour would walk around with five and ten dollar bills sticking out of his hip pockets, with no idea of who had placed them there. From day to day food would arrive from unexpected and anonymous sources to feed the many volunteers who lived or worked at the mission.[68]

One day a wealthy orange grower resisted God's invitation to give a considerable amount of money to an outgoing missionary. The Spirit shook the man off his chair and into the floor. No one knew what was happening with him until he later testified, told the whole story, and said, "Yes, Lord."[69]

Although the revival started among a few who were African-American by race, Holiness by doctrine, and lower to middle in economic class, eventually men and women from all races, creeds and socioeconomic positions worshiped together in the unassuming little mission. While some intoxicated derelicts stumbled into the meeting barely standing on their wobbly legs, the wealthy railroad mogul Carlos P. Huntinton and his wife arrived in a beautiful buggy drawn by "well-groomed" horses.

When A. W. Orwig arrived for his first service in September, he was surprised by the presence of "so many people from the different churches, not a few of them educated and refined." He saw pastors,

---

[67] Sizelove, "Temple," 12; Valdez, 5; Cook, 3; Nelson, 262.
[68] Ewart, 78.
[69] Sizelove, "Temple," 12.

evangelists, foreign missionaries and "others of high positions." And yet, "all took part in the services in one way or another."[70] Even a critic of the movement acknowledged that the Pentecostal message had captured the hearts of "some of the brightest and best."[71]

Cecil Polhill, one of the "Cambridge Seven" who left the university to pledge their lives to missionary service, was baptized in the Holy Spirit at Azusa Street.[72] C. T. Studd, another of the seven; had a brother, George, who taught a Bible class at Azusa.[73] Other veteran missionaries who visited and endorsed the work of the mission include Daniel Awrey, Paul Bettex, and Samuel Mead.[74]

One of the best known attendees was Aldophus S. Worrell, a Baptist scholar and evangelist. Worrell was an extremely colorful character who was a Confederate officer in the Civil War. A graduate of Mercer University, he taught Biblical languages in at least three colleges and was the president of at least three others. Worrell wrote no less than eight books, translated the New Testament and edited several periodicals.[75] Concerning the Azusa revival, Worrell wrote, "There are real gifts

---

[70]Lawrence, 78.

[71]Josephine M. Washburn, *History and Reminiscences of the Holiness Church Work in Southern California and Arizona* (South Pasadena: Record Press, 1912), 383-390.

[72]Gee, 48.

[73]L.F. Wilson, "George B. Studd," in Burgess, *Dictionary*, 834.

[74]Gee, 50; *Heroes of the Faith* (Springfield, MO: Assemblies of God Division of Foreign Missions, 1990), 78; "From a Missionary to Africa," *The Apostolic Faith* [Los Angeles] (September 1906), 3.

[75]John Worrell, letter to Larry Martin, 24 November 1998.

of tongues here in Los Angeles, and other gifts of the Spirit."[76]

Dr. Henry S. Keyes, the president of Los Angeles' Emergency and General Hospital and a member of the First New Testament Church was an early believer. Keyes said he "had been one of the most skeptical . . . and did not wish to be convinced." Yet, in a short time, he was convinced that the gift was "genuine." When his daughter, Lillian, received the baptism of the Holy Spirit at the First New Testament Church, it was front page news in Los Angeles.[77]

"Professor" Carpenter, the head of the math department at Los Angeles High School was also a participant at the meetings.[78] Night after night he would listen to the exhorting of a spiritual leader with no formal education. The contradiction is obvious.

Educated and illiterate, rich and poor, brown, black and white all worshiped together. A witness said, "Divine love was wonderfully manifest in the meetings. They would not even allow an unkind word said against their opposition, or the churches. The message was the love of God. It was a sort of 'first love' of the early church returned." "We only recognized God . . . All were equal."[79]

---

[76] A.S. Worrell, "The Movements in Los Angeles, California," *Triumphs of Faith* (December 1906), 256.
[77] "Young Girl Given Gift of Tongues," *The Los Angeles Express* (20 July 1906), 1. See also, "Queer Gift Given Many," *The Los Angeles Daily Times* (23 July 1906), 7.
[78] Horton, "Pentecostal Explosion," 9.
[79] Bartleman, *Azusa*, 54, 58.
[80] Bartleman, *Azusa*, 54.

Frank Bartleman observed, "The 'color line' was washed away in the blood."[80] Other participants remembered, "Nobody ever thought of color" and "everybody went to the altar together."[81] A. G. Osterberg remembered, "In the beginning, color meant nothing to us. There were no blacks and no whites. . .It was God's Spirit welding us together, and that is a kind of unity that you can't define."[82]

The Apostolic Faith reported, "One token of the Lord's coming is that He is melting all races and nations together, and they are filled with the power and glory of God. He is baptizing by one spirit into one body and making up a people that will be ready to meet Him when He comes."[83]

In this respect, Azusa was fulfilling the New Testament pattern of "There is neither Jew nor Gentile, there is neither bond nor free, there is neither male nor female: for ye are all one in Christ Jesus" (Galatians 3:28). Many believe that this unity of the Spirit, more than glossolalia, was Azusa's unique contribution to the Christian church.[84]

What Seymour accomplished was truly phenomenal. In 1906, more black men were lynched in America

---

[81]Nelson, 234; Lovett, "Black Origins," 133.

[82]Jensen and Perkins.

[83]"One token . . .," *The Apostolic Faith* [Los Angeles] (Feb.-March 1907), 7.

[84]Nelson, 13. I disagree with Nelson's contention, "Seymour championed one doctrine above all others: there must be no color line or other division in the church of Jesus Christ because God is no respecter of persons." A reading of all of Seymour's statements and writings does not support this position. I would be more inclined to agree with Bishop J. Ramsey of Gloster, Mississippi who argues that Seymour's message was primarily a call to biblical holiness–the Holy Spirit would only fall on a sanctified life.

than in any other year. Jim Crow laws separated the races and patronized blacks.[85] Los Angeles newspapers were filled with racial epithets and slurs. Blacks were lampooned by reporters and cartoonists.

An editor in Bombay wrote, "Less than fifty years ago Negroes were owned by white people in the United States as slaves. No one but an American can rightly understand how despised the Negro is."[86] Yet, Seymour led an interracial revival that literally changed the world. Frank Ewart said, "His sweet winsome ways broke down all barriers erected by spiritual bigotry, and won the love and trust of the people to such an extent that they forgot their natural animosities.[87]

People were drawn to Azusa Street from all over the world. Pilgrims came from Canada, Africa, China, Japan, and India.[88] Many rode trains for more than 3,000 miles to visit the mission.[89] One family rode a horse-drawn wagon for five hundred miles.[90] Testimonies were given by people who said they felt the power of the revival when their train was still miles out of Los Angeles. Many more said the "atmosphere changed"

---

[85] Cecil M. Robeck, *The Colorline Was Washed Away in the Blood: A Pentecostal Dream for Racial Harmony* (Costa Mesa, CA: Christian Education Press, 1995), 12.

[86] Max Wood Moorhead, "A Short History of the Pentecostal Movement," *Cloud of Witnesses to Pentecost in India* (November 1908), 15.

[87] Ewart, 70.

[88] Seymour, *Doctrines*, 12.

[89] G. B. Cashwell, "Came 3,000 Miles For His Pentecost," *The Apostolic Faith* [Los Angeles] (December 1906), 3; R.J. Scott, "What The Pentecost Did for One Family," *The Apostolic Faith* [Los Angeles] (Feb.-March 1907), 7.

[90] "Some People...," *The Apostolic Faith* [Los Angeles] (December 1906), 3.

when they got within a few blocks of the meeting and the Holy Spirit literally "pulled" them along to the mission.[91]

M. L. Ryan said, "Converts from all quarters of the globe are arriving constantly not knowing why they come nor the impelling cause . . . they are just moved by the Spirit to go to Los Angeles and when there are directed to their destination, the Azusa Street stable."[92]

Bartleman wrote, "Conviction was mightily on the people. They would fly to pieces even on the street, almost without provocation. A very 'dead line' seemed to be drawn around 'Azusa Mission,' by the Spirit. When men came within two or three blocks of the place they were seized with conviction.[93]

Demos Shakarian and his brother-in-law, Magardich Mushegan were walking on San Pedro Street, looking for a job in the nearby stables when they heard the familiar sounds of Pentecostal worship. They did not know there were other people in Los Angeles who spoke in tongues. After inquiring at the door, they were welcomed into the mission.[94]

The Apostolic Faith, the periodical published by Seymour and his staff, grew until it had a worldwide

---

[91]Richard Crayne, *Pentecostal Handbook: A Reference Guide to the Origins, Personalities and Doctrines of the Pentecostal People in the United States of America* (n.p., 1989), 195; Valdez, 5,10; Ewart, 79. Crayne quotes Fred Anderson, an eyewitness. Ewart was an associate of William H. Durham and succeeded him as pastor in Los Angeles.

[92]"Tongues of Fire–Gift of Languages and Holiness Union," *Daily Oregon Statesman* [Salem] (4 October 1906), 6.

[93]Bartleman, *Azusa,* 53.

[94]Shakarian, 24.

circulation of more than 50,000.⁹⁵ Like Paul who sent out prayer cloths from his body, the workers would lay their hands on the papers before they were mailed.⁹⁶ Many who received the periodical were instantly healed, saved, or received the baptism of the Holy Ghost.

A band of volunteers worked on the paper, answered mail, prayed over the hundreds of letters received into the offices, and oversaw the expansion of the organization. Warren and Farrow, who had came from Texas to help Seymour, were regular helpers, but many more were added as the work grew. Glenn A. Cook, a former newspaper man, was the business manager and assistant state manager; Clara Lum was secretary, stenographer and editor of the paper; Hiram Smith was an associate who, along with Seymour, signed ministerial credentials (he was given the title "deacon"); Jennie Moore and Phoebe Sargent were city missionaries; Florence Crawford was state director; G. W. Evans was field director; and Reuben Clark, a Civil War veteran, served as secretary to the board of trustees. Mary Perkins and many, many more worked as needed.⁹⁷

Some of the workers lived in the apartments above the mission while others lived in a small cottage behind the church building. Meals for the mission workers were also prepared, cooked, and served in the

---

⁹⁵Cook, 3.
⁹⁶Fred T. Corum, "Azusa's First Camp-Meeting," *Word and Work* (January 1936), 1.
⁹⁷Cook, 1, 2; Corum, 1; "Sister Mary. . .," *The Apostolic Faith* [Los Angeles] (December 1906), 3; Nils Bloch-Hoell, *The Pentecostal Movement: Its Origin, Development, and Distinctive Character* (Oslo: Scandinavian University Books, 1964), 48.

cottage.[98] After returning from a short tenure as a missionary to Africa, Lucy Farrow had a room in the cottage where she continued to be used by God to pray for visitors to be healed and baptized in the Holy Spirit.[99]

Many of those baptized in the Spirit at Azusa became Pentecostalism's greatest leaders. Soon the message of Pentecost spread from Azusa and circled the globe. Phineas Bresee, the founder of the Church of the Nazarene and an early critic, compared the influence of the Azusa Street revival to a pebble cast into the sea. If such was the case, this small pebble created a spiritual tidal wave.[100]

---

[98]"Portland is Stirred," *The Apostolic Faith* [Los Angeles] (January 1907), 1; "The Lord has...," *The Apostolic Faith* [Los Angeles] (May 1908), 2; Nelson, 234.
[99]"The Lord has...," 2.
[100]"The Gift of Tongues," *The Nazarene Messenger* (13 December 1906), 6.

William H. Durham

Daniel Awrey
Photos used by permission
Flower Pentecostal Heritage Center

The credentials committee

Standing left to right: unidentified woman (Phoebe Sargent?), G.W. Evans, Jennie Evans Moore (later Mrs. Seymour), Glenn Cook, Florence Crawford, unidentified man (Thomas Junk?), Mrs. Prince. Seated: May Evans, Hiram Smith, Mildred Crawford, William J. Seymour, Clara Lum. Except for the little girl, these are the people who prayed (with the laying on of hands) for candidates who were receiving ministerial credentials.

Henry and Emma Cotton
Photos used by permission
Flower Pentecostal Heritage Center

A. C. Valdez, Sr.
Larry Martin Collection

Florence Crawford
Photo used by permission
Apostolic Faith International Headquarters
Portland, Oregon

Frank and Maggie Bowdan
Photos used by permission
Historical Center
United Pentecostal Church International

T. C. McConnell
Larry Martin Collection

George Studd

William Seymour and John G. Lake, front from left
Back row, Mr. Adams, F. F. Bosworth, Tom Hezmalhalch
Photos used by permission
Flower Pentecostal Heritage Center

The first issue of **The Apostolic Faith**

Samuel J. and Ardel K. Mead
Larry Martin Collection

12 The Pilgrims:
Williams, Mason, and Cashwell

Thousands of people visited the Azusa Street Mission from April 1906 through 1908. They came from all over the world. Most left with a burning fire that brought light to the world around them. It would be impossible to tell each of their stories even if volumes were to be written. However, the visits of three men–Ernest Swing Williams, Charles Harrison Mason and Gaston B. Cashwell–were especially important because of the role these men played in the nation's major Pentecostal denominations.

Ernest S. Williams

E. S. Williams was born in 1885 in San Bernardino, California. Williams' parents were common people who could not provide him many material things, not even a good education. Yet, they gave him something much richer, a godly heritage. Williams testified, "It was my happy lot to be taught principles of righteousness."[1]

The Williams family were charter members of the first Holiness church in Southern California. They proudly named their son "Swing" after the founding president of the Southern California and Arizona Holiness Association, James R. Swing.

At the age of 19, Williams became "very concerned" about his soul.[2] He was born again at a Free Methodist meeting.[3] In 1905, he and a friend decided to travel to Chicago to attend Bible school. Their poorly planned adventure ended prematurely in Colorado where, hoping to earn enough money to return to California, both young men found employment on a ranch near Denver.[4] Williams said, "Conscious of the presence and fellowship of the Lord whom I loved, I was yet conscious that there was something still lacking in my experience. But those among whom I worshiped seemed not to shed further light on my pathway than I was walking in."[5]

During the Spring of 1906, Williams' mother began to write about what was happening at Azusa Street. She told about his "old acquaintances" receiving the Holy Spirit baptism and speaking in tongues. One letter

---

[1] Saint Anonymous "My Experience in the Baptism with the Holy Ghost" *The Pentecostal Evangel* (3 January 1931), 2.

[2] Saint Anonymous, 2.

[3] C. M. Robeck, Jr., "Ernest Swing Williams," in Stanley M. Burgess and Gary B. McGee, eds, *Dictionary of Pentecostal and Charismatic Movements* (Grand Rapids: Zondervan Publishing Co., 1988), 886.

[4] Ernest S. Williams, "Forty-Five Years of Pentecostal Revival," *The Pentecostal Evangel* (19 August 1951), 3.

[5] Saint Anonymous, 2.

told how his father had been so touched by God at the meetings that he would break down and weep when he returned thanks at the dining room table. This made "a definite impression" on Williams' heart. He said, "I felt this must be none other than a work of God if it bore such fruits of righteousness and tenderness."

Soon, Williams received a copy of **The Apostolic Faith**. He said, "It would be hard to describe how the Spirit witnessed to my heart . . . it felt . . . something like the soft, warm, dripping of pleasant waters."[6]

In September, Williams and his companion returned to their home in Los Angeles. On his first Sunday back, Williams had his initial taste of Pentecost. He attended the morning worship service at Bartleman's mission at Eighth and Maple Streets. After the service, he walked to Azusa Street where the altar service was in progress. He said, "I wish I could describe what I saw. Prayer and worship were everywhere. The altar area was filled with seekers; some were kneeling; others were prone on the floor; some were speaking in tongues. Everyone was doing something; all seemingly were lost in God. I simply stood and looked, for I had never seen anything like it."[7] Had it not been for his deep hunger for God, Williams said he "might have turned away, for I had been taught that entire

---

[6]Saint Anonymous, 2, 5.
[7]Ernest S. Williams "Memories of Azusa Street Mission," *The Pentecostal Evangel* (24 April 1966), 7.
[8]Ernest S. Williams, "My Personal Experience at the Azusa Mission," in Wayne Warner, ed., *Touched by the Fire: Patriarchs of Pentecost, Their Lives, Their Visions, Their Ministries* (Plainfield, NJ: Logos, 1978), 45.

sanctification and the baptism with the Holy Spirit were one."[8]

Before seeking the baptism, Williams spent a short time studying his Bible, seeking scripture which might teach an experience subsequent to the experience of sanctification. He said, "I did not wish to be led into anything unscriptural; however, much the Azusa Street worshipers might seem divinely blessed. Then the Lord prompted me and I felt I must seek, as my heart was extremely hungry."[9]

Still not rushing into the experience, Williams, who had not been able to regularly attend worship while working in Colorado, prayed that he might be cleansed. A young man met Williams at the altar and told him if he would praise the Lord, he would be filled. Williams' interest, however, was "Search me, O God, and know my heart; try me, and know my thoughts; and see if there be any wicked way in me."[10]

Finally assured of his salvation and sanctification, he began to seek the Holy Spirit baptism. Late in September, Williams had a remarkable experience while praising and worshiping God at the mission. It was late in the evening and only he and two other seekers remained. He said it seemed that the Lord was dealing with his "very physical flesh." A woman, unknown to him, came near and said, "Lord, give this young brother rest." He said he experienced a rest he never expected to know "this side of heaven."

At about midnight, Williams got up from the altar and said, "I have gotten something, what is it?" He was

---

[9]Williams, "Memories . . .," 7.
[10]Williams, "Memories . . .," 7; Saint Anonymous, 2.

told, "You have received the anointing." Williams said he left the mission and walked in "undisturbed spiritual peace," feeling as though he was protected from any invasion by "the hills of God" that rose on both sides of him.[11]

On October 2, Williams received his Holy Spirit baptism. A young man who had received the experience the previous night prayed with Williams and encouraged him to pray with his "mind stayed on Christ." Although he spoke in tongues that night, Williams did not received the "ecstasy" he expected. The next morning in a grove of eucalyptus trees, the "glory met" him. The Holy Spirit not only took his tongue, but his whole being. Williams said that "language after language" rolled from his lips.[12]

Soon Williams entered the ministry, but not without some struggle. Paul Bettex once told him, "I never pitied a young man more than I pitied you when you started out. You seemed so limited in possibilities."[13] Williams, however, resisted discouragement and persisted. Ordained by Seymour, he traveled as an evangelist and pastored a number of churches before being chosen as the General Superintendent of the General Council of the Assemblies of God in 1929. He successfully held the post for twenty years and led the organization in the powerful, yet gentle, spirit of Azusa.[14]

C. H. Mason

Charles Harrison Mason received news of the revival at Azusa Street when F. W. Williams visited Mississippi

---

[11] Williams, "Memories . . .," 7; Saint Anonymous, 2; Williams, "My Personal . . .," 46.
[12] Saint Anonymous, 2.
[13] Williams, "Forty-Five Years . . .," 3.
[14] Robeck, "Williams," 887.

in 1906. Undoubtedly, he also read about the meeting in many of the Holiness papers that were circulating at the time. Mason said, "I saw that I was not above my Master. If He needed the Holy Ghost, I needed it to do the will of God."

Mason was born September 8, 1866, on a farm near Memphis, Tennessee. Mason's parents were members of the Missionary Baptist Church, and he followed them in the faith. At the age of twelve, he accepted Christ as his Savior following a series of visions of heaven and hell. In fact, Mason had many dreams and visions in his youth.[15] The young man prayed that God would give him "a religion like the one he had heard about from the old slaves and had seen demonstrated in their lives."[16]

In 1879, the Masons moved to Arkansas and worked on a plantation, hoping to avoid the yellow fever epidemic in Memphis. Their plans to escape the ravages of the disease were unsuccessful, and Mason's father succumbed to the affliction in 1879.[17] The next year, suffering from fever and chills, Mason, too, was facing death before his fourteenth birthday. On September 5, 1880, the "glory of God" appeared to Mason and he was instantly and completely healed.

More committed to Jesus Christ than ever before, Mason was baptized at Mount Olive Baptist Church

---

[15]E. W. Mason, *The Man . . . Charles Harrison Mason: Sermons of His Early Ministry (1915-1929) and a Biographical Sketch of His Life* (n. p., n.d.), 6,7.

[16]I. C. Clemmons, "Charles Harrison Mason," in Stanley M. Burgess and Gary B. McGee, eds, *Dictionary of Pentecostal and Charismatic Movements* (Grand Rapids: Zondervan Publishing Co., 1988), 585.

[17]Clemmons, "Mason," 586.

near Plummersville, Arkansas, by Pastor I. S. Nelson, his brother-in-law. Young Mason, still only a layman, traveled Southern Arkansas, sharing his testimony and working the altars at summer camp meetings.[18]

Following a call to the ministry, Mason was given a license to preach by Mount Gale Missionary Baptist Church in 1893. He attended Arkansas Baptist College for three months, but left the school believing that there was "no salvation in schools and colleges."[19]

Soon after his ordination, Mason read the autobiography of Amanda Smith, an outstanding black Holiness evangelist. He was deeply impacted.[20] In 1894, he accepted the Holiness doctrine of sanctification and preached the "second work" in Arkansas, Alabama, and Mississippi. The following year, Mason met C. P. Jones in Jackson, Mississippi. The two became fast friends and colleagues in ministry. Their Holiness message, however, was strongly opposed by Mason's former Baptist colleagues. Following a convention in 1897, Mason, Jones, and others founded a new sect, the Church of God in Christ.[21]

Before visiting Azusa Street, Mason, "hungry and thirsty," began preaching the Holy Ghost baptism to his congregation. Late in 1906, according to his own testimony he was "led by the Spirit to go to Los Angeles, California." J. A. Jeter and D. J. Young accompanied Mason on his spiritual pilgrimage.[22]

---

[18] Clemmons, "Mason," 586.
[19] E. W. Mason, 8, 9.
[20] Clemmons, "Mason," 586.
[21] E. W. Mason, 11-13.
[22] E. W. Mason, 14, 16; Witherspoon, 1; C. H. Mason, "Tennessee Evangelist Witnesses," *The Apostolic Faith* [Los Angeles] (March 1907), 7.

When he arrived at the mission, Mason was forty years old. He was a mature believer and seasoned minister of the gospel. After his first service in the mission, Mason said, "I sat by myself, away from those who went with me. I saw and heard some things that did not seem scriptural to me, but at this I did not stumble. I began to thank God in my heart for all things, for when I heard some speak in tongues, I knew it was right."[23]

The curious preacher remembered Seymour and the role he had played in his Holy Spirit baptism: "I also thank God for Elder Seymour who came and preached a wonderful sermon. His words were sweet and powerful and it seems that I can hear them now . . . When he closed his sermon, he said, 'All those that want to be sanctified or baptized with the Holy Ghost, go to the upper room, and all those that want to be healed, go to the prayer room, and all those that want to be justified, come to the altar. I said that (the altar) is the place for me, for it may be that I am not converted and if not, God knows it and can convert me."

Mason and his friends were called from the altar to Seymour's upstairs room in the mission. The pastor welcomed the brethren from the South and told them that God would do great things for them. He also cautioned them not to run around the city looking for worldly pleasures, but to "seek the pleasure of the Lord."

Satan used several people to hinder Mason. Jeter had some doubts about the meeting and criticized what was going on. When Mason met one lady whom he

---

[23] E. W. Mason, 14.

had known previously, he had to apologize for bad thoughts he had had about her.

Despite numerous temptations, Mason pressed on to the baptism. Finally, he said, "The sound of a mighty wind was in me and my soul cried, 'Jesus, only, one like you.' My soul cried and soon I began to die. It seemed that I heard the groanings of Christ on the cross dying for me. All of the work was in me until I died out of the old man. The sound stopped for a little while. My soul cried, 'Oh, God, finish your work in me.' Then the sound broke out in me again. Then I felt something raising me out of my seat without any effort of my own. I said, 'It may be imagination.' Then I looked down to see if it was really so. I saw that I was rising. Then I gave up for the Lord to have His way within me. So there came a wave of glory into me, and all of my being was filled with the glory of the Lord. So when I had gotten myself straight on my feet there came a light which enveloped my entire being above the brightness of the sun. When I opened my mouth to say, 'Glory,' a flame touched my tongue then ran down to me. My language changed and no word could I speak in my own tongue. Oh, I was filled with the glory of my Lord. My soul was then satisfied."[24]

Now baptized in the Holy Spirit, Mason sang in tongues, spoke in tongues, and even preached in tongues. Even the gestures of his hands and the movement of his body were totally yielded to God.[25]

Five weeks after his first service at Old Azusa, Mason and his friends returned to Memphis. Glenn Cook had already arrived in Tennessee and the "fire had fallen."

---

[24] E. W. Mason, 15-19.
[25] C. H. Mason, 7.

For weeks, Mason held services in a small frame church on Wellington Street. The highly successful meetings often lasted from 7:30 in the evening until 6:30 the next morning.[26]

Although C. P. Jones had encouraged Mason to go to Los Angeles and seek the baptism of the Holy Spirit, the two parted fellowship over the necessity of evidentiary tongues. Mason continued to lead the Church of God in Christ until his death. Today, the church is reported to be the largest Pentecostal denomination in the United States.[27]

Gaston B. Cashwell

Gaston B. Cashwell read about the Azusa Street revival in *The Way of Faith*, a Holiness periodical published in Columbia, South Carolina. Frank Bartleman had contributed news of the revival to this and many other Holiness papers. These testimonies created an intense hunger in Cashwell's heart. He reported the Spirit led him "more and more to seek Pentecost." He spent many days weeping and praying as God prepared him for a Pentecostal ministry.[28]

Cashwell was born in Sampson County, North Carolina, in 1862.[29] Early in life, Cashwell was a "prodigal son" who "raised his share of 'hell.'" According to members of his family, he "was an unlikely prospect

---

[26]Hans A. Baer and Merrill Singer, *African-American Religion in the Twentieth Century: Varieties of Protest and Accomodation* (Knoxville: University of Tennessee Press, 1992), 153.

[27]E. W. Mason, 14, 19.

[28]G. B. Cashwell, "Came 3,000 Miles for His Pentecost," *The Apostolic Faith* [Los Angeles] (December 1906), 3.

[29]H. V. Synan, "Gaston Barnabas Cashwell," in Stanley M. Burgess and Gary B. McGee, eds, *Dictionary of Pentecostal and*

for a future preacher, much less one that would ever amount to anything."

On one sojourn in Georgia, Cashwell, always a prankster, had another man write a letter to his grandfather saying he was dead. The trick contained more truth than Cashwell could have realized. He encountered a Georgia evangelist and was converted. The "old" Gaston Cashwell died in Georgia, and a new man was born. When he returned to North Carolina, some joked that the "dead man had come back to life again."[30]

Cashwell entered the ministry soon after his conversion. He was credentialed by the North Carolina Conference of the Methodist Episcopal Church, South.[31]

While working in the Methodist Church, Cashwell came under the influence of Abner B. Crumpler, an attorney and evangelist. Crumpler had left Methodism after adopting the doctrine of sanctification as a second work of God's grace. In 1897, he founded the North Carolina Holiness Association and in 1900, the Pentecostal Holiness Church.[32] In 1903, Cashwell joined Crumpler in the new denomination.

Longing to be in Los Angeles, Cashwell borrowed money and made the western pilgrimage in November 1906. He rode a train 3,000 miles to receive the baptism

---

Charismatic Movements (Grand Rapids: Zondervan Publishing Co., 1988), 109-110.

[30] Joseph T. McCullen, Jr., "Gaston B. Cashwell Once a Prodigal Son," in *The Heritage of Sampson County, North Carolina: 1784-1984* (Winston-Salem: Hunter Publishing, Co., 1984), 87, 88.

[31] Synan, "Cashwell," 110.

[32] Oscar M. Bizzell, "The North Carolina Holiness Association Started Here, 1897," in *The Heritage of Sampson County, North Carolina: 1784-1984* (Winston-Salem: Hunter Publishing, Co., 1984), 85, 86.

in the Holy Spirit. The six-day journey was a time for Cashwell to fast and pray continually.[33]

As Cashwell left for California, members of the Pentecostal Holiness Church were meeting for their annual convention. When Cashwell's nonattendance was noted, Crumpler read a letter in which the absentee stated he had received a new consecration to God. He also apologized to anyone he had offended and announced he was off to Los Angeles "where I shall seek for the baptism of the Holy Ghost."[34]

Arriving at Azusa Street, Cashwell had mixed feelings about the meeting. He thought some things were "fanatical" but believed that by and large "God was in it." The main problem for Cashwell, a proud southerner, was the mixing of the races. He said it caused "chills to go down my spine" when he thought of black people laying hands on him and praying for him. For five days he wrestled with this as he sought God in the upper room of the mission.

Finally, in his hotel room Cashwell experienced a "crucifixion" of his prejudice. He went to the mission and asked Seymour and several black boys to lay hands on him. Returning to the service on the ground floor, he listened as Clara Lum read testimonies from T. B. Barratt and others who had received their Pentecost. Cashwell wrote, "Before I knew it, I began to speak in tongues and praise God . . . He filled me with His Spirit and love, and I am feasting and drinking at the fountain continually and speak as the Spirit gives utterance both

---

[33]Synan, "Cashwell," 110; Cashwell, 3.

[34]Vinson Synan, *The Old Time Power: A History of the Pentecostal Holiness Church* (Franklin Springs, GA: Advocate Press, 1973), 97.

in my own language and in the unknown tongue... The Lord also healed my body. I had been afflicted with rheumatism for years, and at a healing service held here, I was anointed and prayed for and was immediately healed of rheumatism and catarrh and have a sound body and clothed in a right mind."[35]

The good folks at Azusa Street bought Cashwell a new suit and a train ticket back to North Carolina. On December 31, 1906, he started a meeting in his hometown of Dunn. The meeting, held in a three-story tobacco warehouse, lasted a full month and was phenomenal. Over a thousand people, including dozens of Holiness ministers, attended. People came from all over the south to attend the Spirit-filled meetings. The revival has been called "Azusa Street East."

As a direct result of this meeting the Pentecostal Holiness Church, the Fire Baptized Holiness Church and the Pentecostal Free Will Baptist Church all came into the Pentecostal movement. Later, while Cashwell was preaching in Birmingham, Alabama, M. M. Pinson and H. G. Rodgers, instrumental in the founding of the Assemblies of God, were Spirit-baptized.[36]

In 1907, Cashwell began publishing **The Bridegroom's Messenger**, a monthly Pentecostal publication. The paper carried news about the Pentecostal

---

[35]Synan, *The Old Time...*, 97, 98; Cashwell, 3.
[36]Joseph E. Campbell, *The Pentecostal Holiness Church: 1898-1948; Its Background and History* (Franklin Springs, GA: The Publishing House of the Pentecostal Holiness Church, 1951), 239-243; Vinson Synan, *The Holiness-Pentecostal Tradition: Chraismatic Movements inthe Twentieth Century* (Grand Rapids: William B. Eerdmans, Publishing Co., 1997), 112-122; Synan, *The Old Time...*, 99-104; Synan, "Cashwell," 110.

revival at Azusa Street, in the south and around the world.

A. J. Tomlinson, General Overseer of the Church of God invited Cashwell to Cleveland, Tennessee, in January of 1908. Tomlinson said, "By the close of the year, I was so hungry for the Holy Ghost that I scarcely cared for food, friendship, or anything else. I wanted one thing—the baptism with the Holy Ghost." On Sunday, January 12, while Cashwell preached, Tomlinson received the Holy Spirit and spoke in ten languages that were unknown to him. He testified, ". . . a peculiar sensation took hold of me, and almost unconsciously I slipped off my chair in a heap on the rostrum at Brother Cashwell's feet. I did not know what such an experience meant . . . As I lay there great joy flooded my soul. The happiest moment I had ever known up to that time. I never knew what real joy was before."[37]

In only a year, G. B. Cashwell had been used of God to bring four Holiness denominations into the Pentecostal movement and had seen the conversion to the faith of future leaders of a fifth, not yet established, denomination, the Assemblies of God.

---

[37] Charles W. Conn, *Like a Mighty Army Moves the Church of God*, (Cleveland: Church of God Publishing House, 1955), 84, 85.

Rev. and Mrs. Ernest Swing Williams
Photo used by permission
Flower Pentecostal Heritage Center

Elder Charles Harrison Mason
Photo used by permission
Flower Pentecostal Heritage Center

G. B. Cashwell

Photo used by permission.
Archives and Research Center
(International Pentecostal Holiness Church)

Downtown Dunn, North Carolina near the time of
G. B. Cashwell's revival
Larry Martin Collection
Courtesy of Sandra Bass

The cotton market in Dunn
The three-story building in the far background is likely the site of Cashwell's revival.
Larry Martin Collection
Courtesy of Sandra Bass

13 The Commission: Into All the World

O spread the tidings 'round,
Wherever man is found,
Wherever human hearts
And human woes abound;
Let ev'ry Christian tongue
Proclaim the joyful sound;
The Comforter has come![1]

Early, in the first year of the revival, a visiting preacher said, "The Lord has shown me that this movement will soon blow over."[2] If there is any element of truth in his lame prophecy, it is the fact that the breath

---

[1]"The Comforter Has Come" in *Azusa Street Mission: Fourteenth Anniversary of the Outpouring of the Holy Spirit In Los Angeles*, California, (Los Angeles: W.H Giles, 1920), 6.

[2]Lawrence, *Apostolic Faith Restored*, 80.

of God soon blew the movement all over the world. In fact, the missionary outreach from Azusa was almost unbelievable. First, workers began to go out in the area surrounding Los Angeles. Then they branched out further and further until many were ready and willing to take the message all the way around the world.

Miss Nancy Starret of Cincinnati, Ohio, visited a friend, Clara Pierce, in Los Angeles. Both received the Holy Spirit baptism and returned to Cincinnati with the Pentecostal message. Two thirds of Starret's home church, Christian Assembly, received the baptism.[3] Lucy Farrow took the message to Portsmouth, Virginia, where 150 received the Holy Ghost.[4]

After receiving the baptism in Los Angeles, Edward Vinton and his wife started a mission in Cambridge, Massachusetts. God gave Mrs. Vinton a vision of the building they were to use for services. Following the leadership of the Holy Spirit, they secured a former Presbyterian church on Hampshire Street and began preaching Pentecost.[5]

Miss Iva Campbell took Pentecost to Akron, Cleveland, and Alliance, Ohio. A Los Angeles newspaper called her "the 'gift of tongues' missionary." She caused such a stir in Akron that the ministers of the city passed resolutions "denouncing her."[6]

---

[3]James L. Dodd, III, letter to Larry Martin, 17 December 1998, with photocopies of a history of First Christian Assembly of God.
[4]"Pentecost in Portsmouth" (*The Apostolic Faith* [Los Angeles] December 1906), 1.
[5]Conrad Dottin, "How Pentecost Came to Cambridge, Mass.," *Apostolic Messenger* (December 1920), 12.
[6]"Converts Claim Strange Powers," *The Evening Review* [East Liverpool, Ohio] (7 January 1907), 1, 3; "'Gift of Tongues' is Satan's Work," *Los Angeles Record* (10 January 1907), 2.

Adolpha de Rosa and Harmon Clifford went to Oakland. Ophelia Wiley, Lulu Miller, Florence Crawford, C. W. Solkeld and G.W. Evans, Thomas Junk, and their wives went to Oregon.[7] Wiley and Miller were black, and the others in the party were white, demonstrating attempts to export the racial unity that characterized the Azusa Street services.[8] Wiley, a leader in the group, was a preacher, singer, and songwriter.[9]

Ansel Post went to Santa Barbara; Brigido Perez, to San Diego; Tom Hezmalhalch, to Denver; and Elsie Robinson, to Onawa, Michigan.[10]

When Aldopha de Rosa and Lucy Leatherman preached in Greenwich, Connecticut, in August 1907, they were accused of witchcraft and hypnotism, and met fierce opposition. A member of an angry mob threw an acid bomb into their tent, injuring de Rosa and "almost suffocated those present." The next night the ruffians tore down the missionaries' tent and set a torch to it. Following Jesus' admonition to shake the dust off their feet, Leatherman said, "We will not continue our work further in this locality."[11]

---

[7]"Spreading the Full Gospel" (*The Apostolic Faith* [Los Angeles] November 1906), 1; "Slow to Arrive," *Daily Oregon Statesman* [Salem] (10 October 1906), 2; "Sister Crawford Departs "*Daily Capital Journal* [Salem] (29 December 1906), 5; "Healed Blind Woman," *Daily Capital Journal* [Salem] (24 December 1906), 6.

[8]Wiley is actually described as "a mulatto or quadroon" and "yellow." "New Tongues," *Daily Oregon Statesman* [Salem] (20 November 1906), 6; "Healed Blind . . .," 6.

[9]"New Tongues," 6; "Claims Gift of Tongues," *Polk County Observer* [Dallas, Oregon] (28 December 1906), 1; "Sister Crawford . . .," 5; "Healed Blind . . .," 6.

[10]"Spreading . . . ," 1.

[11]"Fear Witchcraft; Mob Missionaries," *The Des Moines Capital* (7 August 1907), 3.

On another occasion, Ophelia Wiley went to Seattle. She "knew no one" in the city but the Holy Spirit led her to a particular house. When she rang the door bell, a woman answered and said she had been praying that God would send someone to her home. Wiley responded, "I'm a missionary, and the Holy Ghost sent me to Seattle."[12]

Lee Hall had ridden to California on a wagon train. To pay his fare, he served the travellers as assistant cook and rode the jenny in front of the chuck wagon to look for holes and obstructions that might hurt the horses that followed. He had been working on a ranch in Hanford when he heard about the revival at the mission. He took a train to Los Angeles where he was saved and baptized in the Holy Ghost. Hall returned to his native Ozarks and, with two other young men shared the Pentecostal message in northern Arkansas.[13]

F. W. Williams was saved and Spirit baptized at the Bonnie Brae meetings. He traveled throughout the South, preaching and planting churches. His first stop was in Jackson, Mississippi, where he had little success, but he was introduced to Charles H. Mason and shared the Pentecostal message with him. The first church he organized, following a tent revival, was in Mobile, Alabama. Returning to Jackson, he preached at a Primitive Baptist Church where the entire congregation adopted Pentecost. Other churches were established by Williams in Birmingham, Alabama; Century, Florida; and even as far away as Chicago, Illinois.

---

[12] Society, Catley.
[13] John Hall, email to Larry Martin, 9 February 1999. There are conflicting family stories about Hall's experience at Azusa Street.

At times Williams faced blistering oppostion. He described his work in Mobile as "a hard battle." Once, in Century, opponents cut his tent down and accused him of casting spells on people. The faithful put the tent up again and continued the services.[14]

This kind of persecution was often the rule for Azusa evangelists. In Salem, Oregon, the violence was so severe, the Pentecostals had to ask for police protection.[15] Saints in Indianapolis faced the same problem as hoodlums disturbed their meetings.[16] Juvenile authorities in Portland tried to take Florence Crawford's daughter, Mildred, away from her mother. They complained that nine-year-old Mildred was "permitted to roll around on the floor among Negroes and white men for a couple of hours every night."[17]

The press, too, was no friendlier to Azusa missionaries than they had been to the home church in Los

---

[14]Witherspoon, 1, 2; "Spreading," 1; "In Mobile," *The Apostolic Faith* [Los Angeles] (Feb.-March 1907), 3; "In Mobile," *The Apostolic Faith* [Los Angeles] (April 1907), 1; Sherry Sherrod DuPree, *African-American Holiness Pentecostal Movement: An Annotated Bibliography* (New York: Garland Publishing, Co., 1996), 246, 247.

[15]"Under Wings of Police," *Daily Capital Journal* [Salem, Oregon] (14 November 1906); "Ask Police Aid," *Daily Oregon Statesman* [Salem] (15, November 1906), 3.

[16]"Young Mob Assails Bluks' Temple," *Indianapolis Star* (17 June 1907), 3; "Bluks Appeal to Police," *Indianapolis Sun* (17 June 1907), 7; Mayor Will Protect 'Gliggy Bluks,'" *Indianapolis News* (19 June 1907), 1.

[17]"Color Line Obliterated," *The Morning Oregonian* [Portland] (31 December 1906), 4; "Padded Cell Religion in Two Forms Is Rampant in Portland," *The Evening Telegram* [Portland] (31 December 1906), 1; "Frazer after Holy Howlers," *The Evening Telegram* [Portland] (1 January 1907), 1; *The Evening Telegram* [Portland] (2 January 1907), 7; "Judge Frazer Issues Ukase," *The Evening Telegram* [Portland] (3 January 1907), 8; "'Bride of the

Angeles. In Salem, Oregon, the newspaper ridiculed and said, "Perhaps some of the 'Tongues of Fire' people who think they are inspired merely have twinges of the dyspepsia, or plain belly ache."[18] The paper also implied that speaking in tongues was "pigs squeak."[19]

Pentecostalism was mockingly called a "padded cell religion" in Portland. The press quoted an angry neighbor who complained, "For the most part, they are ignorant and feeble-minded persons who have gone insane on the subject. The place is worse than a madhouse when they get to going head on." Services were disparagingly described as "orgies."[20]

The stories of traveling ambassadors going out from Azusa with the spreading flame of Pentecost could go on and on. Their tales of hardship, persecution, and success are almost innumerable. The testimonies of thousands are known only in heaven, but those which are known would also number in the thousands.

Sometimes an experience at Azusa would start a chain reaction with tremendous results. When Harry Van Loon and Louis Osterberg received the baptism at Azusa, they persuaded William H. Durham from Chicago to come and seek at the mission. Durham came to Los Angeles, was baptized in the Holy Ghost, as previously noted, and returned home to bring his North Avenue Mission into the Pentecostal movement.

Lord' Has Severe Cold," *The Evening Telegram* [Portland] (4 January 1907), 12.

[18]"Bits for Breakfast," *Daily Oregon Statesman* [Salem] (5 October 1906), 2.

[19]"Pigs Squeak," *Oregon Daily Statesman* [Salem] (21 December 1906), 1.

[20]"Padded Cell...,1.

Pastor Owen Adams from Monrovia, California, also received the baptism at Azusa. He shared the message with Robert Semple. Semple received the baptism in the Holy Ghost in Chicago at Durham's mission. He shared the message with his bride-to-be, Aimee Kennedy, who also received.

Robert and Aimee answered the call to be Pentecostal missionaries in China. Mr. Semple contracted malaria and died in Hong Kong. His young widow returned to the United States and married Harold McPherson. Aimee Semple McPherson was the founder of the International Church of the Foursquare Gospel and one of the Full Gospel's most ardent proponents. In one of her meetings, Dr. Charles S. Price received the Holy Spirit and also became a national Pentecostal leader.[21]

The first missionary to leave the mission for overseas was Andrew G. Johnson. He ministered in Colorado, Illinois, and New York before departing for Spain, Jerusalem, and then Sweden. He was followed by dozens of God called workers, willing to give their all for Christ and the Pentecostal message.[22] Seymour said missionaries "are going almost every day."[23]

---

[21]Nickel, 18; C.M. Robeck, Jr., "Robert James Semple" in Stanley M. Burgess and Gary B. McGee, eds., *Dictionary of Pentecostal and Charismatic Movement*, (Grand Rapids: Zondervan, 1988), 776, 777.

[22]Arthur G. Osterberg, "I Was There," *Voice* (May 1966), 19. "Missionaries to Jerusalem," *The Apostolic Faith* [Los Angeles] (September 1906), 4; Andrew Johnson, "Letter from Brother Johnson," *The Apostolic Faith* [Los Angeles] (October 1906), 3; A.G. Johnson, "From our Brother in Sweden," *The Apostolic Faith* [Los Angeles] (January 1907), 3. Others may have arrived on the foreign field before Johnson since he stayed some time in Colorado, Chicago and New York.

[23]"We cannot give . . .," *The Apostolic Faith* [Los Angeles] (February-March 1907), 1.

On June 16, 1906, A. G. Garr, a Los Angeles pastor, received the Holy Spirit. One week later he was called to be a missionary to India. He had no money and no sponsors. By faith, he stood in the mission and said, "Friends, I believe God wants me to go to India with the message."

Almost instantly a man stood and offered $500 for the trip. A woman then gave $200 and another man gave $100. Within fifteen minutes and without mentioning an offering, the money was raised to send five people to India. Three weeks after he received the baptism, Garr left Los Angeles, heading east on his way to India.[24]

By October, 1906, eight foreign missionaries and thirty home missionaries had been sent out from the mission.[25] Yet, Florence Crawford could not have been more correct when she shared a vision that God had given her that fall. She saw a "beautiful bouquet of flowers" still in the bud. God spoke to her and said, "This movement is just in the bud."[26]

Julia Hutchins, who had received her baptism, her recently-converted husband, and Lucy Farrow led a large group on a short-term mission to Liberia, West Africa.[27]

---

[24]"Good News from Danville," *The Apostolic Faith* [Los Angeles] (September 1906), 4; William A. Ward, *The Trailblazer* (N.p., n.d.), 9.

[25]"Fire Still Falling," *The Apostolic Faith* [Los Angeles] (October 1906), 1.

[26]"Sister Florence Crawford...," *The Apostolic Faith* [Los Angeles] (November 1906), 2.

[27]"Testimonies of Outgoing Missionaries," *The Apostolic Faith* [Los Angeles] (October 1906), 1; "From Los Angeles to Home and Foreign Fields," *The Apostolic Faith* Los Angeles (December 1906), 4; "Latest Report from our Missionaries to Africa," *The Apostolic Faith* [Los Angeles] (January 1907), 3.

Lucy M. Leatherman, the widow of a medical doctor went to Jerusalem to minister to the Arabic population. A. G. Garr left India to work in China in the fall of 1907. He arrived in Hong Kong on October 9. M. L. Ryan had also led a party of fifteen or more to the Far East. In his group were two single women, May Law and Rosa Pittman, headed for China. The duo arrived just three days after the Garrs. After losing a child to the plague, the Garrs returned to the United States in 1908.

Two other members of Ryan's party, Bertha Milligan and Cora Fritsch, left their work in Japan to join Law and Pittman. The work in China was soon joined by Thomas Junk, Brent Berntsen, Roy Hess, Hector and Sigrid McClean, and several more Azusa Street veterans.[28]

Within two years the Pentecostal message had spread around the globe as an innumerable host of missionaries left for the foreign field. This is not to say that Azusa's missionaries did not face serious setbacks. Charles Parham originally believed that the gift of tongues would allow Spirit baptized missionaries to preach in foreign countries without learning the native language. Scholars call this xenoglossa. Seymour, following his lead, preached the same thing at Azusa Street. Faith in this phenomenon increased as many visitors at the mission testified that men and women spoke in their native tongue.

For example, Samuel K. and Ardel Mead, well-known pioneer Methodist missionaries to Africa, visited the mission and both received the Holy Ghost baptism.

---

[28]David Bays, "Missionary Establishment and Pentecostalism," in Edith L. Blumhofer, Russell P. Splittler and Grant A. Wacker, *Pentecostal Currents in American Protestantism* (Champaign, IL: University of Illinois Press, 1999), 53-56.

They documented many examples of people speaking in African dialects.[29] Although there were a few remarkable instances where this also took place on the mission field, for the most part, the gift of tongues was of little xenoglossaic value.

This inability to communicate with the nationals was not the only challenge faced by these missionaries. Many faced such desperate circumstances, as famine, disease and hostiliy. Not a few died and were buried in the land of their labors. Of the group that accompanied Lucy Farrow and Julia Hutchins to Liberia, seven perished, apparently from black fever. Those who gave their lives for the gospel included the entire family of G. W. Batman, his wife, and their three children.[30]

Paul Bettex left Los Angeles for China in 1910. He had no promised support. His only "outfit" was a Bible and a songbook. His wife Nellie died in 1912, after two years of malnutrition and near starvation. Bettex was martyred in 1916, his bullet-riddled body found in a shallow grave.[31]

Despite the hardships, the seeds of Pentecost were received into fertile soil almost everywhere the

---

[29] William Taylor, *The Flaming Torch in Darkest Africa*, (New York, Eaton and Mains, 1898), 485; "From a Missionary to Africa," *The Apostolic Faith* [Los Angeles] (September 1906), 3. "New Tongued Missionaries for Africa," *The Apostolic Faith* [Los Angeles] (November 1906), 3. Taylor the bishop of Africa said, "If there were a thousand such trainers as Samuel Mead and Ardel, his wife, there would in a few years be twenty thousand native evangelists and pastors in Africa under the leadership of our all conquering King."

[30] Robeck, "The Impact of the Azusa Street Revival: The Impact on Pentecostal Missionary Vision."

[31] *Heroes of the Faith* (Springfield, MO: Assemblies of God Division of Foreign Missions, 1990), 78-84.

message was preached. Within two and one half years Pentecost had been established in 50 countries.[32]

When the mission started publishing **The Apostolic Faith** in September 1906, it also went around the world as a Pentecostal catalyst. After M. L. Ryan, the editor of a religious periodical in Salem, Oregon, received the paper for the first time, he said, "I fell on my knees and agonized Godward a bursting soul of appreciation; a great and blessed conviction seized me, and I rushed out of the office shouting and praising God. The fire had struck my soul."[33]

A lady in New York wrote, "As soon as I began to read your paper, I began to shout and praise God and began to shake so I could not read for some time." She also testified of a wonderful experience in the Holy Spirit although she was still tarrying for tongues.[34]

A. W. Orwig received a paper and was convinced that the work was of God. He told his wife, "I am going to Azusa Street Mission on Sunday and see and hear for myself." On the first day, he stayed for six hours and left even more convinced. Soon he adopted the faith.[35]

When E. S. Hanson of Dallas, Oregon, received the paper, he carefully read it and then said, "The Spirit testified with my spirit that it was the true teaching of the gospel." After examining the scriptures he began to seek God for the Pentecostal gift. In a short time

---

[32] Nelson, 1.
[33] "An editor...," *The Apostolic Faith* [Los Angeles] (September 1906), 2.
[34] "As soon as...," *The Apostolic Faith* [Los Angeles] (January 1908), 4.
[35] Lawrence, 77.

and after receiving prayer from Pentecostal workers, the Holy Spirit came upon him. He said the Holy Ghost "took possession of my face and jaws and began moving them sideways, back and forth, and I began to speak in other tongues, as the Spirit gave utterance, saying only a few words in each, and then began to chant in the Spirit." He described the moment as "wonderful thrilling of joy sweeping all over me of such a sweetness of love that it is impossible for tongue to describe it."[36]

Thomas Ball Barratt was a very successful Methodist pastor, publisher, and church leader in Oslo, Norway, when he visited the United States on a fund-raising mission in 1906. Barratt had hoped to secure enough monetary support to build a "City Mission" upon his return. He went back to Norway without the finances he had hoped for, but in the good economy of God, he had received something much better. He described it as "a blessing of greater worth than every cent in America!"

In September, 1906, Barratt, who had always stood for "holiness and the baptism of the Holy Ghost," read about the Los Angeles revival in **The Apostolic Faith**. A great hunger entered his heart and he began written communications with the workers in Los Angeles. Mrs. I. May Throop wrote him from the mission encouraging him to stay in a "receptive attitude." She shared some secrets about receiving the baptism such as "Be nothing, that He may be all in all." Finally she closed, "When we have this baptism, we are very different from what we were before—and we would do

---

[36]E.S. Hanson, "Called and Baptized," *Apostolic Light* (19 November 1906), 2.

nothing to lose it . . . May God bestow the wonderful baptism upon you most speedily is our earnest prayer."

The fire of God fell on Barratt's soul on October 7, 1906. He continued to seek the fullness of God and corresponded with Glenn A. Cook at Azusa. Cook wrote, "The speaking in tongues should follow the baptism." In a later letter, Cook said, "The more earnestly we covet a gift from God and the more we sacrifice to obtain it, the more highly we will prize it when it is obtained."

On November 15, Barratt attended services at a small mission in New York. Lucy Leatherman and others from Azusa were in New York on their way to the foreign field. Barratt received the "full Pentecostal baptism." He said, "Immediately I was filled with light and such a power that I began to shout as loud as I could in a foreign language. Between that and four o'clock in the morning, I must have spoken seven or eight languages . . . I stood erect at times preaching in one foreign tongue after another, and I know for the strength of my voice that 10,000 might easily have heard all I said." Those who prayed for him saw a crown of light over his head and cloven tongues like fire in front of the crown.[37]

Barratt became one of the Pentecostal movement's most tireless leaders. He established Filadelfia Church in Oslo and helped spread the message across Europe and around the world.

---

[37]"Baptized in New York," *The Apostolic Faith* [Los Angeles] (December 1906), 3; "Missionaries to Jerusalem," *The Apostolic Faith* [Los Angeles] (September 1906), 4; Thomas Ball Barratt, *When the Fire Fell and an Outline of My Life* (Oslo: Alfons, Hansen and Soner, 1927), 98-130.

Soon after his return from the United States, Barratt was visited by Alexander A. Boddy. Boddy was the vicar of All Saints Church in Sunderland, England. He, too, was hungry for more of God. When Barratt visited All Saints in September 1907, the fire fell in England. On October 28, the pastor of Bowland Street Mission in Bradford received his baptism. This master plumber and pastor, Smith Wigglesworth, would be one of the greatest Pentecostal ambassadors. He traveled on five continents preaching and healing the sick.[38]

These stories, too, could be repeated thousands of times. Only the faces and places would change. An early participant in the revival wrote: "This great movement is like a little mustard seed planted in Los Angeles. It took root in a humble place which proved to be good soil and watered with rivers from heaven, it soon put forth its branches to nearby towns as Long Beach and out to Oakland. Soon the limbs spread north and far over the eastern states, and then clear over into Sweden and India. Now it is spreading all over he world, and how beautiful and green it is, and how the birds are coming to lodge in its branches."[39]

---

[38] Gee, 20-25.
[39] "This great . . .," *The Apostolic Faith* [Los Angeles] September 1907), 1.

William J. Seymour
Photo used by permission
Flower Pentecostal Heritage Center

Lee Hall
Larry Martin Collection
Courtesy of John Hall

A newspaper sketch of Iva Campbell
Used by permission
Flower Pentecostal Heritage Center

Mrs. A. G. (Lillian) Garr (right) and Lillian Denny

F. M. Britton and S. D. Page at the front door of the mission (note the 312 over the door)
Photos used by permission
Flower Pentecostal Heritage Center

245

Tom and Mrs. Hezmalhalch M. L. and Mrs. Ryan Lucy Leatherman

Azusa Street missionaries
Larry Martin Collection
Courtesy of Grace and Glory

**Alexander A. Boddy (Seated, right) with
Thomas B. Barratt of Norway (Seated, left) (Ca. 1907)**
Photos used by permission
Flower Pentecostal Heritage Center

Smith Wigglesworth
Larry Martin Collection

14 The First Challenge: Opposition

Despite all that God was doing at Azusa Street, there were still critics, skeptics and scoffers. **The Apostolic Faith** reported, "The religion of Jesus Christ is no more popular now than it was when Jesus was here. Many are rejecting the truth and are not going to receive it. The word not only says that signs shall follow them that believe, but that 'They that live godly in Christ Jesus shall suffer persecution.' This is also being fulfilled."[1] Another observer wrote, "It would be unlike Satan not to stir up derision and opposition."[2]

Secular newspapers had a field day. The first reporter to visit the mission described a "wild scene last night on Azusa Street." Another called the faith "weird

---

[1] "The religion," *The Apostolic Faith* [Los Angeles] (November 1906), 1.
[2] Lawrence, 79.

fanaticism." A cartoon ridiculed the worshipers as "holy rollers," "holy jumpers," and "holy kickers."[3]

When Della Cline, a "pretty" 23-year-old Los Angelean received the baptism of the Holy Spirit, the *Los Angeles Daily Times* carried a front page story with the headline, "Weird Fanaticism Fools Young Girl." According to the report, before attending services at Azusa Street, Miss Cline "thought but little on religious matters." After she received the baptism evidenced by tongues, she spent so much time in her room waiting on more of God that her "friends" became worried about her.[4]

The following newspaper account of what took place in the mission is especially descriptive, "Disgraceful intermingling of the races, they cry and make howling noises all day and into the night. They run, jump, shake all over, shout to the top of their voice, spin around in circles, fall out on the sawdust blanketed floor jerking, kicking and rolling all over it. Some of them pass out and do not move for hours as though they were dead. These people appear to be mad, mentally deranged, or under a spell. They claim to be filled with the spirit. They have a one-eyed, illiterate, Negro as their preacher who stays on his knees much of the time with his head hidden between wooden milk crates. He doesn't talk very much but at times he can be heard shouting 'Repent,' and he's supposed to be

---

[3]"Weird Babel of Tongues," *Los Angeles Daily Times* (18 April 1906), 1; "Weird Fanaticism Fools Young Girl," *Los Angeles Daily Times* (12 July 1906), 1; "Summer Solstice Sees Strenuous Sects Sashaying," *Los Angeles Examiner* (23 July 1906), 1.

[4]"Weird Fanaticism Fools Young Girl," *The Los Angeles Daily Times* (12 July 1906), 1.

running the thing . . . They repeatedly sing the same song, 'The Comforter Has Come.'"[5]

Another article in the **Los Angeles Daily Times** was especially critical of the racial make up of what the reporter called "the strangest service ever held in this city." Seymour is described as "the one-eyed Negro leader" who was surrounded by a motley company who shouted and moaned, screeched and prayed themselves hoarse in their frenzy.

According to the article, one young white woman "engaged in whispered conversation with the black leader and appeared to press her face against his perspiring chops in her eagerness to tell her story." The reporter said, "Pandemonium reigned supreme when the meeting was practically turned over to the Negroes at 10 o'clock. Black wenches threw themselves on the floor and cackled and gabbled." The obvious racial bias is evident throughout the article. The author even criticized because "whites and Negroes clasped hands and sang together." His greatest surprise was that "any respectable white person would attend such meetings as are being conducted on Azusa Street."[6]

Some items reported in the press went beyond the ridiculous. **The Los Angeles Express** repeated a "rumor" that Pentecostals in Monrovia were contemplating "making sacrifices of children, to appease the wrath of God." According to the paper, "timid" women were keeping a close watch over their children.[7]

---

[5] Art Glass, "The Comforter Has Come;" available from http://www.bonniebrae.org.html; Internet; accessed December 1998.
[6] "Women with Men," 11.
[7] Young Girl," 1.

Reporters who came to critique the services were sometimes caught by surprise. One such newsman was sent by his editors to write a comical description of the services. After witnessing the power of God on the service, his attitudes changed dramatically. During the service, a woman stood and began to speak in tongues. She had no idea what she was saying, but she spoke in the native language of the immigrant reporter. Looking straight at him, she described his sinful life in a "holy torrent of truth."

After the meeting he pressed his way through the crowd and asked the woman if she knew the language she had spoken. "Not a word," was her response. At first, he doubted her honesty but was finally convinced by both her sincerity and the grammatical perfection and fluency of her speech. He told her what she had said and that he believed it was God's call for his salvation, a call that he pledged to answer.

Returning to the newspaper, he told his boss he could not deliver the type of article he had been sent to write. He would, on the other hand, be glad to submit a truthful piece on the virtues of the meeting. Not only was he not allowed to give a positive report, he was informed of his dismissal from the paper.

Bartleman wrote, "The newspapers began to ridicule and abuse the meetings, thus giving us much free advertising. This brought the crowds. The devil overdid himself again."[8] Another writer commenting on the critical reports said hungry people came because they understood "the devil would not fight a thing unless God was in it."[9]

---

[8]Bartleman, *Azusa*, 48.
[9]"The secular papers," *The Apostolic Faith* [Los Angeles] (September 1906), 1.

Azusa Street worshipers were cursed, jailed and physically assaulted. Owen "Irish" Lee was a rough customer before he was saved in the mission. This former Catholic had been a bartender and street fighter both in his homeland of Ireland and later in New York City. Once he fought four police officers because he had seen them abuse a drunkard.

After his conversion, a Catholic woman and her "giant" accomplice came to the mission with a stout rope to hang Irish from a street lamp. They were upset that he had left his old religion and accepted Christ as his savior. The man spit in Irish's face and then punched him in the face. By the grace of God, Irish turned the other cheek.

When the man tried to hit Irish again, his fist was stopped by the power of God, which then threw him backwards into the gutter. Irish prayed for his enemies and was thrilled a few night later when he saw them both enter the mission and receive salvation from their sins.[10]

In the face of growing opposition, the mission's periodical courageously proclaimed, "We are ready, not only to go to prison, but to give our lives for Jesus." This was not just cheap talk. Many, many, of the Azusa faithful were arrested for their faith. According to **The Los Angeles Express**, the entire congregation had been "subject to threats of arrest for the disturbances made."[11]

When one man was taken into custody, a witness saw an angel stand by him as he stood in the court. When another couple were arrested for holding a

---

[10] Valdez, 12.
[11] "Young Girl," 1.

street meeting in Los Angeles, the lady sang all the way to jail and shouted and prayed while they were there. The authorities were "anxious to get rid of them."

One brother was arrested for speaking in tongues before two police officers. Convinced that he was "crazy," they put him in the emergency hospital and brought insanity charges against him. At the police station, the emergency room, and later in the county hospital and courtroom, he continued to speak in tongues. Some, including the judge, recognized the language he was speaking. Although several came to testify in his behalf, he was released without needing to call a single witness.

Not long afterwards, the same worker was arrested for disturbing the peace while conducting a street meeting. Among other things that went on in the courthouse, he rebuked the antagonistic city attorney with a message in tongues. The jury deliberated for more than eight hours, but did not reach a verdict. The charges against him were eventually dropped.[12]

Henry Prentice, a black brother, went from Azusa to Whittier where he conducted an open air meeting. Following the Azusa example of not receiving offerings, Prentice could demonstrate no "visible means of support," so the police arrested him for vagrancy.

This was not the first time Prentice had encountered the heavy hand of the law. In June 1906, he was arrested after he disrupted a tent meeting at First and Cummings Streets. Prentice "nearly caused a riot" when he pointed his finger at Emma Robinson, the daughter

---

[12] "Arrested for Jesus' Sake," *The Apostolic Faith* [Los Angeles] (December 1906), 3.

of a white preacher, J. S. Robinson of the Church of God, and told the young lady she was a sinner. Some in the congregation wanted to "hang" Prentice. Someone summoned the police, who arrived and arrested the preacher for disturbing the peace. Prentice was tried and sentenced to thirty days on the chain gang.[13]

Prentice had received only one year of formal education, but on the occasion of his arrest for vagrancy, he insisted on representing himself in a jury trial. He also claimed his legal right to participate in the selection of the jury. He read Matthew 10 to every prospective juror and explained that Jesus told His disciples to go out and preach without taking gold, silver or brass in their purse. He emphasized verses 14 and 15, "And whosoever shall not receive you, nor hear your words, when ye depart out of the house or city, shake off the dust of your feet. Verily I say unto you, it shall be more tolerable for the land of Sodom and Gomorrah in the day of judgment, than for that city."

The judge became exasperated with Prentice and angrily threatened to throw a chair at him. After every outburst from the bench, the defendant would reply, "The Lord bless you, judge."

After Prentice had selected his twelve jurors and read Matthew 10 twelve times, he told the judge to proceed with the trial. The prosecuting attorney, however, had a different plan. He said he would not face Prentice for "all the money in the United States." The case was dismissed and the attorney and judge both

---

[13]"Negro Preacher on Trial in Police Court," *The Los Angeles Express* (12 June 1906), 2; "Abusive Preacher Convicted," *The Los Angeles Express* (13 June 1906), 6; "Negro Preacher to Work in Chain Gang," *The Los Angeles Express* (14 June 1906), 1.

found their way to Azusa where they were born again.[14]

Henry McClain, a husband and father of three little children, did not fare as well as Prentice. He was arrested in Whittier for having a prayer meeting in his home. The police said they were making "unusual noise and disturbing the peace of the neighborhood." McClain was sentenced to 30 days of hard labor on a chain gang.

Not discouraged, he said, "I never had such power of God on me as when I was in that jail." A number of Mexicans were in the jail with McClain, who preached to them in Spanish, a language he did not know. Only after he was through did someone tell him that he had read Isaiah 55, a chapter he also did not know. McClain said, "There was not a one of them but was weeping bitterly."[15]

---

[14]Nickel, 15-18. In 1908, Prentice was working in Indianapolis, Indiana, when he was arrested for interrupting the services at a Methodist church. This was the 23rd time he was arrested for preaching the gospel. Again, Prentice represented himself. About one hundred believers were in the courtroom and sang "I'm on the Hallelujah Side" as the trial began. Prentice interviewed every prospective juror, asking if they were Christians. The jury, however, fined Prentice $25. The judge fined him $10 for calling the Methodist pastor a lawyer and another $25 for contempt for saying, "The Lord bless you." For more details, see "'Tongues' at Allen Chapel," *Indianapolis News* (24 April 1908), 7; "Bluks Invade Allen Chapel and Stop Sermon," *Indianapolis Star* (24 April 1907), 1; "Invade the Bluk's Temple," *Indianapolis Star* (25 April 1907), 1; "'Gliggy Bluks' Are Fined," *Indianapolis Star* (26 April 1907), 3; "For Disturbing Service," *Indianapolis News* (4 March 1908), 7; "Gliggy Bluk Pleads Own Case and Pays 3 Fines," *Indianapolis Star* (5 March 1908), 1; "Gliggy Bluk Preacher Fined for Contempt," *Indianapolis News* (5 March 1908), 16.

[15]"Arrested," 3; "In Jail for Jesus' Sake," *The Apostolic Faith* [Los Angeles] (November 1906), 4.

In Pasadena, Ansel Post and his Household of Faith congregation were harassed by the civil authorities after neighbors complained of the noises coming from their "big tent." It was reported that the "'Householders' hold meetings frequently until after midnight and that they make so much noise that it is impossible for anyone within two blocks to sleep. One of the features of their services is the casting out of devils. These devils invariably depart from the bodies of their victims to the accompaniment of unearthly shrieks and groans."

At first the authorities gave them three days to tone down their services or move their tent. Defiant, Post announced, "We have received a message from the Lord and He tells us not to move our tent." Their injunction ignored, police raided the tent on July 12. Post was arrested, hauled into court, ordered to take the tent down and fined fifty dollars.[16] When Post moved the tent, the **Pasadena Daily News** reported "Buffeted about from pillar to post, with no one caring for their presence in the vicinity, followed by crowds of the curious and, according to their complaint, 'beset by ruffians on all sides,' the members of the 'Household of God' sect are now without home and friends and minus a place to lay their heads, figuratively speaking."[17]

---

[16]"Says House of God Is Noisy," *Pasadena Daily News* (3 July 1906), 1;"Tongues Gift Given Many," *Pasadena Daily News* (5 July 1906), 1; "Lord's Advice Hold the Fort," *Pasadena Daily News* (9 July 1906), 1; "Council Orders Tent of Houshold Moved," *Pasadena Daily News* (10 July 1906), 1; "Heed Divine Injunction," *Pasadena Daily News* (12 July 1906), 10; "Head of Sect Is Disturber," *Pasadena Daily News* (13 July 1906), 12; "Sect Leader Is Fined $50," *The Los Angeles Express* (13 July 1906), 15.

[17]"Household Is On Move Again," *Pasadena Daily News* (18 July 1906), 12.

Yet, the most stinging attacks did not come from the secular media or law enforcement, but from the Christian community. E. P. Ryland, pastor of Trinity Methodist Episcopal South Church and president of the Los Angeles Church Federation, visited the mission and reported to the newspaper that what was going on was nothing worse than "modern religious fanaticism." Ryland expressed his concern, however, that "certain of the enthusiasts might lose their reason through over zeal and become dangerous."[18]

The Azusa meetings did, however, have a positive impact on the established churches in Los Angeles. In response to the Azusa success, the denominational churches operating as the Church Federation began a series of street meetings and campaigns in the summer of 1906. The **Los Angeles Express** reported, "This movement is an outgrowth of a sentiment on the part of Rev. Ryland and his associates, that the orthodox churches are falling behind other religious organizations in missionary effort, and that, for this reason, the people are drawn away from the beaten paths of established faiths." The paper also reported that it was the revival at Azusa Street and Smale's church that "aroused the federation to action."

Ryland commented, "This effort must not be construed into a fight against the new creeds ... New creeds are springing up here and there, and the promoters are imbued with the spirit of missionary work to such an extent that they never rest. On the other hand the orthodox churches in many cases are content with enjoying the light they have received."[19]

---

[18]"Young Girl," 1.

[19]"Churches Aroused to Action," *Los Angeles Express* (July 18, 1906), 12. See also "Church Census for City," *Los Angeles Express*

Holiness churches, Baptist churches and conservatives that lost so many members to the Pentecostal movement were even harsher critics. Holiness papers called the Pentecostals "deluded," "heretical," "counterfeits," "fad worshippers" and much worse.[20] Many church members were asked to leave their churches for visiting Azusa Street.[21]

When William Pendleton, pastor of Hawthorne Street Holiness Church, and some of his members received the Pentecostal experience, the church had a visit from W. M. Kelly, an overseer, who informed them they had "obtained strange fire and had thereby come under the influence of a deceiving, lying spirit and were under a strong delusion." Soon afterwards a denominational meeting was held at the church, and Pendleton was told not to teach "a third blessing."

A few weeks later, Kelly returned and found the Spirit moving, with people lying in the floor and others speaking in tongues. They asked him if he wanted to receive the baptism of the Holy Spirit and he replied,

---

(July 13, 1906), 6; "Church Workers to Meet Tonight," *Los Angeles Express* (July 24, 1906), 12; "Praying Bands for Churches," *Los Angeles Express* (July 25, 1906), 6; "Open-air Service at Trinity Successful," *Los Angeles Express* (July 31, 1906), 4; "Praying Bands Are Forming," *Los Angeles Express* (August 1, 1906), 7; "Open-air Meeting at Trinity Tonight," *Los Angeles Express* (August 2, 1906), 3; ""Plan for Religious Crusade," *Los Angeles Express* (August 3, 1906), 7; "Outdoor Religious Services in Westlake," *Los Angeles Express* (August 4, 1906), 15.

[20]"The Gift of Tongues," 6; "About Tongues," *The Church Herald and Holiness Banner* (27 July 1907); R. L. Averill, "The Apostolic Faith Movement," *The Holiness Evangel* (1 January 1907), 1. There are literally more cases than can be cited. For a few examples, watch for Larry Martin, ed., *Holy Ghost Revival on Azusa Street: Skeptics and Scoffers* (Christian Life Books).

[21]Valdez, 10.

"Another Holy Ghost? No. I would have to deny Him who is living in my heart, to receive another." Mrs. McGowan, of the congregation, shook her finger at him and rebuked him while speaking in tongues. A Mrs. Lemoine said the Spirit was grieved. Kelly stayed until the meeting ended at 5 A. M., but was convinced that he had seen the fulfillment of 2 Thessalonians 2:11, "And for this cause God shall send them a strange delusion, that they should believe a lie."

On August 27, 1906, the elders of the church, led by Asa Adams, forced Pendleton and twenty-eight members to withdraw from the Holiness church, "being out of harmony with the doctrines and rules of the church, they holding that the evidence of receiving the baptism of the Holy Spirit was always the gift of languages; also teaching that the disciples were sanctified before the day of Pentecost, and did not receive the baptism of the Holy Ghost until receiving the gift of tongues, this being in direct opposition to the teaching of the Holiness Church as set forth in the book of rules . . ." According to the Holiness leaders, Pendleton and the other Pentecostals "denied their faith."[22]

The Burning Bush lambasted A. G. Garr when he received his baptism. According to the editor, Garr was "led away by the people known in Los Angeles as the 'Tongues' people, who profess to receive unknown tongues as an evidence of a third blessing." Further it was reported, ". . .the light has left the eye, the fire is gone and we can see clearly that he has lost the Holy Ghost." The editorial concluded, "It is with great personal regret we record this downfall of a man of good gifts and success as a soul winner."[23]

---

[22] Washburn, 383-390.
[23] "A. G. Garr," *The Burning Bush* (19 July 1906), 4.

W. M. Collins, a Baptist preacher, reflected on his Pentecostal experience in **The Upper Room**, a periodical published by Elmer Fisher in 1910. He wrote, "What has it meant to me? On the one hand it has meant *loss*—loss of friends, loss of money, loss of position, loss of reputation. On the other hand *gain*. Here I fail. I cannot tell the heights, the depths, the lengths, the breadths of the riches which this blessing has brought into my experience."[24]

It seems paradoxical that those who had the most in common with the Azusa worshipers were the most critical and violently opposed to the outpouring of the Holy Spirit. Donald Gee, a leader of the Pentecostal movement in Europe once wrote, ". . . there seems to be a law which students are compelled to observe, that the last wave of spiritual revival in the church nearly always seems to offer the greatest opposition to the oncoming wave of blessing and advance."[25]

Before the great revival began in Los Angeles, a resident of the city had a very descriptive vision of the coming movement. He saw individual fires springing up and then gathering together to form a solid wall of flames. A preacher was trying to put the fire out with a gunny sack, but his futile labors were useless against the growing inferno. **The Apostolic Faith** reported the vision and commented, "The man with the wet gunny sack is here also, but his efforts only call attention to the fire."[26]

---

[24]Reprinted in "Impressions of Pentecost 35 Years Ago," *The Pentecostal Evangel* (24 February 1945), 2.
[25]Gee, 19.
[26]"Before the fire," *The Apostolic Faith* [Los Angeles] (November 1906), 1.

"Summer Solstice Sees Strenuous Sects Sashaying"
The Evening News

261

**This cartoon depicts a service at the
First New Testament Church**
Caption: "Types of those who claim to have received the 'gift of tongues' at
the New Testament Church."
(Sketches of Bartleman, Smale, Keyes and others)
The Los Angeles Times
July 23, 1906

Della Cline
Larry Martin Collection

The Azusa Street Mission
Photo used by permission
Flower Pentecostal Heritage Center

This cartoon from the cover of *The Burning Bush* demonstrates the attitude of the Holiness movement toward Pentecostals. "Tongues" are one of the bubbles blown by the devil. The caption for the cartoon was "Satanic Delusions."
November 15, 1906

A few examples from dozens of Christian periodicals that published articles attacking the work of the mission. A comprehensive collection is contained in another book in the Complete Azusa Street Library, *Skeptics and Scoffers*.

William Joseph Seymour (Ca. 1915),
pastor of
the Apostolic Faith Gospel Mission

Photo used by permission.
Apostolic Faith International Headquarters
Portland, Oregon

A. G. Osterberg and Owen "Irish" Lee
Larry Martin Collection
(Courtesy of Dean Osterberg)

Phineas F. Bresee
Larry Martin Collection

15 The Second Challenge: Division

Anna Hall, one of Charles Parham's workers, came to Los Angeles from Texas in the summer of 1906. She was soon followed by the Walter J. Oyler family and Mr. and Mrs. Quinton.[1] The Oylers were residents of Orchard, Texas, and had visited Parham's meetings in Galena, Kansas. Both had received the baptism of the Holy Ghost and asked that a worker accompany them to Texas to assist in spreading the Pentecostal message. Parham sent Anna Hall, the first missionary of the Apostolic Faith to enter this southern state. Later, the Oylers also extended an invitation to Parham to preach the Apostolic Faith message at Orchard. He accepted and began his successful Texas mission.[2] These were people who Parham trusted and, no doubt, they were sent to the west coast as his representatives.

---

[1]Parham, *Life*, 148; "Bible Pentecost," 1.
[2]Goff, 94.

267

This, however, did not satisfy Seymour who was anxious for Parham, his "father in this gospel of the Kingdom," to visit Los Angeles and put his stamp of approval on the work.[3] Seymour wrote the Apostolic Faith offices in Texas on July 12, 1906, requesting ministerial credentials. W. F. Carothers sent a note to Parham that the credentials had been sent and noted this was the "first colored mission."[4]

In August, Seymour wrote Parham, acknowledging Hall's arrival and inviting him to Los Angeles for a large meeting. He was expecting a spiritual "earthquake" as God would shake the city.[5] The faithful at Azusa also looked forward to Parham's visit. One remarked that he wanted to see the white "father of the black son."[6]

There was hope that Parham would arrive in Los Angeles on September 15 and conduct the city-wide revival in the early fall.[7] When he agreed to the campaign, the Azusa paper heralded his coming. He was announced as "God's leader of the Apostolic Faith Movement."[8] Parham, however, was giving his attention to ministry in Zion, Illinois, and the Midwest and postponed his visit to Los Angeles.

When Parham finally arrived at Azusa Street in late October, to say that he was not pleased is a gross

---

[3]J.G. Campbell, "History of the Apostolic Faith Movement: Origin, Projector, etc.," *The Apostolic Faith* [Goose Creek, TX] (May 1921), 7. Campbell is quoting K. Brower, from a 1909 letter from Los Angeles.
[4]William J. Seymour to Warren F. Carothers, 12 July 1906.
[5]Parham, *Life*, 154, 155.
[6]Campbell, 6.
[7]Parham, *Life*, 154.
[8]"Letter from Brother Parham," *The Apostolic Faith* [Los Angeles] (September 1906), 1.

understatement. Before entering the building he heard "chatterings, jabberings and screams." Without being introduced, Parham walked to the front of the mission, greeted Seymour and pronounced, "God is sick at His stomach!"[9] This was not what the Californians had expected!

No doubt, Parham was turned off by the emotionalism at the mission. This, however, does not completely explain his repulsion. Early in Parham's meetings there were manifestations of emotion, including violent shaking.[10] Parham, who by today's standards would probably be considered a racist, was most offended by the interracial composition of the meetings.[11] He described the Azusa upper room by saying ". . . men and women, whites and blacks, knelt together or fell across one another; frequently a white woman, perhaps of wealth and culture, could be seen thrown back in the arms of a big 'buck n-----,' and held tightly thus as she shivered in freak imitation of Pentecost."

Later, Parham wrote that the worship at Azusa was a "cross between the old-fashioned Negro worship of the South, and Holy-Rollerism."[12] Through the

---

[9] Shumway, "Study," 178.

[10] For one such example, see Lawrence, 60.

[11] Although it offends some, it is hard for this author to refer to Parham as anything less than racist. He held to a British-Israelism theory that amounted to little less than white supremacy. His doctrinal positions condemned interracial marriages, and he apparently denied that blacks could be part of the bride of Christ. In later years he associated with the Ku Klux Klan. In fairness, it should also be noted that Goff, Parham's biographer, argues that Parham's view of blacks was not racist, but patronizing. He admits, however, that his prejudices increased as he grew older.

[12] Charles F. Parham, "Free Love," *The Apostolic Faith* [Baxter Springs] (December 1912), 4; Charles F. Parham, *The Everlasting Gospel* (Baxter Springs: n.p., n.d.), 118.

remainder of his life, he never ceased to criticize the work of the Los Angeles mission.

The congregation was as unhappy with Parham as he was with them. A. G. Osterberg said, "We didn't like that he told us that he was above us."[13] It was reported by Glenn Cook that Parham almost "discouraged" Lucy Farrow by telling her that blacks could not be part of the bride of Christ.[14] After only a couple of services, two of the elders at Azusa asked Parham to leave and Seymour "closed the door" against him.[15] According to E. S. Williams, in the only reference Seymour ever made to race, he lamented, "You know, it is my color."[16]

Parham started another mission at the Women's Temperance Christian Union building at Broadway and Temple Streets in Los Angeles and drew away some of the Azusa devotees.[17] When Parham left California, W. F. Carothers was placed in charge of his mission. This Texas lawyer's racial views were even more extreme than Parham's. He believed that hatred and animosity between the races was a work of the Holy Spirit, a gift of God to prevent mixing of racial groups.[18] Though the ministerial work of both Parham and his successor in California was largely unsuccessful, the founder of the Apostolic Faith had succeeded in causing the first major division at Azusa.

Seymour totally severed his relationship with Parham and the parent organization, incorporating as "the Apostolic Faith Mission." An interracial group,

---

[13] Jensen and Perkins.
[14] Campbell, 6.
[15] Campbell, 6; Parham, *Life*, 163.
[16] Tinney interview of Williams.
[17] Parham, *Life*, 163.
[18] Goff, 109, quoting *The Apostolic Faith* [Melrose-Houston] (March 1906), 12.

Richard Asbery, Louis Osterberg, James Alexander, John Hughes and Reuben Clark served as the incorporating trustees. According to the Articles of Incorporation, the organization was formed "to do evangelistic work; conduct, maintain and control missions, revivals, campmeetings, street and prison work."[19]

Carothers wrote, "... The work in Los Angeles separated from us, under circumstances which the present writer believes justified them, but about which it would be painful to write."[20] On another occasion he wrote, "We have felt that God's permissive providence was in all of this. They discovered before we did that the man we all supposed to be an apostle raised up to lead in the great work of restoration manifestly in progress was not an apostle..."[21]

The Azusa Street Mission began to issue credentials and recognized the ordination of many ministers, including E. S. Williams.[22] Although these early Pentecostal ministers were highly suspect of any organization and especially hierarchic authority, they gladly accepted ordination because it gave them a discount with the railroads.

In July 1907, Parham was arrested in San Antonio, Texas, and charged with sodomy.[23] Although he denied the accusations until his death, his ministry never fully recovered. Carothers and Howard Goss disfellowshipped Parham from the organization he had

---

[19] Articles of Incorporation, Apostolic Faith Mission, Los Angeles County, California, 9 March 1907.
[20] Carothers, 1.
[21] W.F. Carothers, *Church Government* (Houston: n. p., 1909), 62.
[22] Tinney interview of Williams.
[23] Goff, 136.

founded.[24] For decades, Pentecostal historians did not even mention his name.[25]

Even before Parham's visit, Frank Bartleman had left the Azusa Mission on August 12, 1906, and started a work at Eighth and Maple. He rented a building that had been occupied by The Pillar of Fire Church, some of Pentecost's most vociferous critics. Always an independent, Bartleman was offended when Azusa elected elders and began to "organize." He was also offended when he saw a sign, "Apostolic Faith Mission" outside the building. This, to Bartleman, was the evidence of a "party" spirit, that he said God showed him would come to Azusa.[26] Bartleman was soon joined by William Pendleton who, with several in his congregation, had been turned out of the Hawthorne Street Holiness Church for embracing the Holy Spirit baptism evidenced by tongues.[27]

Elmer Fisher, the pastor of Glendale's First Baptist Church, received the baptism on his second visit to Azusa Street. He continued to work with his friend, Pastor Smale at the New Testament Church and Bishop Seymour at Azusa. Fisher led the Azusa Mission for four months while Seymour conducted his mission in the South. Fisher's motto was "Exalt Jesus Christ; honor the Holy Ghost."

When a group of people left the First New Testament Church, Fisher joined them in starting The Upper Room

---

[24]Lawrence, 67.

[25]For an example, see Stanley H. Frodsham, *With Signs Following* (Springfield, MO: Gospel Publishing House, 1946). Frodsham actually edited the Parham name out of quotations.

[26]Bartleman, *Azusa*, 67-69.

[27]"Spreads the Fire," *The Apostolic Faith* [Los Angeles] (October 1906), 4; Bartleman, *Azusa*, 82.

Mission. After the revival first exploded at Azusa, so many of Smale's members were worshiping at the mission that he had to go there to look them up. Smale invited his congregation back and promised them greater "liberty" in the Spirit.

One of Smale's members reported, "They drove our pastor... from the First Baptist Church because he had the power and now he has brought it to us. We are speaking with tongues and we are enjoying the religion those numbered in the big church might have had if they had not turned that good man out."[28]

Smale became a strong advocate of the Pentecostal message and wrote a pamphlet, *A Tract for our Times*, endorsing the movement. Later, unfortunately, Smale recanted and became an even stronger critic forcing the "baptized" members to leave the First New Testament Church.

Fisher's Upper Room Mission, meeting in an upstairs hall at 327 1/2 South Spring Street, not only received the remnant from the First New Testament Church, but also drew "most" of the whites away from Seymour. George Studd joined Fisher and taught a morning Bible study at the new mission.[29]

By the end of 1906, the movement that was founded on unity and love was already becoming

---

[28]"Rolling on Floor in Smale's Church," *Los Angeles Daily Times* (14 July 1906), II, 1.

[29]Shumway, "Study," 176; Bartleman, *Azusa*, 54, 84; Horton, "Twentieth-Century...," 18; Stanley Horton, "Elmer Kirk Fisher," in Burgess, *Dictionary*, 310; Carter, "I Remember," 1; Carter, "Notes;" Ruth Carter, "An Unusual Experience in the Upper Room Mission," *The Pentecostal Evangel* (7 August 1966), 9. Smale's First New Testament Church became Temple Baptist Church and later he founded Grace Baptist Church.

splintered. A critic wrote, ". . . some were saying 'We are with Seymour;' others were saying, 'We are with Parham;' and still others, 'We are with Bartleman.'"[30]

Early in 1907, the mission faced another major challenge. The Stevens A. M. E. Church continued to make the building available for purchase. In fact, for some time the "For Sale" sign remained on the structure. With the real estate market booming in Los Angeles, the faithful were concerned that if they did not move expeditiously to buy the old Azusa Street building, another interested party might acquire the property, forcing them to vacate quickly and leaving them without an alternative house of worship.

The landholders requested that $15,000 be paid in three years. Late in 1906, some money had been given towards either purchasing the mission or relocating, but the reserves were not sufficient to meet the owners' demands. However, within days of Seymour's announcement of the need, $4,000 was raised for a down payment on the purchase. In less than two years the building was completely debt free.[31] Cecil Polhill gave the last 1,500 dollars on February 2, 1908.[32] Despite this great blessing from God, some attendees were offended because a tradition had been broken: money had been mentioned in the mission, and an offering had been received.[33]

---

[30]"Speaking with Tongues," *The Church Herald and Holiness Banner* (15 December 1906), 1.

[31]Clara E. Lum, "Wonderful News from Los Angeles," *Apostolic Light* (19 November 1906), 3; "The Purchase of the Azusa Mission," *The Apostolic Faith* [Los Angeles] (Feb-March 1907), 2; "What God Hath Wrought," *The Apostolic Faith* [Los Angeles] (May 1908), 1.

[32]George B. Studd, Personal Diary, Flower Pentecostal Heritage Center.

[33]Sizelove, "Temple," 10.

Perhaps the first serious internal challenge to Seymour's leadership came from one of the trustees, Professor Carpenter. Carpenter insisted that Seymour give an account for all the funds that had been given to the mission. The money had flowed so freely that Seymour had not kept any books, not even "the scratch of a pen." A full accounting was impossible. Seymour said, "I have done the best I could with the funds. I can't remember where it was all spent." He could recall giving $100 dollars to one effort and perhaps $500 to another. He mentioned as many as fifty names that had received offerings but could not "cover all the ground." Certainly uncomfortable trying to defend himself, Seymour said, "I sent it out as the Lord told me and as the need required, and before God, I never misspent or kept one cent of it."

Seymour never owned property and lived and died in near poverty, yet Carpenter was not satisfied. He continued to insist on a full accounting, causing a "different spirit" to creep in—a spirit that was "destructive to the place."[34]

New ground was broken in the summer of 1907, when Azusa sponsored a camp meeting. One can only imagine how uncomfortable the Southern California summers would have been in the crowded mission. This testimony described the previous summer, ". . . during the hot days when the crowds would fill Azusa Mission all day, people would often get up and say they praised God for what He was doing 'this morning;' not realizing that the sun was going down in the evening. They had not eaten all day, and yet they were

---

[34] Osterberg, "From the," 3; Jensen and Perkins.

so taken up with sitting at the feet of Jesus that they lost track of the time and would sit there in the heat, wiping the perspiration from their faces."[35] For the summer of 1907 the mission would provide more comfortable quarters.

The idea of a camp meeting originated with Rachel Sizelove. She dreamed one night that she saw many white tents pitched at the foot of a hill in Hermon, where she lived. She shared the dream with a group at the mission. R. J. Scott, a Canadian who had been Holy Spirit baptized at the mission, became a principle organizer of the event.[36]

The camp meeting, at Arroyo Seco, near Hermon, was attended by thousands. They erected a tabernacle to seat 1,000 and also had an "upper room" tent for seekers. More than 200 living tents and a number of large tents were set up for pilgrims. Blacks and whites had separate accommodations but worshiped together as they did at Azusa. Many were saved, healed, and baptized in the Holy Ghost. Over 100 converts were baptized in a nearby stream.

The power of God was evident throughout the camp. An attendee actually saw fire "issuing out of the tabernacle." One morning after breakfast, ten praying workers were slain in the Spirit. They could not get away until noon."[37]

In the meantime, services continued all summer at Azusa, affectionately called, "the old manger home."

---

[35]"Los Angeles Campmeeting of the Apostolic Faith," *The Apostolic Faith* [Los Angeles] (May 1907), 1.

[36]Fred Corum, "Azusa's First Camp-Meeting," *Word and Work* (January 1936), 1.

[37]Carter, "Notes;" "Everywhere Preaching the Word," *The Apostolic Faith* [Los Angeles] (September 1907), 1.

An observer who attended the regular services held back at the mission wrote, "The pillar of fire still rests there."[38]

Early in 1908 the church reported, "The meetings have been going on every day since the work started and God's Word and the Holy Spirit are just as fresh and new as ever." Nevertheless, another group of dissenters had left the mission because of Seymour's hard preaching on divorce.[39] The pastor not only believed that divorced people could not remarry without committing adultery, but he also held that those couples who had been previously divorced and remarried should separate and live apart.[40]

On May 13, 1908, over the objections and protests of some of his helpers, Seymour married Jennie Evans Moore. According to their marriage license, Seymour was 38, and Jennie was also in her thirties. They were united by one of their most faithful friends, Edward S. Lee. Edward's wife, Mattie and Richard Asbery witnessed the happy event.[41] Seymour had preached several sermons on marriage, perhaps getting the congregation ready for what was ahead, and **The Apostolic Faith** had printed an article that explicitly

---

[38] "Everywhere," 1.

[39] "From Azusa Mission," *The Apostolic Faith* [Los Angeles] (January 1908), 1.

[40] "The Marriage Tie," (*The Apostolic Faith* [Los Angeles] (September 1907), 3.

[41] William Joseph Seymour and Jennie Evans Moore, *Certificate of Marriage*: California State Board of Health, 13 May 1908; *Marriage License*, 27 May 1908, Los Angeles County. The marriage license says Jennie was 30. According to her death certificate, she would have been 34. According to the 1900 census she would have been 32.

stated, "It is no sin to marry."⁴² Despite these preparatory efforts, several workers left the mission.⁴³

One of the first missionaries to leave Azusa was Florence Crawford. She first preached in Portland, Oregon, on Christmas Day, 1906. Two years later she gave up her home in Los Angeles, returned to Portland, established a mission, and spent the remainder of her life there.⁴⁴ The Portland Apostolic Faith Mission accused the Azusa Street Mission of letting "down the standard of holiness" and ceasing to teach sanctification as a second work of grace. No basis are given for these charges, and they appear to be blatantly false, at least by any established standards of holiness.⁴⁵

---

⁴²"Bible Teaching on Marriage and Divorce," *The Apostolic Faith* [Los Angeles] (January 1907), 3.

⁴³There is a theory that Clara Lum and Florence Crawford, both white women, left the mission because they had romantic feelings toward Seymour and felt rejected when he married Moore. I have seen no evidence of this. Clemmons does say that in 1908 Seymour met with C. H. Mason who advised him not to marry a white woman. See Ithiel Clemmons, "True Koinonia: Pentecostal Hopes and Historical Realities," *Pneuma: The Journal of the Society for Pentecostal Studies* (Spring 1982), 54. Two other possibilities for the fissure seem more reasonable. First, many early Pentecostals felt that it was not advisable to marry because of the nearness of Christ's coming (1 Corinthians 7). There could also have been a conflict between the departing women and Mrs. Seymour. E. S. Williams described Florence Crawford as "a strong minded woman." He said of Mrs. Seymour, "She was the backbone of his trying to push himself" and she "wanted to put Brother Seymour in his place." See Tinney interview of Williams.

⁴⁴Crawford, *Light,* 11,12; "Azusa to Portland," A Moment in History Revisited," *Higher Way* (November-December 1996), 7.

⁴⁵*A Historical Account of the Apostolic Faith: A Trinitarian-Fundamental Evangelistic Organization,* (Portland: Apostolic Faith, 1965), 70. Until his death, Seymour was a strong proponent of sanctification. See the end of this chapter for the division with William Durham. Further, how could anyone accuse this pious

After Seymour's marriage, Clara Lum, who had served as the editor of **The Apostolic Faith**, left Los Angeles to assist Crawford. In June 1908, the fourteenth edition of the paper, was printed without the familiar "Apostolic Faith" mast on the front page. The second page of the paper carried this message, "For the next issues of this paper address: The Apostolic Faith Campmeeting, Portland, Oregon."[46] Lum wrote the following in the July/August edition, "We have moved the paper which the Lord laid on us to begin at Los Angeles to Portland, Oregon, which will now be its headquarters." She also asked that money should be sent to the Apostolic Faith in Portland. An article on the front page described the outpouring of the Holy Spirit in Los Angeles, but Seymour's role was conveniently omitted.[47] By late 1908, the entire publication was moved to Portland.[48]

Without permission, Clara Lum had removed the paper and more importantly, the national and

---

man of compromising on holiness? No moral stain was ever found on his spotless record. Some feel this compromise could have been his decision to marry. Since Bartleman was offended by a church sign and others were offended when an offering was taken to pay for the building, these charges could amount to nothing. Allowing the readers to draw their own conclusions, it is also interesting to note that the Upper Room Mission, which from the natural point of view would be a serious competitor to Azusa, was very supportive of the Portland work. See "We are glad to see . . .," *The Upper Room* (August 1910), 2; "Portland, Oregon," *The Upper Room* (May 1910).

[46] *"For the next. . . .," The Apostolic Faith* [Portland, OR] (June 1908), 2.

[47] "We have moved . . .," *The Apostolic Faith* [Portland, OR] (July/August 1908), 2; "The Promised Latter Rain," *The Apostolic Faith* [Portland, OR] (July/August 1908), 1.

[48] Number 18, the January 1909 edition, says, "The last paper . . . was the first to be published in Portland." The author has not seen Number 17.

international mailing lists to Portland.[49] This was devastating to the Los Angeles work. Seymour tried to print at least one edition, and perhaps more, of the paper, but it was impossible to continue without the mailing lists or the financial contributions that had been misdirected to Portland. In an October/November 1908 edition published in Los Angeles, Seymour said, "I must for the salvation of souls let it be known that the editor is still in Los Angeles, . . . and will not remove **The Apostolic Faith** from Los Angeles, without letting subscribers and field workers know.

"This was a sad thing to our hearts for a worker to attempt to take the paper which is the property of the Azusa Street Mission to another city without consent, after being warned by the elders not to do so."[50]

---

[49]J. C. Vanzandt, *Speaking in Tongues* (Portland, OR: Vanzandt, 1926), 34-37. Some argue that Lum had permission to move the paper. This cannot be the case. They cite the incorporation papers of the Portland Apostolic Faith which say, "vested by said mission with authority to publish at various times issues of the official organ, "Apostolic Faith," a paper devoted to principles and doctrines of said cause and distributed without charge." There are two major problems with this argument. First, these articles were dated 11 October 1909, nearly a year and a half after Lum moved the paper. Furthermore, these articles were signed by Jennie Seymour and Edward Doak, Azusa workers—not Lum or Crawford. It seems to me this was an attempt by the Azusa workers to reclaim the work in Portland. The articles say the Portland work is "auxiliary spiritually" to the mission in Los Angeles. This harmonizes with Allan V. McPherson who remembered, "Mr. Seymour came to Portland, Oregon, about 1911, with some of his helpers and tried to take over Sister Crawford's work at Front and Burnside Street, but met with complete failure." See Crayne, 203.

[50]Vanzandt, *Speaking*, 37. To the author's knowledge no copy of this Los Angeles paper exists. Some have said that because Vanzandt is a critic of Pentecostalism he created this story. This is not plausible. Vanzandt first wrote in 1911 when his work could

In the summer of 1910, the Portland paper carried a weak apology, "This paper would be No. 21 from the beginning in Los Angeles, but it is No. 7 of Portland. We said it was moved from Los Angeles when we should have stated we were starting a new **Apostolic Faith** in Portland."[51] Neither the paper, nor the mailing lists were returned to Los Angeles. The revival at the mission never fully recovered from the loss.

Seymour journeyed to Portland during the period of crisis trying to bring the mission back into the fold but was met by resistance from Florence Crawford and Will Trotter, the former leader of a rescue mission in Los Angeles and a former participant at Azusa Street. When leaving the mission without reaching a reconciliation, Seymour met E. S. Williams on the stairs and asked him, "Are you going to continue to preach here?"

When Williams answered, "Yes," Seymour said, "I'll have the railroad take away your clergy book."

"If that is necessary," Williams replied. The fact that the usually conciliatory Seymour followed through with his threat is an indication of the depth of the pain caused by the split.[52]

George Studd regularly attended the Azusa Street Mission and the other Pentecostal missions throughout 1908 and his daily diary gives some detail as to the services. He was at Azusa when Cecil Polhill gave the great offering to pay off the mortgage. He wrote, "What a Sunday at Azusa! Dispute as to taking collection. How

---

have been validated or invalidated by the participants. Further, he is accurate when quoting the Portland paper.
[51]Vanzandt, *Speaking*, 36.
[52]Tinney interview of Williams.

the devil tried to get in and how the Lord defeated him!"

On February 16, he said there were "very good meetings all day." Studd was "greatly blessed" and the meeting was "packed to the doors at night." Sunday, March 15, found Studd at the mission at 10:30 A. M. He tarried at the altar until 3 o'clock.

Most often, Studd described the services as "pretty good," "good," "splendid," "excellent" or "very good." Only on one occasion, March 21, he reported "meeting not very good."

On April 9, the mission celebrated the second anniversary of Pentecost in Los Angeles. Studd said there were "many good solid testimonies." In the afternoon service, Studd, himself, was given "great liberty" in his testimony.

Studd joined Richard Asbery and Joseph Warren at the Security Savings Bank on April 16. They finished legal work on the deed to the Azusa property.[53] That night he met with the board of trustees. The following Sunday, April 19 was Easter. Seymour and Edward Lee were in charge of the services at Azusa.

Studd said that Seymour "spoke well" in the morning meeting on May 3. The message was followed by a "good time 'tarrying' in upper room." A week later, Studd said the pastor, "seemed to throw away his message (if he had one)." Seymour had opened the service "for everyone to talk." Studd complained, ". . .and some did, too."

---

[53] According to the Los Angeles County Records, the sale of the property was originally recorded on December 1906 and finalized April 15, 1908. See pages 266, 267 of Los Angeles County Records, photocopies in Azusa Street File, Flower Pentecostal Heritage Center.

A Mrs. Kallaway spoke at the mission on Sunday May 17. She "spoke splendidly with great power and unction." Brother Seymour also delivered a message, speaking of his "wedding and wife."

Lucy Farrow left the mission on May 20, and there was a farewell service for her. There was a good time of tarrying for the Lord in what Studd called the "after meeting."

Seymour and a Brother Stewart from Phoenix spoke on Sunday June 28. Stewart spoke from the fifteenth chapter of John.[54]

During the summer and fall, Studd's visits to the mission became much less frequent. Azusa Street is hardly mentioned in his diary. In August, he wrote to *Confidence* and reported that even though white people still attended the services, the mission was "entirely controlled (humanly speaking)" by blacks.[55]

Bartleman visited the mission in March of 1909 and said, "The Lord met me in great power." He attended Azusa regularly and preached or testified often. By the end of the year, however, he reported that the mission had "lost out greatly." Despite his criticism and failure to support the work, when Bartleman left for a trip to Europe, Azusa was the only mission in Los Angeles that gave him an offering.[56]

Greek scholar and translator W. B. Godbey visited Los Angeles in 1909 and found the city "all electrified" with the Pentecostal movement. The meetings at

---

[54]Studd, Diary.
[55]George B. Studd, "Los Angeles," *Confidence* (15 August 1908), 10.
[56]Bartleman, *Azusa*, 143-146.

Azusa were still running night and day without intermission. Workers from the mission stayed at the depot watching the trains at all hours to receive guests visiting the revival. They would ask visitors, "Have you received the baptism of the Holy Ghost?" If the answer was "Yes," they followed with a direct question about tongues, "Have you the sign?" If the answer was "no," they invited them to the altar and prayed with them to receive.

Godbey refused an invitation from the "runner" at the station, but his ego could not resist when Seymour invited him to speak at the mission. He said there was a "large audience" at the mission. Like all guests, Godbey was asked if he had received the sign of the Holy Ghost. He responded, "I can say with Paul, 'I thank God I speak with tongues more than you all.'" From his own knowledge of biblical languages, "*Johannes Baptistes tinxit, Petros tinxit et Christus misit suos Apolstolos ut gentes tingerent.*"

Godbey sarcastically reported that the people "shouted over" him and wanted to put him at the "front" of the movement.[57] It is unfortunate that he perpetrated this sham on the people, gleefully bragged about it, and then used it as fodder in a critical cannon that blasted the movement. Is it difficult to ascertain who had a Christlike spirit, the humble pastor that shared his pulpit with this skeptic, or the arrogant guest that took advantage of his host?

Paul Bettex, a former missionary to South America, attended the mission in early 1910 where he was "basking in the presence of God." While there he felt God

---

[57] White, *Demons*, 119-121.

calling him to China, and he soon departed as a faith missionary.[58]

In April, 1910, Bishop and Mrs. Seymour lived at the crowded mission along with J. A. Warren, Samuel Murphy, Mack Jonas, a Mrs. Jones from Oklahoma, Phebe Conway and her four children, Emma, Wanda, Elenore and Albert and Johanna Eibinfeldt, a Hungarian immigrant who was serving as an Apostolic Faith missionary.[59]

During the same year, George N. Eldridge said he "became interested in the old Azusa Street Pentecostal work." Although he was initially cautious, he and his wife were both baptized in the Holy Spirit. They established Bethel Temple in Los Angeles.[60]

Despite the continued presence of God at Azusa Street, four years after the opening of the mission, there were 25 Pentecostal churches in greater Los Angeles.[61] The movement had drifted far from the vision of nonsectarian harmony originally espoused by William J. Seymour.

Canadian A. W. Frodsham, brother of Stanley Frodsham, was in Los Angeles in late 1910 or very early in 1911. He visited Azusa where blacks and whites continued to "worship freely together." He also said, "The mission has not been flourishing of late, but now there are signs of abundance of rain, and many are being blessed."[62]

---

[58] *Heroes*, 78.
[59] United States Census, Los Angeles County, CA, 1910.
[60] George N. Eldridge, *Personal Reminiscences* (Los Angeles: West Coast Publishing, Co., 1930), 40, 41.
[61] Thrapp, III, 11.
[62] A. W. Frodsham, "A Pentecostal Journey in Canada, British Columbia, and the Western States," *Confidence* (June 1911), 139.

On February 14, 1911, while Seymour was on a missionary trip to the East, the mission opened its pulpit to William H. Durham, the Chicago pastor who received his Holy Spirit baptism at Azusa in 1907.[63] In the years following 1907, Durham had formed his own association, providing ministerial credentials from his Chicago church.[64]

Durham had been denied the pulpit at the Upper Room Mission because he had developed and was preaching a new doctrine of sanctification. Durham's baptistic view emphasized the finished work of Calvary and argued that sanctification was instantaneous at conversion and continuing with spiritual maturity.[65] This position was a direct contradiction to the Holiness doctrine endorsed by Seymour and the Apostolic Faith Mission.

Despite the controversy, Durham had great success at the mission. Many of the original participants returned to the mission as huge crowds gathered. Durham was endorsed by H. S. Covington who had seen him in a dream before he arrived in Los Angeles. Covington went to the station, saw Durham and said, "This is the man I saw last night in a dream."[66]

Many souls were saved and an average of ten a week were receiving the Holy Spirit. In one week more

---

[63]William H. Durham, "The Great Revival at Azusa Street—How it Began and How it Ended" (*Pentecostal Testimony* n. d., Volume I, Number 8), 3.

[64]Arthur G. Osterberg, *Certificate of Ordination*, Full Gospel Assembly, 25 September 1909.

[65]For a fuller treatment on Durham, see Larry Martin, *In the Beginning* (Duncan, OK: Christian Life Books, 1995), 31-36.

[66]Untitled brochure published by A. C. Driscoll, 1, Historical Center, United Pentecostal Church.

than twenty came through to the experience.⁶⁷ On Sundays the building was filled and hundreds were turned away. Bartleman said, "The fire began to fall at old Azusa as at the beginning."⁶⁸

The Azusa faithful were disturbed that Durham's doctrine conflicted with their strongly held position on sanctification. Previously, Sister Rubley at the mission had had a vision about the conflict. She saw the devil and his demons seated at a large table discussing the problems they were having with all the Pentecostal people and what they should do about it. Various demons suggested remedies like taking the Pentecostal people's joy or peace. But the devil responded they would still have the Holy Ghost. Finally, a demon suggested, "I have it; give them the baptism on the unsanctified life." The demons all clapped and roared.⁶⁹ Now, through the ministry of Durham, they believed the vision was being fulfilled.

The elders wrote Seymour and asked him to come home and handle the volatile situation. Receiving their reports, he wired Los Angeles for the money to return to the church. Upon his arrival, he met with Durham and asked him to stop preaching the "finished work" at Azusa. Seymour also informed Durham that "this was his work." Apparently Durham tried to block Seymour from preaching in his own pulpit.

Instead of submitting to the pastor of the local assembly, Durham went before the congregation on Sunday morning and asked the people to vote on whether they wanted him to continue the work or

---

⁶⁷Durham, "Great," 3.
⁶⁸Bartleman, 150.
⁶⁹Crayne, 207, 208.

turn it back to Seymour. Durham said only "ten or less" voted with Seymour. How Durham could have participated in this unethical and egotistical spiritual *coup d'etat* is unimaginable.

Seymour faced this challenge to his authority without flinching. He consulted with the leaders of the mission and on May 2, 1911, without notice he locked Durham and his followers out of the mission.[70] For years, the doors had never been locked. Louis Osterberg and four other members of the board tried unsuccessfully to dissuade Seymour from locking the doors against Durham. In protest, Osterberg, a long-time friend of Azusa, resigned his position as a trustee.[71]

Durham said, "While we were preaching, praying and seeking God in the mission, Seymour had been scheming and planning as to how he could get possession of the building." How unfortunate that Seymour would be accused of "scheming" to regain control of his own pulpit after his pastoral authority had been usurped by a former friend.

Frank Bartleman secured a mission on Kohler Street as a temporary home to Durham's meeting, and then his followers opened their own mission in a large

---

[70] Durham, "Great," 4; Shumway, "Study," 179; Max A. X. Clark, *Latter Rain and Holy Fire: The Beginnings of the Pentecostal Movement* (n. p., n. d.), 28.

[71] Osterberg, "From the Personal," 4; "Notes from A. G. Osterberg-May 24, 1956," typescript, Flower Pentecostal Heritage Center. A. G. Osterberg remembered the dispute as a racial issue. He said, ". . . the colored folks began to fight the whites because they said the whites were going to try to come in and take over Azusa." He added that, "Seymour himself was very humble about it." Laying the blame at Mrs. Seymour's feet he said she "antagonized all the colored people. The colored folks believed in an inter-racial church as long as they had a Negro pastor."

building on the corner of Seventh and Los Angeles and his crowds followed him. One commentator said, "Azusa leadership had failed God."[72] Bartleman, the Osterbergs, and other Pentecostal leaders in Los Angeles gave their support to Durham. On Sundays, one thousand would attend his meetings. Unfortunately, the Apostolic Faith Mission was devastated. Bartleman said the place became "deserted."[73]

Durham was not satisfied to practically empty the mission; he personally attacked Seymour through his periodical, **The Pentecostal Testimony**. He spoke of Seymour's "failures and blunders" and said "the power of God had entirely left him, and that he was no longer worthy of the confidence and respect of the saints." After all but destroying Seymour's work in Los Angeles and questioning his leadership, Durham lamented that all this character assassination was his "unpleasant duty."[74]

Charles Parham was also incensed by Durham's sanctification doctrine. In January 1912, he prayed that God would show the world which teaching was correct by taking the life of the teacher who was in error. That summer Durham died of tuberculosis. Parham believed that God had answered his prayer and the "finished work" controversy was over.[75] Durham's message, however, outlived the messenger and has become the predominant Pentecostal position.

Sad to say, this was not the last division to strike the fledgling Pentecostal movement. In 1913, R. J. Scott led in the planning of another camp meeting at Arroyo

---

[72]Clark, 29; Shumway, "Study," 179.
[73]Bartleman, *Azusa*, 151.
[74]Durham, "Great," 4.
[75]Goff, 152.

Seco. Noted faith healer, Maria Woodworth-Etter was the featured speaker. Brother Seymour attended the meeting but "only as a spectator."

As was often the case in Etter's meetings, many were healed and saved. A water baptismal service was scheduled, and R. A. McAlister, a Canadian who had been Holy Ghost baptized at Azusa, was invited to teach. McAlister discussed baptismal formulas and suggested that the disciples baptized in "Jesus' name" and the words "Father, Son and Holy Ghost were never used by the early church in Christian baptism."

That evening, John G. Scheppe meditated on McAlister's remarks and the wonderful healings performed as Woodworth-Etter prayed in Jesus' name. The following morning, Scheppe ran through the camp shouting that God had given him a revelation that believers were to baptized in the name of "Jesus Only."

Frank Ewart, a former associate of William Durham, attended the meeting and was taken with the idea of the "Jesus Only" issue. He, along with McAlister and Glenn A. Cook, developed the idea of rebaptizing in Jesus' name. Within two years the Pentecostal movement that was already divided over sanctification, was again splintered between Trinitarian and oneness believers.[76]

In April 1914, at an opera house in Hot Springs, Arkansas the Assemblies of God denomination was born. Although C. H. Mason, the black founder of the

---

[76]Shumway, "Study," 191; Edith L. Blumhoffer, *The Assemblies of God: A Chapter in the Story of American Pentecostalism*, vol. 1 (Springfield: Gospel Publishing, 1989), 222, 223; D. A. Reed, "Oneness Pentecostalism," in Burgess, *Dictionary*, 644; J. L. Hall, "Frank J. Ewart," in Burgess, *Dictionary*, 290; Anderson, *Vision*, 177.

Church of God in Christ, spoke at the first general council it was obvious that the Assemblies of God, with very few exceptions, would be a white denomination.[77] Two other major Pentecostal denominations, the Church of God in Cleveland, Tennessee and Pentecostal Holiness were also predominantly white. Mason's group would remain almost exclusively black.

Racial segregation that disappeared when the Spirit was poured out at Old Azusa was now institutionalized. Pentecostalism, that began with a utopian dream of New Testament unity was now divided by sect, doctrine and race.

---

[77]Former General Superintendent E. S. Williams says a decision was made to discourage the ordanation of blacks to appease Southern pastors who questioned having to share their pulpits with African-Americans. They feared this would cause an uproar in the strictly-segregated Southern states. See Tinney interview.

The Azusa Street Mission
Photo used by permission
Flower Pentecostal Heritage Center

Early Azusa Street Mission Letterhead
Notice that W. J. Seymour is pastor and Charles Parham is projector.
Larry Martin Collection

This cartoon from the *Burning Bush* bafoons the dispute between Parham and Seymour.
Larry Martin Collection

Charles Parham in Robes
Used by Permission
Apostolic Faith Report

Frank Bartleman

The Eighth and Maple Mission
Photos used by permission
Flower Pentecostal Heritage Center

Elmer Fisher

The Upper Room Mission
Photos used by permission
Flower Pentecostal Heritage Center

The sign on the Azusa Street Mission

Rachel Sizelove
Photos used by permission
Flower Pentecostal Heritage Center

More of the Azusa Faithful

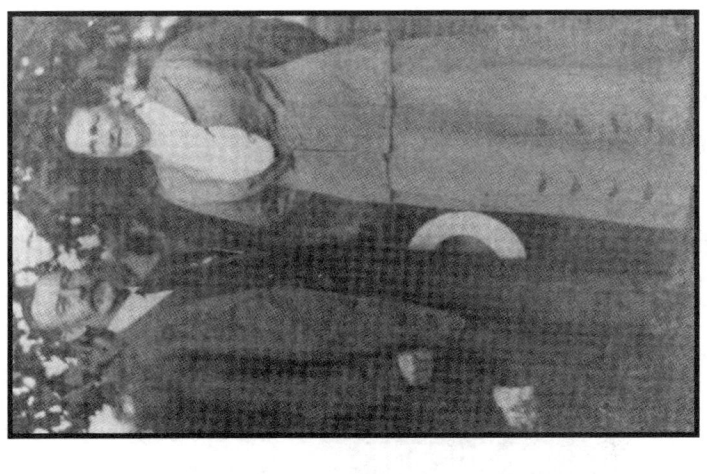

Mr. and Mrs. Edward Doake

Julia Carney
Larry Martin Collection

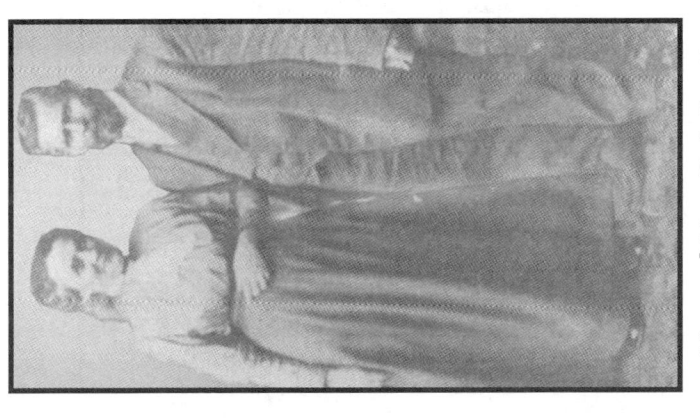

Mr. and Mrs. R. J. Scott

William J. and Jennie Evans Moore Seymour
Photo used by permission
Flower Pentecostal Heritage Center

Moore and Seymour Marriage License

George Eldridge
Photo used by permission
Flower Pentecostal Heritage Center

Elder and Mrs. Covington
Photo used by permission
Historical Center
United Pentecostal Church International

William H. Durham
(Center of photo, praying for someone)
Photo used by permission
Flower Pentecostal Heritage Center

R. E. McAlister
Larry Martin Collection
(Courtesy of the Pentecostal Assemblies of Canada)

16 The Apostolic Ministry: Seymour's Travels

As the news of the meetings at Azusa Street spread, Seymour was invited to travel and take the revival to other areas. He evangelized, established churches and ordained ministers much like Paul and the first century apostles.

In November 1906, he traveled to Oakland; in the next few months, he was in San Francisco and San Jose; Spring 1907, he was in Texas, the South and Midwest; in the summer of 1907, he went to Chicago; Indianapolis; Zion, Illinois; and points further east.[1]

More information is probably available on the Indianapolis meetings than all of Seymour's other

---

[1] "Spreading the Full Gospel," *The Apostolic Faith* [Los Angeles] (October 1906), 4; "Pentecost Both Sides the Ocean," *The Apostolic Faith* [Los Angeles] (Feb.-March 1907), 1; "Missions in Los Angeles," *The Apostolic Faith* [Los Angeles] (April 1907), 1; Corum, "Azusa's," 1.

evangelistic ministry. Thomas Hezmalhalch (called Brother Tom because his name was so difficult) and Glenn A. Cook started the Pentecostal work in Indianapolis. They were soon joined by J. O. Lehman, Celia Smock, Elnora Hall and a "Brother Harry."

In April 1907, a newspaper reporter visited the meetings held in the Murphy League Hall at Alabama and New York Streets and listened to the Pentecostals speak in tongues. What he heard sounded like gibberish to him and he coined the name "Gliggy Bluk" to refer to the city's Apostolic Faith believers and their strange gift of tongues. The name stuck and for years the newspapers used the title when referring to the group.[2]

One of the early believers in Indianapolis was Alice Reynolds, a pretty sixteen-year-old student at Shortridge High School. The **Indianapolis Morning Star** reported her involvement with the Pentecostals, including her speaking in tongues, lying prostrate on the floor and coming "under the power."[3] One reporter said her "manipulation of the strange tongue is really a feature of the meetings." When she would rise to speak, there would be a "craning of necks" and

---

[2]"Seek New Religious Speech," *Indianapolis Morning Star* (1 February 1907), 5; "Gliggy Bluks Meet," *Indianapolis Morning Star* (17 April 1907), 1; "Stutterer Speaks at 'Glug' Service," *Indianapolis Morning Star* (18 April 1"907), 15; "'Bluks' Pay No Rent," *Indianapolis Morning Star* (19 April 1907), 1, 3; "Trance Followed Sermon by Cook," *Indianapolis Morning Star* (24 April 1907), 3. See also "'Bluk' Followers Grow," *Indianapolis Morning Star* (22 April 1907), 7; "Bluk's Faith Fades," *Indianapolis Morning Star* (23 April 1907), 11; and other articles appearing almost daily in Indianapolis newspapers.

[3]"Stutterer Speaks . . .," 15; Young Girls, Mere Children, Speak 'Tongue' of the Bluks," *Indianapolis Morning Star* (19 May 1907), 40; "Bluk Crowd Runs Over," *Indianapolis Star* (10 June 1907), 12.

spectators would rise in their seats.[4] Later Reynolds married J. Roswell Flower, who became an early official in the Assemblies of God. Their son, Joseph, also served as General Secretary for the organization. The Assemblies of God Archives is named the Flower Pentecostal Heritage Center after this influential family.

The Indianapolis Pentecostals received regular attention from the secular press and the police department. A riot nearly erupted in their mission when a black convert, Ernest Lloyd, tried to exorcise an evil spirit from a twelve-year-old white girl, Naomi Groves. Lloyd rushed to the girl, seized her by the hair with both hands and shook her violently. Cook said Naomi had a demon, and Lloyd was trying to shake it out. All this attention frightened the young girl who began to scream hysterically.

Naomi's screams aroused a group of unbelievers who attended the meeting as skeptical observers. The angry mob shouted racial epitaphs and demanded that Lloyd leave. One man said, "Religion is religion, but it is another thing for a burly n----- to grab a little girl and frighten her to death." A number of policemen were called and soon order was restored. The paper reported that the white believers associated freely with Lloyd and even took him with them "when they go to restaurants to get their meals."[5] It is clear that racial tolerance was not only practiced at Azusa, but exported by missionaries who left Los Angeles to preach in other areas.

---

[4]"Tongues Crush Idols," *Indianapolis Morning Star* (27 April 1907), 5.

[5]"Negro Bluk Beats Demon from Girl," *Indianapolis Morning Star* (5 May 1907), 1.

About a week later the police were called again when several people fell into "trances." The lawmen threatened the believers with arrest, declaring that if they were called to the meeting again "somebody would get a ride in the patrol wagon."[6]

Seymour was invited to Indianapolis by Sarah Cripe, one of the local worshippers. Apparently she also financed his trip. Cripe was a "massage doctor" with considerable wealth. The Pentecostal leaders in Indianapolis lived rent free in Cripe's home at 2341 Fletcher and were supported by her generosity. In terms that would seem patronizing by today's standards, Cripe announced, "Brother Seymour is a good man. He is a Negro, but he is the discoverer of this great faith. He met with a little band in a stable in Los Angeles and discovered the wonderful power. And now just to think that this wonderful Negro is coming right here to be with us."[7]

After a long wait, the highly anticipated visit began on June 2, 1907. Seymour arrived at the mission with the E. H. Cummings family from Los Angeles. Mr. and Mrs. Cummings were traveling to Liberia, South Africa with their eight children, Emma, Bessie, Frank, Ida May, Mattie Belle, John C., Marjorie and Ardell.

When Seymour entered the hall, he was greeted by Cook with a hug and a kiss. A kiss on the cheek from a member of the same sex, or the "holy kiss" as it was called, was a hallmark of the Evening Light Saints and adopted by many early Pentecostals. Not everyone

---

[6]"Police Visit 'Bluks,'" *Indianapolis Morning Star* (13 May 1907), 12.

[7]"'Bluks' Pay . . . ," *Indianapolis Morning Star*, 1; "Gives Bluks $8,000," *Indianapolis Morning Star* (21 April 1907), 1, 7; "Negro Bluk Coming," *Indianapolis Morning Star* (5 May 1907), 3.

in Indianapolis was accustomed to this embrace and one girl in the audience gasped, "Oh, that white fellow kissed the Negro."

Cook introduced the Los Angeles leader as "my brother, Seymour." In a voice that "shook the church" Seymour said, "Let's sing 'The Comforter Has Come,'" a favorite hymn at Azusa Street. Afterwards, he announced, "I have come to spread the gospel over Indianapolis."

A visiting reporter gave one of the most complete contemporary descriptions of the preacher available anywhere. He wrote, "This founder of the sect stands full six feet in height. He wears a rubber collar, decorated by no sign of a necktie. Adorning his mouth is one massive gold tooth, ranked by rows of other teeth, perfectly straight and white. The beard that he wears could be called a flowing one if it was longer. It flows–what there is of it. His voice is like the roaring of a cannon, and of all his most striking characteristics, he has but one eye."[8]

Although the believers were "wonderfully impressed by his power," Seymour's visit was marked by controversy from the beginning. Ida May Oddy of 1720 West Washington Street, wife of Tom Oddy a prominent grain dealer, testified that her husband was going to leave her if she continued to attend the services. Oddy played the organ and sang for the meetings. She had also received the baptism in the Holy Spirit.

Seymour addressed Oddy's problem in his message on June 3, and told of one man who was "struck down" by God because he didn't want his wife to attend the

---

[8]"Negro Bluk Kissed," 3.

meetings. A tearful Oddy also bowed on her knees before Seymour who took her by the hand and prayed for her.

Oddy's comments in the service indicate that her husband's real complaint was the racial composition of the meetings. Referring to Seymour, she said, "This brother is a man of God. And after all we should not hesitate to associate spiritually with Negroes. In the great beyond the Negroes and whites will be together. We need not associate with Negroes here except spiritually. I must associate with these people, for you know what the Bible says about the man who hid his talent under a bushel."

Oddy's husband filed for divorce, claiming his wife stayed away from home from 2:00 p.m. until 11:00 p.m. every evening to attend the services. He said she could have the choice of "quitting the Bluks or quitting him." Mrs. Cummings told the church that she was not surprised by the turn of events. "Way out there in California," she said, "lots of families were torn up because the women came to our meetings."[9]

Another controversy arose when Arthur Scott, a young man residing at 3313 Graceland Avenue came under the power while working at Van Camp Packing Company. Scott shook so violently that the dispensary ambulance was called. "Don't touch me," the man told a doctor, "this is the power of God."

The skeptical doctor replied, "If that is the power of God it is giving you a devil of a shaking." Soon, the

---

[9]"Bluks Divide Home," *Indianapolis Morning Star* (4 June 1907), 1; "Negro Bluk 'Blows,'" *Indianapolis Star* (5 June 1907), 20; "Woman Sticks to Bluks; Husband Asks Divorce," *Indianapolis News* (5 June 1907), 4; "Oddy Asks Divorce Because of Bluks," *Indianapolis Morning Star* (6 June 1907), 3.

manifestation subsided and Scott went home shouting "Hallelujah" and "Glory."[10]

Local police attended the meetings regularly after Seymour's arrival. The chief reported he had received "many complaints" even though the offended parties did not want it known that they had attended the meetings. One protest concerned the fact that "white women of good appearance attend the meeting and mingle with Negroes freely, holding hands while they call each other 'brother' and 'sister.'" Referring to the integrated meeting, one police officer said, they found things "pretty mixed up there."

On one occasion, the police refused to leave when the meeting was over and several women were still prostrate in the floor. The faithful prayed for over an hour for the "police demons."

During another meeting, Detective Billy Holtz went to the altar to feel the pulse of a young girl in a "trance." Brother Seymour explained that "It's the power of the Lord," but the policeman would not accept the explanation, choosing to believe the girl was under some kind of "hypnotic" power.[11]

Seymour and the Cummings family participated in the Indianapolis meetings for weeks. The Cummings children would give messages in tongues and then interpret their meaning. Mrs. Cummings also spoke out frequently.

---

[10] "Oddy Asks...," 3.
[11] "Bluks Fail in Efforts to Rout 'Police Demon,'" *Indianapolis Star* (9 June 1907), 16; "Police Are Spectators at 'Bluks' Meeting," *Indianapolis News* (11 June 1907), 4; "Police after Bluks," *Indianapolis Star* (11 June 1907), 15.

On June 9, the crowd was so large that two meetings had to be held. Seymour preached to a large assembly upstairs and Cook spoke in the main hall. Still the throng kept coming until Cook had to request, "Will some one please go down and stop the crowd that's comin' in so that no one will get hurt?" After the preaching, the congregation merged in the upper chamber for prayer.

During the same meeting, Alice Reynolds received considerable attention when she "conversed long and earnestly" with "Frank Cummings, Negro." The newspaper also noted that during the service Cummings sat "with a white young man on one side of him and a white girl on the other."[12]

Opposition to the meetings became so determined that Cook found himself in the reversed role of asking the police to come to the meetings and provide protection from rowdy intruders. This protection was needed as crowds grew more hostile. On one occasion, Cook was "hit several times about the head."[13]

Saturday, June 15, was an especially important day for the Pentecostals. At 2:00 p.m., between two and three hundred believers and spectators gathered at Fall Creek near Indiana Avenue for a baptismal service. Seymour performed the baptism, assisted by Cook. Cook entered the waters first, and waited as Seymour exhorted from the book of Luke and conducted a service consisting of hymns and prayers. Seymour said, "People say they don't understand this strange language. No wonder, they can't understand it until they

---

[12]"Bluk Crowd ...," 12.
[13]"Brother Cook Was a Real Bad Man," *Indianapolis Star* (15 June 1907), 3; "Hit Brother Cook," *Indianapolis Sun* (17 June 1907), 3.

are baptized in the Holy Ghost and fire." He proclaimed there were not enough devils in Indianapolis, heaven or hell, to destroy the faith of the Pentecostal believers.

Both Seymour and Cook were dressed in long black robes. One reporter said the former resembled "authentic portraits of the King of Abyseinia."

Thirteen people were immersed in the muddy waters. They were assisted through the dangerous current by E. H. Cummings and Joseph Ingland. Mrs. Oddy was the first baptized. Seymour gave the declaration and with Cook's help, dipped her deep into the water. She came up speaking in tongues.

Others following the Lord in baptism were Cummings, Ingland, Lloyd and Cripe, plus Ada Willey, Mabel Cook, Naomi Groves, Nelda Kelso, Grace Harrison, Luella McCarty, Elizabeth Shaw and Bennett Lawrence.

After the baptism, the faithful returned to Murphy Hall for a foot washing service. Visitors were not allowed in the room as about one hundred believers washed each other's feet. Four large tubs of water were carried into the hall for the service and men and women were discretely separated to opposite ends of the room. Men washed men's feet and women, women's. Afterwards, the men hugged each other and shared the holy kiss. Women in the front of the hall did the same. Once again, the secular press made an issue of blacks and whites hugging, kissing and showing affection to one another.

When the fellowship ended, Seymour announced, "Now we will have the Lord's Supper. Praise God!"[14]

---

[14]"Bluks to Wash Feet," *Indianapolis Star* (12 June 1907), 3; "Bluk Feet, Little and Big, Scubbed," *Indianapolis Star* (16 June 1907),

Seymour, following another tradition of the Evening Light Saints, taught that baptism, foot washing and communion were all mandatory church ordinances.[15]

News of the Saturday services brought more opposition to the meetings. Neighbors from around the hall presented a signed petition to the Board of Public Safety, asking them to close the mission. A group of 200 "hooting, jeering" protesters surrounded the meeting threatening the safety of Cook and others inside. The police had to be called at least six times.[16]

The mayor of the city, Mr. Hookwaiter, visited the meetings and determined the group was not a nuisance and that they deserved the protection of the police. Hookwaiter said, "I want to say that I have seen just such actions as theirs indulged in hundreds of revivals and many, many prayer-meetings. True, they get worked up in their religious frenzy until they do not seem to understand what they are doing, but they do not harm anyone and they do not interfere with any of the neighbors." The mayor also said he saw no inappropriate familiarity between races and "I did not see a man place his finger on a woman."[17]

The Cummings family left Indianapolis for their missionary trip on June 18, and the mission hosted a

---

10; ""Gliggy Bluks Bathed in Fall Creek Waters," *Indianapolis News* (17 June 1907), 7.

[15]Seymour, *Doctrines.*

[16]"Desire the 'Bluks' to Go," *Indianapolis News* (17 June 1907), 1; "Young Mob Assails Bluks' Temple," *Indianapolis Star* (17 June 1907), 3; "Bluks Appeal to Police," *Indianapolis Sun* (17 June 1907), 7.

[17]"Mayor Will Protect 'Gliggy Bluks,'" *Indianapolis News* (19 June 1907), 1; "Police Have No Power to Stop Bluks' Meetings," *Indianapolis News* (20 June 1907), 18.

farewell service.[18] The time of Seymour's departure is not known, but it must have been soon thereafter.

Later that year, Glenn Cook invited Henry Prentice to come to the city from Los Angeles and lead the work. With the help of Oddous Barber, they soon converted Garfield Thomas Haywood who became a prominent Pentecostal pioneer and respected church leader.[19]

On the same Eastern journey, while ministering with Tom Hezmalhalch in Zion, Illinois, Seymour sent this glowing report back to the mission, "People here receive the baptism in their pews while the service is going on and sometimes scores of them receive it. It is the sweetest thing you want to see. It reminds me of old Azusa ten months ago. The people that receive the baptism seem so happy, they remind me of our people at home. There are little children from six years and on up who have the baptism with the Holy Ghost, just as we have it in Los Angeles. Praise our God. This is another Azusa. It would do you good to hear these people speak under the power of the Holy Ghost. Some of them converse in tongues. Brother Tom has never lost the spirit of the Azusa. He is still fired up the same as ever. Everywhere I have traveled among our baptized souls they seem to have such joy and freedom in the Holy Ghost."[20]

Often neglected and almost forgotten in Los Angeles, Seymour was still well-received across the country, and he continued to travel throughout his life.

---

[18] "Hit Brother Cook," 2.

[19] Victoria M. Peagler, "Garfield Thomas Haywood-1880-1931: From a Migrant's Son to an Internationally Reknowned Churchman," dissertation, Wright State University, 1993, 10-14.

[20] "In the Last Days" *The Apostolic Faith* [Los Angeles] (June to September 1907), 1.

In the years between 1906 and 1922, he conducted preaching tours in many American cities including, but not limited to, Indianapolis, Chicago, Cincinnati, New York, Washington, Baltimore, and Houston.

On more than one of his many Eastern trips, Seymour held revivals, issued ministerial credentials, and planted new churches. In 1911, in Handsome, Virginia, Elder Charles W. Lowe, a carpenter, was left in charge of one such mission. Seymour appointed Lowe "Senior Bishop and Chief Apostle of the Apostolic Faith Mission." Under Lowe's leadership the group expanded into North Carolina, Maryland, Ohio, Pennsylvania, New York, New Jersey and Liberia, West Africa. After Lowe, the church was led by John Thomas Cox, Robert Clarence Butts and Oree Keyes. The fruit of Lowe's and his successors' labors continue until today in the fellowship known as the Apostolic Faith Church of God.[21]

Over the decades, the Eastern churches founded by Seymour and his surrogates suffered many schisms and divisions, but in 1987 several churches with ties to Seymour's ministry formed a loose knit and very fragile federation of church groups affiliated under the name The Azusa Street Mission Churches. Cooperating churches include Apostolic Faith Holiness Church of God, Apostolic Faith Churches of God, Apostolic Faith Church of God in Christ, Apostolic Faith Church of God Live On, The Church of Christ Holiness Unto the Lord, Inc., Saints of Runney Mede Holiness Church and Sweet Haven Church.[22]

---

[21]DuPree, *African-American*, 138-140; Otis J. Smith and Oree Keyes, *Manual of the Apostolic Faith Church of God* (Franklin, VA: General Assembly AFCOG, n. d.), 8,9.

[22]DuPree, *African-American*, 138-140. The author made dozens of telephone calls, wrote many letters and even visited

Seymour was back in Centerville in the Fall of 1912. He, along with his siblings, received $5.00 from the Iberia, St. Mary, and Eastern Railroad Company for a right of way across the family farm. Phillis, who was staying with Jennie at the mission in Los Angeles, received $25.00 for her interest.[23]

In 1918, Seymour returned to Virginia again, preaching at the Holiness church attended by Estella Cobb. The church enthusiastically received the Pentecostal message. Cobb remembered that the people "rushed" to hear Seymour.[24]

On at least one occasion, Seymour ministered with his friend, John G. Lake, in the Pacific Northwest. Lake said "the glory and power of God was upon his spirit" as Seymour preached to more than 10,000 people. The impact on the audience was phenomenal as men "shook and trembled and cried to God."[25]

Seymour was a frequent visitor at the annual convocations of the Church of God in Christ. He was an honored guest of his dear friend, Bishop Mason. He

---

Franklin, VA to learn more about this federation and the history of Seymour's eastern ministry. Unfortunately, the sparse history, if any exists, is guarded more securely than Fort Knox. The one pleasant exception was Bishop Oree Keyes who sent a copy of the group's manual with important photographs of Seymour and Lowe, and copies of the most recent convention programs. He has promised to share more information in the future.

[23] St. Mary Parish, Louisiana, *Book "3H" of Conveyances,* 93, 24 October 1912; St. Mary Parish, Louisiana, *Book "3H" of Conveyances,* 93, 12 November 1912.

[24] DuPree, *African-American,* 473.

[25] *John G. Lake: His Life . . .*, 88. Lake does not say if this was at his church in Portland (1914-1920) or later when he moved to Spokane (1920–).

attended several meetings in Memphis and at least one in Chicago, probably in January 1921.[26]

In 1921, on one of his last missionary journeys, Seymour preached several weeks at the Christian and Missionary Alliance Church in Columbus, Ohio. Some of the last memories of the bishop came from Mrs. Georgiana Aycock nee Pepsico of Columbus. She said, "The glow would be on that man's face. He looked like an angel from heaven. So many wanted to hear him, they had heard of him . . . He was no man to exalt himself, but a humble man. When you'd meet him at the door you could just feel . . . he was a real man of God . . . He didn't talk much. He was not a conversationalist. He'd get off about the Lord, being true to God."[27]

Perhaps on the same trip, Seymour ministered in the New York City area. Bishop Frank Clemmons met Seymour at the corner of 135th Street and Lenox Avenue in Harlem. Since Clemmons was affiliated with the Church of God in Christ, Seymour asked him if he knew Mason. Clemmons answered, "Yes, as a matter of fact, Bishop Mason is in New Jersey now attending meetings." When Seymour asked to see Mason, Clemmons took him to East Orange, New Jersey. These two gospel soldiers met, for what would probably be the last time, at the home of Elder James Wells, pastor of the Old Tabernacle Church of God in Christ. Clemmons saw the two giants "weeping on each other's shoulders and praising God in power and glory."[28]

---

[26]Sherry DuPree, personal interview, 26 February 1999. The dates and circumstances of these meetings cannot be confirmed. Unfortunately, the minutes from many of the Church of God in Christ convocations were destroyed in a recent flood.
[27]Nelson, 269.
[28]Clemmons, 55.

At his death, Seymour's supporters reported correctly, "The world was his parish."[29] The faithful pilgrim and apostle had taken the Pentecostal message far beyond the walls of the Azusa Street Mission.

---

[29]"Brother Seymour Called Home," *The Pentecostal Herald* (1 October 1922), 1.

Seymour often rode the train from Los Angeles to points East.
From the **The Los Angeles Express**

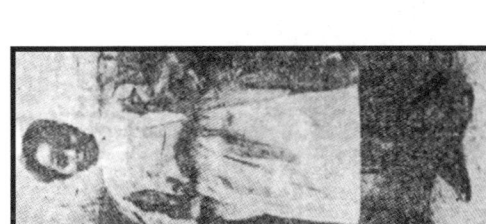

The Cummings children, left to right, John, Frank, Mattie, Majorie and Bessie
Photos used by permission
Indiana State Historical Society

Mrs. Tom Oddy
Photo used by permission
Indiana State Historical Society

The Indianapolis baptismal service.
Glenn Cook is on the right, in the water.

Mrs. Oddy is assisted from the baptismal waters
by Joseph Ingland and Frank Cummings
Photos used by permission
Indiana State Historical Society

320

SPRAY FROM THE GLIGGY BLUKS' WATER CARNIVAL

This newspaper cartoon gives sketches of Seymour and Cook at the baptismal service.
Larry Martin Collection
From the **The Indianapolis Star**

Glenn A. Cook
Larry Martin Collection

Murphy League Hall and Glenn Cook inside
Photos used by permission
Flower Pentecostal Heritage Center

Charles W. Lowe

Manual of the Apostolic Faith Church of God
Photos courtesy of Bishop Oree Keyes

17 The End: Disappointment and Death

One of the last detailed looks at the mission was in 1912 when English publisher, A. A. Boddy visited. Seymour was on one of his evangelistic trips in the East, but Mrs. Seymour greeted Boddy at the mission. Seymour's aged mother, Phillis, J. A. Warren, and his wife also lived in the upstairs apartments.[1] Boddy noticed a sign protruding from the building with the words "Jesus Saves" and a transparency that said, "You shall know the truth and the truth shall make you free." There was also a chalkboard near the front door announcing service times.

Boddy was invited to preach in the mission and described the service in detail. Mrs. Seymour led the

---

[1] Boddy, "At Los Angeles," 232-234. Phillis lived in Los Angeles for some time. In 1915 she listed 312 Azusa as her address when asking for an increase in her widow's pension. See, *Widow's*

hymn singing, exhorting between each song. She also led the assembly in prayer and prayed "as one who knew God." The singing was "very earnest" and was without musical accompaniment. The meeting was "orderly" and both blacks and whites attended the service.

The building was "brightly lit up," clean and comfortable. A board floor had been added to the sanctuary and the building was "nicely furnished."

After Boddy's sermon, many "seekers" came to the altar. One man was delivered from the "demon of drink" and some were healed and baptized in the Holy Spirit. Boddy said, "I am greatly drawn to these dear colored people."[2]

By 1914, C. H. Mason sent Eddie R. Driver to organize a Church of God in Christ church in Los Angeles. The church experienced a great revival with souls saved, sanctified and baptized.[3] Although Mason and Seymour remained fast friends, it could not possibly have strengthened Seymour's work to have yet another black Pentecostal mission in the city.

Pension, 472, 276, Simon Semour Pension File, National Archives and Records Administration. She returned to Verdunville when she became ill. Her daughter Julia apparently traveled to California to bring her home. Phillis died January 30,1940 from chronic myocarditis, a heart ailment. Also see Interview, Lucille Seymour; St. Mary Parish, Louisiana, *Book "3H" of Conveyances,* 93, 12 November 1912; and Phillis Seymour, *Standard Certificate of Death,* 3 February 1940.

[2]Boddy, "At Los Angeles," 232-234; A. A. Boddy, "A Meeting at the Azusa Street Mission, Los Angeles," *Confidence* (November 1912), 244, 245.

[3]Aaron Howard, "Southern California Is the Cradle of our Rich Pentecostal Heritage" (May 28, 1998); available from http://www.bonniebrae.org/article.htm; Internet; accessed 12 December 1998, 3.

On May 19, 1914, the mission held a business meeting, amended the articles of incorporation, and elected trustees. In addition to Bishop and Mrs. Seymour, the church chose Richard Asbery, Spencer James, and James Ross to serve as the official board. The new constitution required that the bishop, vice-bishop, and all trustees were to be "people of color." Seymour reluctantly excluded whites from leadership in the church, "not for discrimination, but for peace."[4]

At this time less than twenty people attended the Apostolic Faith Mission, most of them the original seekers from Bonnie Brae.[5] There is little doubt that racial prejudice contributed to the diminished role that Seymour would play in the future of the movement. Yet, he was never bitter. An old black proverb says, "There is no medicine for hate," and Seymour lived his life with this in mind.[6] Considering the Spirit's work and not his own feelings, he wrote, ". . . division came through some of our brethren, and the Holy Spirit was grieved."[7]

Seymour wrote and collected a 95-page book in 1915, **The Doctrines and Discipline of the Azusa Street Apostolic Faith Mission of Los Angeles.** He wrote about "all the trouble we have had with some of our white brethren," but said, "We love our white brethren and sisters and welcome them." He went on to say, "Our colored brethren must love our white brethren and respect them in the truth so that the

---

[4]Seymour, *Doctrines*, 12, 48, 49; Articles of Incorporation, Apostolic Faith Mission, Los Angeles County, California, 3 June 1914.
[5]Shumway, "Study," 179.
[6]A. O. Stafford, "The Mind of the African Negro as reflected in his Proverbs," *The Journal of Negro History* (January 1916), 46.
[7]Seymour, *Doctrines*, 12.

Word of God can have free course, and our white brethren must love their colored brethren and respect them in the truth so that the Holy Spirit won't be grieved. I hope we won't have any more trouble and division spirit."[8]

It is obvious that much of the discipline was borrowed from other sources with Seymour editing the material to fit the needs of the mission. For example, the "Articles of Religion," "Rules for a Preacher's Conduct" and several other passages in the book were taken from **The Doctrines and Discipline of the African Methodist Episcopal Zion Church**. Seymour omitted several passages including information about infant baptism from the A. M. E. Zion book. He also added a note on foot washing as a church ordinance.[9] The collecting and editing from other sources and adding of original material for the publication of this book would require more education and ability on Seymour's part than many historians are willing to acknowledge.

Long-time friend F. W. Williams broke with Seymour and the Los Angeles organization in October 1915. He changed the name of the churches he founded to Apostolic Faith Mission Church of God.[10]

About 1917 or 1918, Seymour called a meeting for restoring unity to the Pentecostal movement. Although he invited all of the Los Angeles leaders to attend, only two showed up for the meeting. A disappointed

---

[8] Seymour, *Doctrines*, 10, 12, 13.
[9] G. L. Blackwell, ed., *The Doctrines and Discipline of the African Methodist Episcopal Zion Church*, (Charlotte: A. M. E. Zion Publication House, 1916), 25-34.
[10] Witherspoon, 2.

Seymour laments, "He has done what little he could to help the movement."[11]

The meetings at Azusa Street were cut back to only one day a week, and only a couple dozen attended. Seymour taught with a blackboard and chalk and sometimes visitors from the glory days would stop by and visit.[12]

Money at the mission became scarce. Sometimes Seymour would have to receive a second offering just to cover mission expenses. Mrs. Seymour had to return to secular employment to help the couple make ends meet.[13]

Aimee Semple McPherson arrived in California late in 1918. Her biographer said, "the Azusa Street Revival was little more than a memory." When she held her first campaign in Los Angeles in 1918, Seymour attended. He told a friend that "he had not been feeling completely well; his heart had been hurting him."[14]

Fourteen years after the fire fell, Azusa held an anniversary service and Bible conference. Unlike the revival of 1906, the 1920 meeting was more liturgical with a printed program for the services. The rapture of the church was the theme for the meeting, but teaching on repentance, conversion, sanctification, the baptism of the Holy Spirit, healing, and doctrines of baptisms were also included. The selected songs for the service were a mixture of traditional hymns, revival

---

[11] Nelson, 41.
[12] Nelson, 261, 262.
[13] Nelson, 62.
[14] Daniel Mark Epstein, *Sister Aimee: The Life of Aimee Semple McPherson* (New York: Harcourt Brace Jovanovich, Publishers, 1993), 152; Nelson, 267.

songs and black spirituals. The Azusa Street favorite, "The Comforter Has Come," was also included.[15]

Some of the most important players in the Los Angeles story were still in the city and may have participated in the anniversary service. Joseph A. Warren, now 69, was living with his sister and brother-in-law at 1445 W. 36th Street.

Edward S. Lee, 60, and his wife Mattie, 37, lived at 3624 Western. An eleven-year-old niece, Mary Ann Wiley, lived with the couple.

Richard and Ruth Asbery still lived in the house where the fire fell, but the city had renumbered the street, changing their address to 216 Bonnie Brae. Their daughter Willie Ella and two grandchildren, Ruth E. and Marian E. Pruden, lived with them in the home. Their son Morton and his wife, Julya, lived on the same block, at 228 1/2 Bonnie Brae. One son, Richard, Jr., an eyewitness to Pentecost, apparently strayed from God and appears to have been incarcerated at San Quentin. At age 61, Richard maintained his position as a janitor.[16]

Lucy Farrow, the other major player in the outpouring, had returned to Texas to join her son and his family. After suffering from intestinal tuberculosis, she was promoted to her heavenly reward on February 21, 1911.[17]

---

[15] *Azusa Street Mission: Fourteenth Anniversary of the Outpouring of the Holy Spirit In Los Angeles, California* (Los Angeles: W. H. Giles, 1920), 6.

[16] United States Census, Los Angeles County, California, 1920. The prison did not respond to the author's request for confirmation.

[17] Anne Douglass to Larry Martin, 9 June 1999; Lucy Farrow, *Standard Certificate of Death*, 22 February 1911. Farrow's son died on April 14, 1929. See James M. Pointer, *Standard Certificate of Death*, 16 April 1929.

Frank Bartleman continued to do mission work in Los Angeles. He had traveled the world preaching Pentecost. Bartleman joined the "Oneness" Pentecostals and was rebaptized in "Jesus Name." He was then ostracized by most of his Trinitarian friends. He continued, nevertheless, to be an avid author, writing *My Story: "The Latter Rain"* (1909); *From Plow to Pulpit: From Maine to California* (1924); *Two Years Mission Work in Europe Just before the World War* (1924); *Around the World by Faith, with Six Weeks in the Holy Land* (1925); *The Deity of Christ* (1926); and the widely read *How Pentecost Came to Los Angeles* (1925).

Korsets Seier, a periodical from Norway carried a report on the mission in 1920. They said the church had been through "stirring times." Their report that Seymour had returned to the mission and the work was "resumed" led European historian Nils Bloch-Hoell to erroneously presume that the mission had been closed for a time. More probably, Mrs. Seymour or another worker was in charge of the mission while Seymour took another of his mission trips. The magazine noted, "The Mission is independent. It cannot compromise. When people have tried to impose a new doctrine they have been rejected."[18]

John Matthews, a noted critic of the tongues movement, attended a convention in Los Angeles in the summer of 1922. He noticed an aged black man in the audience. When he inquired as to his identity, he was informed that the visitor was Seymour, the "man who had introduced 'tongues' on the Western Coast." He described Seymour, who was in his early fifties, as looking "worn, tired, (and) decrepit."[19]

---

[18] Bloch-Hoell, 54.
[19] John Matthews, *Speaking in Tongues* (n.p., 1925), 14.

On September 28, 1922, Seymour suffered serious chest pains and shortness of breath. Dr. Walter M. Boyd was called to the mission for a single visit. At 5 P. M., Bishop Seymour was called home to be with the Lord he loved. His vision never waned; his last message was "a plea for love among the brethren everywhere." He spent his last day with his beloved Jennie, praying, singing, praising God, and planning for the work.[20]

Seymour died without a struggle. Smiling radiantly he spoke his last words, "I love my Jesus so." His followers reported his death and stated, "His life was a crowning example of the believer in word and deed, self-denial and whole consecration to God. He was true to the end, never failing in faith or lowering the standards, but standing against every tide in firm allegiance to God and the truth. He so often said, 'Never doubt your God and never disappoint him.' He walked in closest communion and fellowship, looking unto Jesus, his never failing source of comfort and strength."[21]

Seymour's funeral on October 2 was attended by about 200 people, mostly black. After a long service with many testimonials, Mrs. Seymour brought the service to a close. His earthly remains were laid to rest in Evergreen Cemetery in a simple wooden casket. A few weeks later, he was disinterred and his body was placed in a concrete vault. Admirers purchased a simple headstone that reads, "Our Pastor."[22]

G. T. Haywood of Indianapolis, by then a leader in the "Jesus Only" movement and a man who differed

---

[20]"Brother Seymour," 1; "Home-going of Rev. W. J. Seymore," *The Bridegroom's Messenger* (November and December 1922), 3; Nelson, 270; W.J. Seymour, *Standard Certificate of Death*.
[21]"Brother Seymour," 1.
[22]Nelson, 270.

with Seymour on both his sanctification and Trinitarian views, wrote, "Though he did not agree with the brethren in many things yet he was loved and respected."[23] The ancient writer of the biblical Proverbs said, "When a man's ways please the Lord, he maketh even his enemies to be at peace with him" (Proverbs 16:7).

After Seymour's death, his faithful wife, who was herself "an evangelist of power and note greatly loved by all," continued as pastor of the mission. Seymour had "placed" the work into her hands before his death.[24]

Lewi Pethrus, a noted Pentecostal leader from Sweden, visited Los Angeles in 1924. He reported to Swedish readers of **Evangelii Harold** that the work of the mission was continuing. Very little else is known of the work of the mission for nearly ten years after Seymour's death.[25]

R. C. Griffith, a white man, tried to gain control of the mission in 1930. Claiming to be a Coptic priest, Griffith showed up one day for a prayer meeting at the mission. His request to join in the intercession was granted and the people were impressed by the fervency of his prayer. Griffith was invited back and began to attend daily, "ingratiating himself in the affection of the membership."

To the surprise of Mrs. Seymour, Griffith announced that he had canvassed the congregation and a majority wanted him to replace her and assume the pastorate. Once again, a white man was trying to take the

---

[23]"Death of W. J. Seymour," *The Voice in the Wilderness* (Volume 2, No. 13 n.d.), 7
[24]"Brother Seymour," 1.
[25]Bloch Hoell, 54.

work from its God-ordained leadership. Sad to say, the remaining white element in the church had joined him in this evil plot. The resulting "fight" became so bitter that the police padlocked the mission on January 16, 1931. Worshipers were not readmitted until their problems were settled in a secular courtroom.

Finally, Judge Guerin ruled in favor of Mrs. Seymour and she was able to retain the property.[26] The legal battle took a heavy financial toll on the church. Late in 1930, the corporation borrowed $2,000 from Mrs. Seymour, who took a six-year mortgage on the property. Long-time supporter, Richard Asbery signed the mortgage as church trustee. Florence M. Ludden was the mission's secretary.[27]

In April 8, 1931, the members of the church amended their bylaws once again. There were twenty members present. They were "a majority of the voting power of the membership of said corporation" since the total membership was no more than "twenty-seven." The president of the corporation was N. H. Barragar. Jay P. Nix served as secretary.

The changes appear to weaken the office of bishop and give the power to the trustees.[28] The amendments, however, were of little consequence. After the business meeting, there were not many more meetings held at 312 Azusa.

The City of Los Angeles took advantage of the problems at Azusa Street and condemned the building as a fire hazard. According to Stanley Frodsham, the

---

[26] Bass, 25,26.
[27] Mortgage, 31 December 1930, Los Angeles County.
[28] Articles of Incorporation, Apostolic Faith Mission, Los Angeles County, California, 14 May 1931.

building was offered to the Assemblies of God. They rejected the offer, because they were not interested in "relics."[29] The Apostolic Faith Gospel Mission was razed in 1931. Frank Bartleman visited the demolition site and took the numbers "312" that had marked the building and placed them on the wall of his Los Angeles home.[30]

Mrs. Seymour continued meetings with the faithful in her home on Bonnie Brae. The movement that began as a cottage meeting on Bonnie Brae had made the full circle and returned to the street where it had begun twenty-five years earlier.

Mrs. Seymour remained as pastor of the small group until June 1933.[31] In difficult financial times, she sold the mortgage on the Azusa Street property to a Los Angeles Bank and also mortgaged her home. Because she could not make the payments or pay past due taxes, the bank foreclosed on the property on January 13, 1936.[32]

Jennie Seymour became ill and was admitted to Rancho Los Amigos County Hospital on February 3, 1936.[33] Realizing her weakening physical condition, on June 12, Mrs. Seymour gave her brother, Henry R. Moore, power of attorney to conduct her business.[34] Just over two weeks later on July 2, 1936, she joined her husband and her Lord Jesus Christ in heaven.[35]

---

[29] Bloch-Hoell, 39.
[30] Nelson, 273.
[31] Jennie Evans Seymour, *Standard Certificate of Death*.
[32] Nelson, 43, 45, 273, 274.
[33] Nelson, 45, 274.
[34] Power of Attorney, 12 June 1936, Book 14128, p. 288, Los Angeles County, California.
[35] J. E. Seymour, *Standard Certificate of Death*.

After lengthy legal wrangling, the bank received the mission property on June 10, 1938. 312 Azusa Street, in the possession of Security First National Bank was turned into a parking lot.[36]

At one point, Bishop A. C. Driscoll and Elder H. S. Covington attempted to revive the mission, announcing the "reopening of Azusa Apostolic Faith Mission now located at 9411 Parmelee Avenue." A brochure carried testimonies from Azusa Street and pictures of the mission and Seymour. Driscoll even proclaimed himself as the successor to Seymour. Their efforts, however well intentioned, were largely unsuccessful.[37]

On at least three occasions, celebrations have been held to commemorate the Azusa Street revival. April 9-26, 1936, a 30th anniversary celebration was held at the Saints Home Church and Angelus Temple. Emma Cotton was "manager" for the event. Osterberg, Bartleman, and a number of the other Azusa faithful joined Aimee Semple McPherson and more than twenty other pastors in sponsoring the event. Guests were invited to come praying "that the Lord will send a mighty revival." A memorial service was held for "all the saints that have gone to be with the Lord these 30 years."[38]

Elder Henry and Mrs. Henry (Emma) Cotton also held a 39th anniversary meeting in 1945 at Azusa Pentecostal Tabernacle, a church they pastored at 1001 East 27th Street in Los Angeles.[39] A much larger and

---

[36]Nelson, 45, 274.
[37]Driscoll, 4.
[38]Great Anniversary, flyer, Flower Pentecostal Heritage Center.
[39]The Golden Anniversary, flyer, Flower Pentecostal Heritage Center; Tharp, "Pentecostal Sects . . .," III, 2;Nickel, 20-27.

more spectacular event was scheduled during the golden anniversary of the revival. Angelus Temple was the site for this meeting that brought together some of the world's leading Pentecostals and surviving Azusa Street participants. Oral Roberts, William Branham, Jack Coe, David Nunn, Gordon Lindsey, and many others hosted services attended by thousands.[40]

In 1975, the students of Howard University chose the name "William Seymour Pentecostal Fellowship" to identify an ecumenical Pentecostal campus ministry. This was probably the first organization to honor the leader.[41]

The Assemblies of God dedicated the first permanent home for their denominational seminary in Springfield, Missouri In 1998. To honor the Azusa Street leader, the chapel was named the William J. Seymour Chapel. A stained glass window depicting Seymour and the fire that fell at Azusa Street adorns the facility. A memorial plaque reads, "William J. Seymour, pastor of the Azusa Street Mission played a formative role in the worldwide expansion of the Pentecostal movement. The ministry of the son of former slaves was marked by sound judgment, spiritual balance, personal integrity, and faithfulness. He encouraged every member of his congregation to minister, to testify, and to share the gospel whenever God led them, regardless of race, class, gender, or age.

"He demonstrated the value of racial unity and cultural harmony, exhorting his congregation to seek God

---

[40] Great 39th Anniversary of "Old Azusa," flyer, Flower Pentecostal Heritage Center.

[41] Tenney, 223, 224; "Seymour House: Intercollegiate Pentecostal Conference-International, Inc.," *Jet* (18 May 1987), 14.

about all things, to exhibit the fruit of the Spirit even as they exercised the Spirit's gifts, and to measure all doctrine and experience by the word of God. He remains an eloquent model for Pentecostal ministry."

Today, the former 312 Azusa is part of Los Angeles' "Little Tokyo." In February 1998, a Walk of Remembrance led by Azusa scholar Cecil M. Robeck ended with a rally at the site. Those gathered committed themselves to erect a memorial wall and historical marker to commemorate W. J. Seymour and the Azusa revival.[42]

Finally, on February 13, 1999, a memorial plaque was placed at the site. The ceremony was attended by participants from a number of ethnic groups and Christian denominations. Fred and Wilma Berry led worship, Cecil M. Robeck presented the history of the mission, and a number of local pastors greeted the assembly before a ribbon was cut and the marker unveiled.[43]

Visitors can find the marker in Nagouchi Plaza, the entrance to the Japanese-American community. Before the Pentecostal World Conference is held in Los Angeles in 2001, the Azusa Street Memorial Committee hopes to expand the memorial by creating "an interactive site including historic photographs and video terminals describing key events."[44]

To some it would appear that the Azusa fires were slowly extinguished by time, division, and opposition.

---

[42] Takeshi Nakayama, "African American Roots of Little Tokyo," *The Rafu Shimpo* 13 (February 1998), 1, 4.

[43] Available from http://www.Joshuam.org/bonnie.htm; Internet; accessed 7 July 1999.

[44] "Azusa Street Memorial Site Dedicated in Los Angeles," *The Pentecostal Evangel* (28 March 1999), 24.

This, however, could only be the view of the nearsighted or narrow-minded. The Holy Ghost fires ignited at Azusa have not gone out; the breath of God merely blew them to other locations, both near and far. Today, the Spirit of Azusa continues to blaze in places like Toronto, Ontario; Pensacola, Florida; Smithton, Missouri; and even unto the uttermost parts of the earth. Like a prairie fire swept by a West Texas sirocco, the winds of God will continue to spread the flaming inferno of Pentecostal fire until Jesus returns to welcome all of His children home.

W. J. Seymour in his senior years
Photo used by permission
Dixon Pentecostal Research Center

This series of photos were taken by Alexander A. Boddy in August 1912

Photos used by permission.
Flower Pentecostal Heritage Center
(Assemblies of God Archives)

Photo taken by Donald Gee
This is probably the most published and perhaps most popular picture of the mission.
Photo used by permission
Flower Pentecostal Heritage Center

Later view of the mission
Photo used by permission
Apostolic Faith International Headquarters
Portland, Oregon

More late views of the mission
Photos used by permission
Apostolic Faith International Headquarters
Portland, Oregon

Missionary Frank Bartleman
Larry Martin Collection

Frank Bartleman in his senior years
Photo used by permission
Flower Pentecostal Heritage Center

William J. Seymour's grave
Larry Martin Collection

A memorial plaque placed on the grave by the Apostolic Faith Church of God, founded by Seymour
Larry Martin Collection

Thirtieth anniversary flyer
Used by permission
Flower Pentecostal Heritage Center

Thirty-ninth anniversary flyer
Used by permission
Flower Pentecostal Heritage Center

Fiftieth anniversary banner
Photo used by permission
Flower Pentecostal Heritage Center

Fiftieth anniversary promotional flyer
Used by permission
Flower Pentecostal Heritage Center

Today in downtown Los Angeles,
312 Azusa Street is now part of a plaza adjoining the
Japanese Cultural Center.

Larry Martin Collection

Stained-glass window in William J. Seymour Chapel
Assemblies of God Theological Seminary
Photo used by permission
Flower Pentecostal Heritage Center

The 1999 dedication service and ribbon cutting for the new memorial plaque at Azusa Street

Praise and worship led by Fred and Wilma Berry and Rochelle Lander

Front row: Mel Robeck, Elliott Mason and Fred Berry
Photos used by permission
Joshua Ministries

Commemorative Plaque

Inscription: "This plaque commemorates the site of the Azusa Street Mission which was located at 312 Azusa Street. Formally known as the Apostolic Faith Mission, it served as a fountainhead for the international Pentecostal Movement from 1906-1931. Pastor William J. Seymour oversaw the 'Azusa Street Revival.' He preached a message of salvation, holiness, and power, and welcomed visitors from around the world, transformed the congregation into a multicultural center of worship, and commissioned pastors, evangelists, and missionaries to take the message of 'Pentecost' (Acts 2:1-4) to the world. Today, members of the Pentecostal/Charismatic Movement number half a billion worldwide."

The Larry Martin Collection

Epilogue

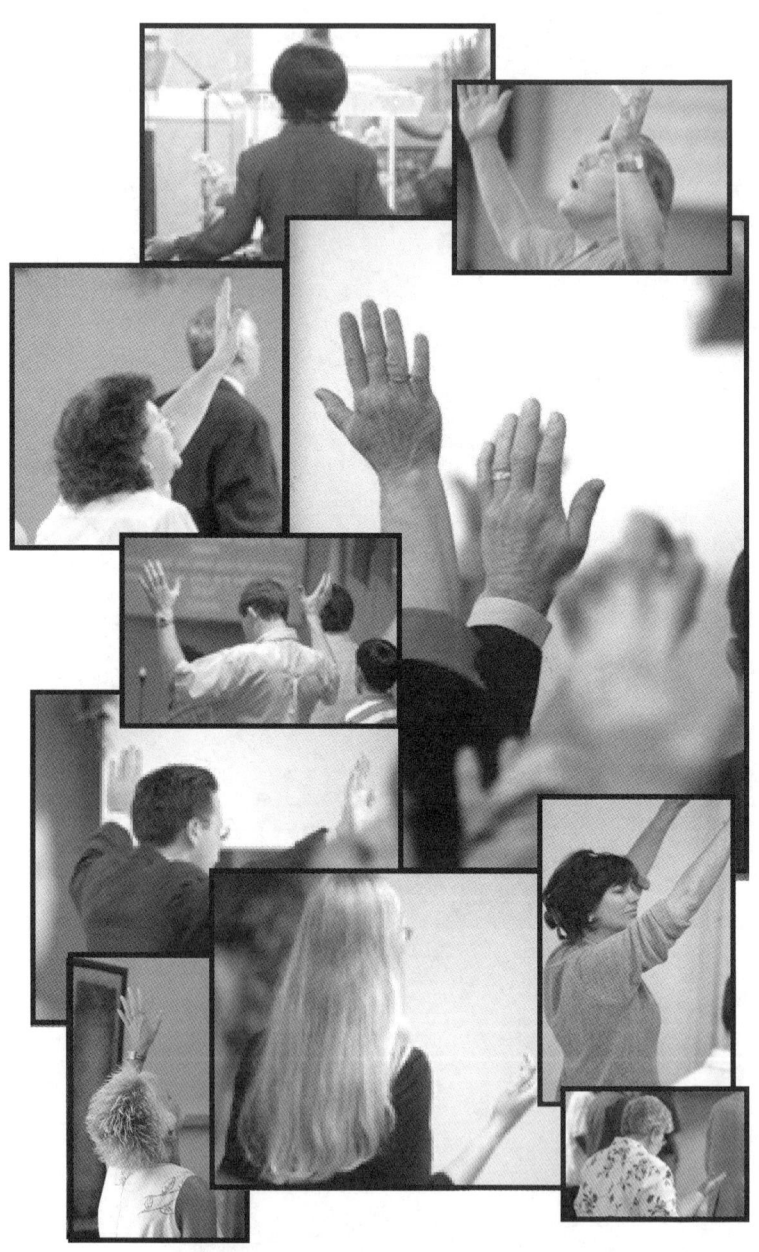

The cry for revival continues!
Pensacola Revival Church
Photos courtesy of Richie Wood

Opportunity once passed is lost forever. There is a time when the tide is sweeping by our door. We may then plunge in and be carried to glorious blessing, success and victory. To stand shivering on the bank, timid or paralyzed with stupor, at such a time, is to miss all, and most miserably fail, both for time and for eternity. Oh, our responsibility! The mighty tide of God's grace and favor is even now sweeping by us, in its prayer-directed course. There is a river (of salvation) the streams whereof make glad the city of God (Psalm 46:4). It is time to "get together," and plunge in, individually and collectively. We are baptized "in one Spirit, into one body" (1 Cor. 12:13). Let us lay aside all carnal contentions and divisions, that separate us from each other and from God. If we are of His body, we are "one body." The opportunity of a lifetime, of centuries, is at our door, to be eternally gained or lost. There is no time to hesitate. Act quickly, lest another take thy crown. Oh, church of Christ, awake! Be baptized with power. Then fly to rescue others. And to meet your Lord.

Frank Bartleman
Gospel Tract
June, 1906

Once again America stands on the verge of a great spiritual awakening. The river is rising across the nation. Let us not allow this mighty torrent to pass us by. Pray, church, pray! May the same Spirit that flooded Azusa Street now flood every street from Pennsylvania Avenue to Wall Street to Main Street to your street. Please, God, send revival to the United States of America.

Larry Martin
September 1998

The favorite song of the Azusa faithful

Index

Adams, Asa, 258
Adams, Mr., 206pl.
Adams, Owen, 233
Africa, 72, 198, 201, 235
African languages, 236
African Methodist Episcopal, 104, 155, 156
African Methodist Episcopal Zion, 104
Akron, OH, 228
Alabama, 87, 215
Alexander, James, 271
Alliance, OH, 228
All Saints Church, Sunderland, England, 240
Anderson, C. H., 128, 137pl.
Anderson College School of Theology, See **Anderson University**
Anderson, IN, 77
Anderson, Robert, 125
Anderson University, 14, 78
Angelus Temple, Los Angeles, 334, 335
Anglo-Israelism, 24

The Apostolic Faith, Los Angeles, 19, 188, 197, 199, 207pl., 211, 237, 247, 259, 277-280
The Apostolic Faith, Charles Parham's paper, 19, 23
The Apostolic Faith, Portland, 281
Apostolic Faith Church, Baxter Springs, KS, 14
Apostolic Faith Church of God, 312, 322pl.
Apostolic Faith Churches of God, 312
Apostolic Faith Church of God in Christ, 312
Apostolic Faith Church of God Live On, 312
Apostolic Faith Gospel Mission (Azusa Street Mission),Los Angeles, *Also See Los Angeles, 312 Azusa Street,* 20pl., 21, 79, 163pl., 165, 166, 170pl., 178, 189, 199, 209, 237, 238, 262pl., 270-275, 278, 280, 281, 283, 286, 289, 292pl., 296pl., 312, 315, 323,

355

325, 335, 339pl., 340pl., 341pl., 350pl.
Apostolic Faith Holiness Church of God, 312, 333, 334
Apostolic Faith International Headquarters, Portland, OR
Apostolic Faith Mission, Portland, OR, 14, 278
Apostolic Faith Mission Church of God, 326
Apostolic Faith Movement, 21, 26, 27, 72, 90, 94, 98pl., 267, 268, 270, 279, 285, 302
Apalachicola, FL, 51
Arizona, 126
Arkansas, 87, 214, 215, 230
Arkansas Baptist College, 87, 215
Around the World by Faith, with Six Weeks in the Holy Land, 329
Arroyo Seco, CA, 276, 289
Assemblies of God, 14, 213, 221, 222, 290, 291, 303, 333, 335
Assemblies of God Archives, See Flower Pentecostal Heritage Center
Assemblies of God Theological Seminary, 14, 348pl.
Asbery, Julia, 328
Asbery, Morton, 129, 148, 328
Asbery, Richard, 129, 131, 138pl., 144, 147,152pl., 271, 277, 282, 325, 328, 332
Asbery, Richard, Jr., 129, 328
Asbery, Robert, 129
Asbery, Ruth, 129, 131
Asbery, Willie Ella, 129, 147, 152pl.
Atteberry, Thomas G., 127
Austin, TX, 129
Awrey, Daniel, 195, 202pl.
Aycock, Georgiana P., See Pepsico, Georgiana

Azusa Mission, See Apostolic Faith Gospel Mission
Azusa Pentecostal Tabernacle, Los Angeles, 334
Azusa Street, See 312 Azusa Street
Azusa Street Memorial Committee, 336
Azusa Street Mission, See Apostolic Faith Gospel Mission
Azusa Street Mission Churches, 312
Baltimore, MD, 312
Baptism of the Holy Ghost, 24-27, 90, 91, 93-95, 127, 130, 131, 139-142, 144, 145, 147, 148, 166, 180, 182, 184, 185, 190, 192, 193, 200, 201, 210, 212, 213, 215-218, 220-222, 228, 230, 232-235, 237-240, 248, 257, 258, 267, 272, 276, 284, 286, 287, 290, 305, 309, 311, 324, 327
Baptist, 58, 87, 88, 120, 121, 127, 166, 195, 215, 257, 259
Barber, Oddous, 311
Barragar, N. H., 332
Barrancas, FL, 51
Barratt, T.B., 220, 238-240, 246pl.
Bartleman, Frank, 13, 19, 119, 120, 123-125, 132pl., 144, 160, 167, 168, 173pl., 181, 182, 187, 197, 199, 211, 218, 250, 261pl., 272, 283, 287, 288, 89, 294pl., 329, 333, 334, 342pl., 353
Bass, Charlotta, 107
Bass, Sandra, 15
Bates Hotel, Indianapolis, 70, 85pl.
Batman, G.W., 236
Baton Rouge, LA, 14, 67
Baxter Springs, KS, 27

Bayou Sale, 51
Bayou Teche, 32, 42pl., 55
Beckworth, Jim, 104
Belle of Memphis, 82pl.
Bernsten, Brent, 235
Berry, Fred and Wilma, 336, 349pl.
Berwick City, LA, 51
Bethel Bible College, Topeka, KS, 25, 26, 30pl.
Bethel Healing Home, Topeka, KS, 23
Bethel Temple, Los Angeles, 285
Bettex, Nellie, 236
Bettex, Paul, 195, 213, 236, 284
Bible Proofs of a Second Work of Grace, 78
The Bible Training School, Houston, TX, 27, 99pl.
Birmingham, AL, 221, 230
Blanchard, James, 50
Bloch-Hoell, Nils, 329
Bocage, 43pl.
Boddy, Alexander A., 240, 246pl., 323, 324, 339
Boehmer, Brother,
Bombay, India, 198
Bosworth, F. F., 206pl.
Bowdan, Frank, 192
Bowdan, William & Maggie, 192, 205pl.
Bowens, Charles, 53
Bowens, Morris, 47n.1
Bowland Street Mission, Bradford, England, 240
Boyd, Walter M., 330
Bradford, England, 240
Branham, William, 325
Brashear City, LA, 50
Bresee, Phineas, 201, 266pl.
The Bridegroom's Messenger, 221
Britton, F. M., 244pl.
Brother Harry, 301
Brown, Charles, 53

Brownsville Assembly of God, Pensacola, FL, 10
Bryan Hall, Houston, 91, 98pl.
Bunche, Ralph, 105
Burbank Hall, Los Angeles, 124, 165
Burbank Theater, Los Angeles, 124
The Burning Bush, 258, 263pl.
Burning Bush Hall, Los Angeles, 127
Burning Bush Movement, 168
Butler, Benjamin F., 49
Butts, Robert Clarence, 312
Caledonia Hall, Houston, 91
California, 14, 94, 102-104, 106, 121, 147, 155, 156, 167, 190, 210, 220, 230, 269, 270, 275, 306, 327
Cambridge, MA, 228
Hampshire Street, 228
Campbell, Iva, 228, 243pl.
Canada, 13, 198, 276, 285, 290
Cape Girardeau, MO, 14
Carlin, Adilard, 51-53, 61pl.
Carlin, Carmilite, 52
Carney, Julia, 297pl.
Carothers, Warren Faye, 92, 94, 100pl., 268, 270, 271
Carpenter, Professor, 196, 275
Carter, Howard, 181
Carversville, PA, 120
Cashwell, G. B., 209, 218-222, 225pl.
Catholic, **See Roman Catholic**
Catley, Lawrence, 179, 193
Celle, Joseph, 67
Centerville, LA, 31-33, 41pl., 43pl., 51, 55, 58, 66, 89n.9, 313
Century, FL, 230, 231
Chicago, IL, 14, 68n.9, 73-75, 84pl., 120, 127, 178, 210, 230, 232, 233, 286
2329 Dearborn, 74

Clark and Dearborn, 74
China, 198, 233, 235, 236
Christ for the Nations, 14
Christian and Missionary Alliance Church, Columbus, OH, 334
Christian Assembly, Cincinnati, OH, 228
Christian Catholic Church, Chicago, 74
Christian Theological Seminary, Indianapolis, 14
Christie, Tammy, 16
Christ Methodist Church, Indianapolis, 71
Christ's Association of Mississippi of Baptized Believers, 88
Church of the Assumption, Franklin, LA, 14, 53
Church of Christ Holiness, 88, 97pl.
The Church of England, 80
The Church of God, Cleveland, TN, 14, 222, 291
Church of God Holiness, 14
Church of God Holiness unto the Lord, 312
The Church of God in Christ, 88, 146n.31, 215, 218, 291, 313, 314, 324
Church of God, Los Angeles, 253
Church of God Reformation, 77-80, 90, 304, 310
Church of the Nazarene, 14, 201
Cincinnati, OH, 14, 68n.9, 75, 76, 79-81, 228, 312
   23 Longworth, 75
   437 Carlisle Avenue, 75
Civil War, 31-33, 35, 36, 49, 50, 66, 195, 200
Clark, Reuben, 200, 271
Clemmons, Frank, 314
Cleveland, OH, 14, 228
Cleveland, TN, 222
Clifford, Harmon, 229
Cline, Della, 248, 262pl.
Cline, Walter B., 130
Cloud, David, 15
Cobb, Estella, 313
Coe, Jack, 335
Coffin, Levi, 75
Coleman, David, 15, 20pl.
College Park, MD, 14
Collins, Harold, 13
Collins, George G., 13
Collins, W. M., 259
Colorado, 210, 212, 233
Columbia International University, 14
Columbia, SC, 218
Columbus, OH, 14, 81, 89n.10
   315 W. 8th, 81
   413 King, 81
Comanche, OK, 5
The Comforter Has Come, 179, 227, 249, 305, 328, 354pl.
Communion, See The Lord's Supper
Confidence, 283
Conversion, See Salvation,
Conway, Phebe, Emma, Wanda, Elanore, & Albert, 285
Cook, Glenn A., 200, 203pl., 270, 290, 302-305, 308-311, 319pl., 320pl., 321pl.
Cook, Mabel, 309
Cook, Raymond, 15, 18pl.
Coptic Religion, 331
Corps de Afrique, 50, 60pl.
Corum, James F., 15
Cotton, Emma, 145, 191, 203pl., 334
Cotton, Henry, 203pl., 334
Covington, H. S., 286, 299pl., 334
Crawford, Florence, 186, 191, 203pl., 204pl., 229, 231, 234, 278, 279, 280n.49, 281
Crawford, Mildred, 203pl., 231

Crayne, Richard, 15
Cripe, Sarah, 304, 309
Crocker Street Hospital, Los Angeles, 149
Crumpler, Abner B., 219, 220
Cunningham, Johnny, 15
Cummings, Ardell, Bessie, Emma, Ida May, John C., Marjorie, and Mattie Belle, 304, 307, 310, 317pl.
Cummings, E.H., 304, 307, 309
Cummings, Frank, 304, 307, 308, 310, 317pl., 319pl.
Cummings, Mrs. E.H., 304, 305, 307
Dallas, Oregon, 237
Davis, John, 107
The Deity of Christ, 329
Demons, 193, 255, 287, 303, 307, 309, 310
de Neve, Don Felipe, 102
Denison Hotel, Indianapolis, 70, 85pl.
Denny, Lillian, 244pl.
Deno, Vivian, 15
Denver, CO, 95, 96n.35, 210, 229
DePauw University, 14
de Rosa, Adolpha, 229
Devil, **See Satan**
Devils, **See Demons**
Dillon, Dan, 15
Dillon, David, 15
Diossy, R. K., 52
Doak, Edward, 280n.49, 297pl.
The Doctrines and Discipline of the Azusa Street Apostolic Faith Mission of Los Angeles, 13, 325
The Doctrines and Discipline of the African Methodist Episcopal Zion Church, 326
Dodd, James L., 15
Dodd, Judith, 15

Dodge, Brother, 149
Douglass, Frederick, 72, 89
Dowie, John Alexander, 23, 74, 75
Downey, CA, 127
Dozier, Melville and Barton, 123, 133pl.
Driscoll, A. C., 334
Driver, Eddie, 324
Dunn, NC, 221, 226pl.
Dupree, Sherry S., 15
Durham, ME, 24
Durham, Calvin, 15
Durham, William H., 13, 19, 127, 178, 180, 202pl., 232, 233, 286-290, 300pl.
The Eagle, 106
East Orange, NJ, 314
Edwards, J. E., 157
Egypt, 122
Eibinfeldt, Johanna, 285
Eighth and Maple Holiness Church Los Angeles, 211, 272, 294pl.
Eldridge, George, 285, 299pl.
Ellis, Jefferson, 48n.1, 153
Emancipation Proclamation, 49
Emergency and General Hospital, Los Angeles, 196
Emerson, Ralph Waldo, 31
England, 26, 120, 323
English Language, 146, 166
Episcopal Church, 104
Europe, 239, 259, 283
Evangelii Harold, 331
Evans, G.W., 200, 203pl., 229
Evans, May (Mrs. G.W.), 148
Evansville, IN, 14
Evening Light Church of God Holiness, **See Church of God Reformation**
Evergreen Cemetery, Los Angeles, 330
Evertt, Edward, 104

Ewart, Frank, 198, 290
Fall Creek, near Indiana Avenue, Indianapolis, 308
Falling under the power, See Slain in the Spirit
Farrow, Lucy, 89-91, 144, 145, 200, 201, 228, 234, 236, 270, 283, 328
Fasting, 92, 98, 141, 145, 220
Filadelphia Church, Oslo, Norway, 239
Filled with the Holy Ghost, See Baptism of the Holy Ghost
Finney, Charles, 26
Fire Baptized Holiness, 24, 221
First African Methodist Episcopal Church, Los Angeles, 157
First Baptist Church, Glendale, CA, 124, 272
First Baptist Church, Los Angeles, 121-124, 133pl., 273
First Methodist Church, Los Angeles, 125, 261pl.
First New Testament Church, Los Angeles, 124, 165, 196, 272, 273
Fisher, Elmer, 124, 125, 134pl., 181, 190, 259, 272, 273, 295pl.
Fisher, Mrs. Elmer, 126
Fisher, Ruth, 180, 181
Florida, 51
Flower, Alice Reynolds, See Reynolds (Flower), Alice
Flower, Joseph, 303
Flower Pentecostal Heritage Center, 14, 303
Flower, J. Roswell, 303
Foster, Ruth, 15
France, 26
Franklin, LA, 14, 32, 33, 37-39, 50, 52, 53

Franklin, VA, 14
Freedman's Bureau, 36
Free Methodist Church, 120, 210
French Language, 47, 143
Fritsch, Cora, 235
Frodsham, A.W., 285
Frodsham, Stanley, 285, 332
From Plow to Pulpit: From Maine to California, 329
Full Gospel Church (Assembly), Los Angeles, 127, 149
Full Gospel Business Men's Fellowship International, 126
Gabrielino, 101
Galena, KS, 27, 267
Garr, A. G., 127, 134pl., 168, 234, 235, 258
Garr, Lilliam, 244pl
Gee, Donald, 259, 340
Georgia, 219
German Language, 181
Glass, Art, 15
Glenn, Patrolman, 115pl.
Gloster, MS, 197n.84
Godbey, W.B., 283, 284
God's Bible School, Cincinnati, OH, 79
Gohr, Glenn, 14, 15
Gorman Methodist Church, Indianapolis, 71
Gospel Missionary Union, 14
The Gospel Trumpet, 78, 90
Gospel Witness, 19
Goss, Howard A., 92, 99pl., 144, 271
Goss, Lary, 15
Grace and Glory, 14
Grand Hotel, Indianapolis, 70, 85pl., 86pl.
Grant Parish, LA, 40
Graves, A. P., 122
Great Britain, 121, 122
The Great Revival in Wales, 125

Greece, 122
Greek Language, 143, 283
Greenwich, CT, 229
Griffith, R.C., 331
Groves, Naomi, 303, 309
Guerin, Judge, 332
H. & T.C. Yards, Houston, 89
Hagood, Louis M., 71
Haley, Smith, 15
Hall, Anna, 267
Hall, Elnora, 302
Hall, John, 15
Hall, Lee, 230, 242pl.
Hancock County, MS, 156
Handsome, VA, 312
Hanson, E. S., 237
Harlem, NY, 135th Street and Lennox Avenue, 314
Harnais, Father M., 54
Harper's Weekly, 40, 41pl., 45pl.
Harrison, Grace, 309
Harvard University, 104
Harvey, Greg, 16
Hawthorn Street Holiness Church, Los Angeles, 257, 272
Haywood, Garfield Thomas, 311, 330
Healing, 22, 23, 27, 75, 79, 91, 139, 144, 145, 148, 182, 185, 190-193, 200, 201, 214, 216, 221, 240, 276, 290, 324, 327
Heavenly Choir, See Singing in the Spirit
Hebrew Language, 143, 147, 182
Heritage Bible College, 14
Hermon, CA, 276
Hernandez, Vaslin, 56, 57
Hess, Roy, 235
Hezmalhalch, Tom, 206pl., 229, 245pl., 302, 311
Hindustani Language, 143
Holiness Movement, 22, 23, 72, 76, 78, 79, 87-90, 93-95, 96n.36, 119, 120, 127, 130, 131, 139-141, 178, 194, 210, 214, 215, 218, 221, 222, 238, 257, 258, 286, 313
Holler, Brother, 149
Holy Land, 122
Holy Spirit Research Center, ORU, 14
Hong Kong, 233, 235
Hood Theological Seminary, 14
Hookwaiter, Mr., 310
Hope and Sixth Streets, See Los Angeles, CA, Sixth and Hope Streets
Hot Springs, AR, 290
Houma, LA, 32
Household of Faith, 127, 128,
Household of Faith, Pasadena, CA, 255
Household of God, 178
Houston, TX, 14, 21, 27, 81, 89-91, 94, 95, 96n.35, 98pl., 99pl., 131, 141, 144
   503 Rusk Avenue at Brazos, 91
   509 Herndon, 145
   613 Taylor, 144
   812 Robin, 144
   1606 Dart, 90
   1626 Winter, 90
   1717 Edwards, 90
   1806 Clay, 90
   Texas Avenue near Main Street, 91
Houston Trunk Factory, Houston, 144
Howard University, 335
How Pentecost Came to Los Angeles, 17, 329
Hughes, Brother, 146
Hughes, John, 271
Hugh Waddell, Henkle and Pillot, Houston, 144

Huguenots, 26
Hunger for God, 11, 143, 150, 211, 212, 215, 222, 238, 250
Hungary, 285
Huntington Building, Los Angeles, 159
Huntinton, Carlos P., 194
Hutchins, Julia, 94, 128, 140, 234, 236
Iberia, St. Mary, and Eastern Railroad, 6, 313
Illinois, 233
Independence, MO 14
India, 198, 234, 240
Indiana, 14, 78
Indianapolis, IN, 68n.9, 69, 70, 71, 73, 231, 254, 301-305, 307, 309, 310, 312, 319pl., 330
  127 1/2 Indiana Ave., 69
  309 Bird St., 69
  2341 Fletcher, 304
  3313 Graceland Avenue, 306
  1720 West Washington Street, 304
  Alabama and New York Streets, 302
  Howard and Second, 71
  Illinois and Maryland, 70
  Illinois and Washington, 70
  Missouri and Eleventh, 71
  Pennsylvania and Ohio, 70
Indianapolis Morning Star, 302
International Church of the Foursquare Gospel, 14, 233
Ingland, Joseph, 309, 319pl.
International Holiness Union and Prayer League, 79
Interpretation of tongues, 181, 307
In the Beginning, 27
Irvingites, 26
Irwin, Benjamin Hardin, 23

Jackson, MS, 14, 81, 87, 88, 215, 230
James, Spencer, 325
Japan, 198, 235
Jerking, See shaking in the Spirit
Jerusalem, Israel, 233, 235
Jesus Only Movement, 290, 329, 330
Jett, Jerry, 15
Jeter, J.A., 88, 215, 216
Johnson, Andrew G., 233
Jonas, Mack E., 166, 183, 285
Jones, Charles P., 87, 88, 97pl., 215, 218
Jones, Donald, 15
Jones, Mrs., 285
Joplin, MO, 14, 16, 27
Joseph F. Meyer Co., Houston, 144
Junk, Thomas, 203pl., 229, 235
Kallaway, Mrs., 283
Kansas, 11, 21, 23, 27, 90
Kansas City, 14, 90
Kelso, Nelda, 309
Kennedy Aimee, See Aimee Semple McPherson
Kenyon, E. W., 13
Kelly, W. M., 257, 258
Keyes, Henry S., 196, 261pl.
Keyes, Lillian, 196
Keyes, Oree, 312
Kilpatrick, A. J., 78
Kilpatrick, John A., 10
Knapp, Martin Wells, 79, 80
Kol Kare Bomidbar: A Voice Crying in the Wilderness, 27
Korsets Seier, 329
Ku Klux Klan, 38
Knights of Industry of the Hotel Brotherhood, 70
Knights of the White Camellia, 38
Lafayette, LA, 32
Lake Fausse Point, LA, 50

Lake, John G., 19, 141, 189, 206pl., 313
Lander, Rochelle, 349pl.
Latin Language, 143
Law, May, 235
Lawrence, Bennett, 309
Laying on of hands, 95, 143, 145, 150, 192, 220, 221
Leatherman, Lucy, 229, 235, 239, 245pl.
Leaves of Healing, 75
Lee, Edward S., 130, 141-143, 145, 146, 277, 282, 328
Lee, Mattie, 130, 143, 277, 328
Lee, Joyce, 15
Lee, Owen "Irish," 251, 266pl.
Lemoine, Mrs., 258
Liberia, West Africa, 234, 236, 304, 312
Lifting hands to God, 146
Lincoln, Abraham, 49
Lindsey, Gordon, 335
Little Tokyo, Los Angeles, 336
Lloyd, Ernest, 303, 309
Lockett, Samuel H., 32, 33
London, England, 121
London, Jack, 167
Long Beach, CA, 240
The Lord's Supper, 309, 310
Los Angeles, CA, 9, 11, 14, 21, 76, 94, 95, 101, 103-107, 109pl., 126-128, 131, 146, 147, 155, 156, 160, 167, 168, 178, 181, 184, 196, 198, 199, 211, 215, 218-220, 228, 230-232, 234, 236, 238, 240, 248, 252, 256, 259, 267, 268, 270, 271, 274, 278-283, 286-289, 303-305, 311, 313, 316pl., 324, 326, 327, 329, 333, 336, 347pl.
   214 North Bonnie Brae, 129, 130, 138pl., 144-147, 149, 156, 165, 166, 168, 183, 230,325
   216 North Bonnie Brae, 328
   217 North Bonnie Brae, 129, 333
   228 1/2 Bonnie Brae, 328
   312 Azusa Street, 9, 11, 21, 105, 119, 126, 155-158, 160, 161pl., 178, 179, 191, 193, 195, 198, 199, 210, 212, 213, 215, 217, 218, 220, 221, 229, 235, 239, 244pl., 247, 248, 249, 251, 252, 268, 285, 301, 395, 327, 332-334, 336
   919 Boston Street, 126, 135pl.
   1001 East 27th Street, 334
   1445 W. 36th Street, 328
   327 1/2 So. Spring Street, 273
   9411 Parmelee Avenue, 334
   Broadway and Temple Streets, 270
   Eighth Street and Towne Avenue, 157
   First and Bonnie Brae, 128
   First and Cummings Streets, 252
   Grand Avenue, 130
   Kholer Street, 288
   Ninth and Santa Fe Streets, 130, 139
   Seventh and Broadway Streets, 130
   Seventh and Los Angeles Streets, 289
   Seventh and Spring Streets, 130
   Sixth and Hill Streets, 125
   Sixth and Main Streets, 159

Sixty-eighth and Denver Streets, 127
Spring Street between 3rd and 4th, 156
Los Angeles Daily Times, See *Los Angeles Times*
Los Angeles Church Federation, 256
Los Angeles County, CA, 156
Los Angeles Examiner, 260pl.
Los Angeles Express, 110pl., 115pl., 116pl., 117pl., 118pl., 147, 167, 176pl., 249, 251, 256
Los Angeles High School, 196
Los Angeles River, 155
Los Angeles Times, 14, 166, 172pl., 177, 248, 249, 261pl.
Louisiana, 14, 31-38, 40, 47, 49-51, 65
Louisiana State Seminary, 32
Lowe, Charles W., 312, 322pl.
Ludden, Florence M., 332
Lum, Clara, 159, 178, 189, 200, 203pl., 220, 279, 280n.49
McAlister, R.E., 13, 290, 300pl.
McClean, Hector and Sigrid, 235
McGowan, Mrs. W.H., 258
McGowan, W.H., 140, 144
McLain, Henry, 254
McNeil, J.B., 160
McPherson, Aimee Semple, 233, 327, 334
McPherson, Allan V., 280n.49
McPherson, Harold, 233
Maine, 49
Mallinak, John, 15
Manley, William, 127, 128, 178, 185
Maple and Seventh Streets, See Los Angeles, CA, Seventh and Maple
Marshall, R. S., 147

Martin, Larry, 9, 10, 16, 353, 376pl.
Martin, T. J. & Summer, 16
Maryland, 312
Mason, Bridget "Biddy," 156, 162pl.
Mason, Charles H., 88, 209, 213-218, 224pl., 230, 290, 291, 313, 314, 324
Mason, Elliott, 349pl.
Massachusetts, 49
Matthews, John, 329
Mead, Ardel K., 208pl., 235
Mead, Samuel J., 195, 208pl., 235
Memphis, TN, 14, 66-68, 214, 217, 314
32 Jefferson, 68
94 Pontotoc, 68
Mercer University, 195
Methodist, 22, 23, 52, 72, 74, 79, 80, 120, 125, 219, 235, 238, 254
Methodist Episcopal Church South, 219
Mexican, 254
Mexico, 101
Meyer, F.B., 125
Michigan, 127
Miller, Lulu, 229
Milligan, Berha, 235
Minnesota, 26
Missionary Baptist Church, 214
Mississippi, 14, 87, 89, 213, 215
Mississippi River, 66-68
Missouri, 11, 14, 27, 68
Missouri Southern State College, 14
Mitchell, Washington, 52
Mobile, AL, 14, 230, 231
Monrovia, CA, 233, 249
Montgomery, Anita, 15
Moore, Henry R., 233
Moore, Jackson and Eliza, 129

Moore, Jennie Evans, **See Seymour, Jennie E.M.**
Moody D. L., 26, 120, 121
Morette, Charles, 54
Morgan, G. Campbell, 125
Mount Gale Missionary Baptist Church, 215
Mount Olive Baptist Church, Plummersville, AR, 215
Mount Pleasant College, 14
Murphy League Hall, Indianapolis, 302, 309, 321pl.
Murphy, Samuel, 285
Muscatine County, IA, 21
Mushegan, Magardich, 199
My Story: "The Latter Rain," 329
Nagouchi Plaza, Los Angeles, 336
National Archives, 14
National Holiness Association, 78
Native Guard, 49
Nelson, Douglas, 15, 197n.84
Nelson, I. S., 215
New Iberia, LA, 50
New Jersey, 312
Newman Methodist Church, Los Angeles, 147
New Orleans, LA, 14, 50, 56, 58, 67
New Providence Baptist Church, 57, 58
New Testament Church, **See First New Testament Church**
New York, 76, 233, 237, 239, 251, 312, 314
Nix, Jay, 332
North Avenue Mission, Chicago, IL, 127, 232
North Carolina, 26, 219, 221, 312
North Carolina Holiness Association, 219
Northern Indiana Eldership of the Church of God, 77
Norway, 246pl., 329
Nunn, David, 335
Oakes, Carrie, 16
Oakland, CA, 178, 229, 240
Oddy, Ida May, 305, 306, 309, 318pl., 319pl.
Oddy, Tom, 305
Ohio, 75, 88, 312
Ohio District Assemblies of God, 14
Oklahoma, 13, 285
101 Ranch, 13
Old Tabernacle Church of God in Christ, East Orange, NJ, 314
Onawa, MI, 229
Oral Roberts University, 14
Orchard, TX, 27, 267
Oregon, 229
Orwig, A.W., 194, 237
Osterberg, Arthur G., 127, 149, 150, 159, 160, 164pl., 168, 177, 179, 183, 185, 191, 197, 266pl., 270, 289, 334
Osterberg, Dean, 15
Osterberg, Louis and Cena, 127, 137pl., 149, 179, 232, 271, 288, 289
Oyler, Walter J., 267
Ozark Christian College, 14
Ozarks, 230
Ozman, Agnes Nevada, 25
Pacific Ocean, 184
Pacific Pentecostal Association, Los Angeles, 125
Page, S.D., 244pl.
Parham, Charles Fox, 21-27, 28pl., 29pl., 75, 87, 90-94, 97pl., 235 98pl., 130, 131, 140, 141, 267-272, 274, 289, 293
Parham, Claude, 29pl.
Parham, Esther, 29pl.
Parham, Phillip, 29pl.
Parham, Sarah (Mrs. Charles), 29pl., 91, 93

Parham, Wilford, 29pl.
Pasadena, CA, 255
Pasadena Daily News, 255
Payne, Sarah H., 180
Pendleton, William, 127, 257, 258, 272
Peniel Hall, 227 S. Main, Los Angeles, 130, 141
Pennsylvania, 312
Pensacola, FL, 10, 337
Pentecostal Assemblies of the World, 14
The Pentecostal Church of God, 13
The Pentecostal Evangel, 14
The Pentecostal Free-will Baptist, 221
The Pentecostal Holiness Church, 14, 219-221, 291
The Pentecostal Testimony, 289
The Pentecostal World Conference, 336
People's Church, Los Angeles, 127
Pepsico, Georgiana Aycock, 314
Perez, Brigido, 229
Perkins, Mary, 200
Peter, Azelie, 54
Pethrus, Lewi, 331
Philippines, 182
Phillips, Thomas, 12
Phoenix, AZ, 283
Pierce, Clara, 228
Pierson, Darrol, 15
Pillar of Fire Church, 95, 272
Pinson, M.M., 221
Pittman, Rosa, 235
The Planter's Banner, 33, 39
Plummersville, AR, 214
Poe, H. J., 70
Pointer, James and Florence, 89
Polhill, Cecil, 195, 274, 281
Port Hudson, LA, 60pl.
Portland, OR 231, 232, 278-281
Portsmouth, VA, 228
Post, Ansel H., 127, 136pl., 229, 255
Prayer, 12, 25, 71, 72, 75, 88, 91, 92, 95, 119, 122, 124-126, 140-142, 144-146, 149, 150, 179-184, 189-193, 200, 211, 213, 218, 220, 221, 238, 249, 251, 252, 254, 276, 289, 307, 324, 330, 331, 334, 353
Premillennialism, 59, 79, 88, 140
Prentice, Henry, 252-254, 311
Presbyterian, 126, 228
Prescott, AZ, 121
Price, Charles S., 233
Primitive Baptist Church, Jackson, MS, 230
Prince, Mrs., 181, 203pl.
Prophesy, 91, 126, 128, 160, 179, 180, 227
Protestant, 104
Pruden, Marian E. and Ruth E., 328
Puryear, Mr., 69
Quakers, 23
Quaking, See Shaking under the power
Quinton, Mr. and Mrs., 267
Ramos, Brian, 16
Ramsey, J., 15, 197n.84
Rancho Los Amigos County Hospital, Los Angeles, 333
Rapture, See Return of the Lord
Reconstruction, 33, 37, 38, 89
Return of the Lord, 88, 180, 197, 327
Revival in Wales, 125
The Revivalist, 79
Reynolds (Flower), Alice, 302, 303, 308
Robeck, Cecil M., Jr., 15, 336, 349pl.

Roberts, Evan, 122, 125, 184
Roberts, J.M., 140, 141
Roberts, Oral, 335
Robinson, Elsie, 229
Robinson, Emma, 252
Robinson, J.S., 253
Rodgers, H.G. 221
Roman Catholic, 39, 53, 59, 103, 104, 160, 183, 191
Roper, David A., 5
Rosebud Cafe, St. Louis, MO, 69
Ross, James, 325
Rubley, Sister, 287
Ryan, M.L., 199, 235, 237, 245pl.
Ryland, E.P., 256
St. Louis, MO, 14, 68, 69, 83pl.
    205 N. 12th, 69
    820 Market, 69
    Market Street, St. Louis, 69
St. Mary Parish, 14, 32-38, 48, 51
Saints, **See Church of God Reformation**
Saints of Runney Mede Holiness Church, 312
Saints Home Church, Los Angeles, 334
Salabar, Adaline, 52
Salabar, Antirnette, 52
Salabar, Lucy, 51
Salabar, Michael, 51, 53
Salabar, Phillis, **See Seymour, Phillis**
Salabar, Polly, 52
Salt Lake, Utah, 156
Salem, OR, 231, 232, 237
Salvation, 21, 27, 81, 91, 139, 148, 183-185, 189, 200, 212, 214-216, 250, 251, 254, 276, 286, 324, 327
Salvation Army, 120
Sampson County, NC, 218
San Antonio, TX, 271
San Bernardino, CA, 209

Sanctification, 24, 75, 77-79, 81, 87, 90, 91, 128, 139-141, 148, 184, 185, 211, 212, 215, 216, 219, 286, 287, 289, 290, 324, 327, 331, 332
San Diego, 229
Sanford, Frank, 24
San Francisco, 104, 167, 168, 174pl., 175pl., 301
    Eighteenth Street, 175pl.
    Kearney Street, 175pl.
San Gabriel, CA, 101
San Jose, CA, 301
San Pedro Street, 155, 199
San Quentin, CA, 328
Santa Barbara, CA, 229
Sargent, Phoebe, 200, 203pl.
Satan, 216, 250, 263pl., 282, 287
Scheppe, John G., 290
Scott, Arthur, 306, 307
Scott, R.J., 276, 289, 297pl.
Seatle, WA, 230
Second Baptist Church, Los Angeles, 128
Second Coming, **See Return of the Lord**
Security First National Bank, Los Angeles, 334
Security Savings Bank, Los Angeles, 282
Selaba, Michael and Lucy, **See Salabar**
Semmes, Thomas J., 38
Semple, Robert, 233
Seymour, Amos, 54, 57
Seymour, Andrew, 54, 55
Seymour, Benjamin, 54, 55
Seymour, Caleb, 54, 55
Seymour, Emma, 55
Seymour, Henry S., 67
Seymour, Horatio, 38
Seymour, Issac, 54

Seymour, Jacob, 15, 54
Seymour, Jennie E.M., 129, 138pl., 143, 146, 147, 149, 153pl., 179, 200, 277, 280n.49, 285, 288n.71, 298pl., 313, 323, 325, 327, 329-331, 333
Seymour, John Emmuas, 54, 55
Seymour, Julia, 54
Seymour, Lucille, 15, 58
Seymour, Lydia, 67
Seymour, Philis Salabar, 47, 48n.4, 51-53, 56-58, 61pl., 62pl., 313, 323
Seymour, Rosalie, 54
Seymour, Simon, 47, 48, 50, 51-54, 56, 57, 60pl., 62pl.
Seymour, Simon, Jr., 54, 57
Seymour, Van, 15
Seymour, William Joseph, 6pl., 9, 12, 13, 15, 18pl., 19, 21, 32, 35, 37-39, 46, 47, 53-55, 57, 63pl., 65-67, 69-81, 82pl., 85pl., 88, 90-95, 108, 131, 139-143, 145, 146, 148, 149, 151pl., 155, 158, 160, 165, 166, 170pl., 171pl., 180, 184, 185, 188, 189, 191-194, 197, 198, 200, 203pl., 206pl., 216, 220, 233, 235, 241pl., 249, 265pl., 268-270, 272-275, 277, 279-290, 298pl., 301, 304-314, 316pl., 320pl., 323-327, 329-331, 334-336, 338pl., 343pl., 350pl.
Seymour's Knights, 38
Shakarian, Demos, 126
Shakarian, Demos (Grandfather), 126, 135pl., 199
Shaking under the power, 26, 142, 143, 150, 179, 186, 194, 248, 269, 313
Shaw, Elizabeth, 309
Shaw, S. B., 125

Sheridan, Philip, 37
Shepley, General, 37
Shouting, 26, 166, 179, 329, 248, 249, 252, 284
Shumway, Charles, 88, 145
Shortridge High School, Indianapolis, 302
Simpson, A.B., 23
Simpson Chapel Methodist Episcopal Church, Indianapolis, 70
Singing in the Spirit, 150, 179, 187, 217
Sizelove, Maud, Matt, & Snowdie, 192
Sizelove, Rachel A., 168, 169n.15, 192, 276, 296pl.
Slain in the Spirit, 143, 145, 146, 148, 179, 182, 189, 193, 194, 211, 248, 257, 302, 304, 307
Slavery, 33-36, 44pl., 47, 49, 52, 89, 156, 198, 214, 335
Smale, Joseph, 120-125, 133pl., 165, 256, 261pl., 272, 273, 276
Smith, Amanda, 215
Smith, Hiram, 200, 203pl.
Smith, Jedediah Strong, 104
Smith, Joseph, 125
Smithton, MO, 337, 352pl.
Smock, Celia, 302
Solkeld, C. W., 229
South America, 284
South Carolina, 25
Southern Baptist Church Archives, 14
Southern California Holiness Association, 140
Southern California and Arizona Holiness Association, 210
South Union Avenue near First Street, Los Angeles, 130

Southwestern Assemblies of God University, 14
Southwest Baptist University, 14
Southwest Kansas College, 22
Spain, 102, 233
Spaniards, 101
Spanish Language, 143, 254
Speaking in tongues, 25, 26, 88, 90, 93, 126, 130, 131, 139, 140, 143-145, 147-150, 165, 166, 179, 180, 182, 188, 189, 193, 197, 199, 210, 211, 213, 216-218, 220-222, 232, 235-239, 248, 250, 252, 257, 258, 272, 273, 284, 302, 308, 309, 311
Speicher, J. G., 178
Springfield, IL, 14
Springfield, MO, 335
Spurgeon's College, 120
The Star, 103
Starret, Nancy, 228
Steelberg, Wesley, 181
Stevens African Methodist Episcopal Church, Los Angeles, 156, 161pl., 274
Stewart, Brother, 283
Stope, Laura, 16
Stone's Mansion, Topeka, KS, 25, 30pl.
Studd, C.T., 195
Studd, George B., 195, 206pl., 273, 281-283
Sunderland, England, 240
Sweden, 233, 240, 331
Sweet Haven Church, 312
Swing, James R., 210
Synan, Vinson, 15
Tarr, Del, 188
Tears, 26, 150, 183, 186, 187, 211, 218, 314
Tennessee, 26, 217

Tennessee Paper Company, Memphis, 68
Terminal Island, Los Angeles, 184
Terre Haute, IN, 14
Terry, Neely, 94, 131
Testimony, 11, 13, 146, 165, 166, 179, 180, 184, 186, 194, 198, 215, 232, 275, 282, 330, 334, 335
Texas, 11, 14, 26, 88, 89, 93, 94, 106, 107, 129, 140, 141, 156, 200, 267, 268, 270, 301, 328, 337
The Texas Bar, 14
Thistlethwaite, Lillian, 23, 29pl.
Thompson, Harold, 16
Throop, I. May, 238
Tomlison, A.J., 222
Topeka, Kansas, 11, 23, 24, 26, 91, 95
The Topeka Outpouring of 1901, 13
Toronto, Ontario, 337
A Tract for Our Times, 273
Traynor, Sallie, Bud, & Sis, 146, 147
Treaty of Guadelupe Hidalgo, 103
Trinity Methodist Episcopal South Church, Los Angeles, 256
Trotter, Will, 281
Truth, Sojourner, 72
Twelfth Street, St. Louis, MO, 69
Two Years Missions Work in Europe Just before the World War, 329
Under the Blood, 179
Union University, 14
United Pentecostal Church, 14
United Methodist Archives, 14
University of South Carolina, 14
University United Methodist Church, 71
The Upper Room, 259

Upper Room Mission, Los Angeles, 272, 273, 286, 295pl.
Valdez, A.C., Sr., 204pl.
Van Camp Packing Company, Indianapolis, 306
Van Loon, Harry, 232
Verdunville, LA, 55, 58, 64pl.
Vermont, 49
Vinton, Edward, 228
Virginia, 89, 129, 313
Visions, 59, 143, 146, 214, 228, 259, 287
Wales, 12, 122, 125, 184
Walker, E.F., 126
Walton, Rhonda, 15
Warner, Daniel S., 77-79
Warner, Wayne, 15
Warren, Joseph A., 144, 160, 200, 282, 285, 323, 328
Washington, DC, 14, 312
Water baptism, 53, 184, 276, 290, 308-310, 319pl., 320pl., 327
The Way of Faith, 218
W.C.T.U. Building, Broadway and Temple Streets, Los Angeles, 270
Weaver, Brother, 149
Weeping, See Tears
Wegmann, Lucas, 15
Welch, Bridget, 183
Wellington Street, Memphis, TN, 218
Wells, James, 314
Wesleyan Holiness, 24, 120
Wesley, John, 26, 80
West Africa, 188
White, Alma, 95, 100pl.
Whittier, CA, 252, 254
Wigglesworth, Smith, 240, 246pl.
Wiley, Mary Ann, 328
Wiley, Opal Stauffer, 95, 98pl., 229, 230
Willey, Ada, 309
William Jewell College, 14
William J. Seymour Chapel, A.G.T.S., 335, 348pl.
Williams, Ernest S., 185, 187, 190, 209-213, 223pl., 270, 271, 281
William Seymour Pentecostal Fellowship, 335
Williams, Fannie, 73
Williams, F.W., 148, 154pl., 213, 230, 231, 326
Williams, Thomas R., 15
Winebrennerian Church of God, 78
Woodworth-Etter, Maria, 290
Worrell, A.S., 19, 195
Worrell, John, 15
Young, D.J., 215
Zion City, IL, 178, 268

List of Illustrations

The author has tried to find photographs of all Azusa Street players. Unfortunately, many were not located. I hoped for images of Richard and Ruth Asbery, Edward Lee, Lucy Farrow, Joseph Warren, A. S. Worrell and many more. Perhaps some day they will be available. Many of the photos are of poor quality, some are really too flawed to use, but they were the best I could find. I pray the reader will appreciate seeing many of the people about whom they are reading.

William Joseph Seymour Signature	6
William Joseph Seymour Chalk Portrait	18
Charles Fox Parham	28
The Parham Family	29
Stone's Folly	30
A Different View of Stone's Folly	30
Centerville, LA	41
Sugar Cane Harvest	41
Bayou Teche	42
Bocage	42
Confederate Currency	43

Centerville, 1881	43
Slave Sale Announcements	44
Black Men in Swamps	45
Black Family during Reconstruction	46
A Group of the Corp de Afrique	60
United States Colored Troops in Louisiana	60
Simon Seymour's Military Service Record	60
1860 Census	61
Map of Carlin Plantion	61
Marriage License - Simon and Selleba	62
Seymour Relative Bible	62
Baptismal Record - William Simon	63
Catholic Church - Franklin, LA	63
Van Seymour Bar	64
The Seymour Homeplace	64
Post Card - Black Children, Log Cabin	64
An Early Photo of W. J. Seymour	82
The Belle of Memphis	82
Life in the Slums of St. Louis	83
Madison Street in Chicago	84
Three Hotels in Indianapolis	85
Grand Hotel Cafe	86
Cartoon of Black Waiter	86
Charles P. Jones	96
Lucy Farrow Neighborhood	97
Charles F. Parham and Team	97
Parham and Workers at Bryan Hall	98
Howard A. Goss	99
The Bible Training School - Houston	99
Warren F. Carothers	100
Alma White	100
City of Los Angeles	109
Los Angeles Railroad Map	110
Los Angeles Express Clippings	111-114
Patrolman Glenn	115
Racist Advertisment	116
Racist Comics	117
Lynching Clippings	118
Frank Bartleman	132

Joseph Smale	133
First Baptist Church Deacons	133
Elmer Fisher	134
A. G. Garr	134
The Shakarian Family	135
The Boston Street Home Church	135
Ansel and Mrs. Post	136
C. H. Anderson	137
Louis and Cena Osterberg	137
The Richard Asbery Home	138
Jeannie Moore's Home	138
Jennie Evans Moore	138
Seymour, Seated with Table	151
The Asbery Porch	152
The Asbery Home (Later Photo)	152
Bonnie Brae Street Sign	152
The Asbery Piano	153
F. W. and Mrs. Williams	154
Stephens A. M. E. Church	161
Biddy Mason	162
Second and San Pedro	162
Early Azusa Mission	163
A. G. Osterberg	164
The Azusa Street Mission	170
Seymour and the Mission	170
William J. Seymour	171
"Weird Babel of Tongues"	172
Bartleman's Earthquake Tract	173
San Francisco Burning	174
18th Street - San Francisco	175
Kearney Street - San Francisco	175
Grim Reaper	176
William H. Durham	202
Daniel Awrey	202
The Credentials Committee	203
Henry and Emma Cotton	203
A. C. Valdez, Sr.	204
Florence Crawford	204

Frank Bowdan	205
Maggie Bowdan	205
T. C. McConnell	205
George Studd	206
John G. Lake & Co.	206
The Apostolic Faith	207
Samuel J. and Ardel K. Mead	208
Rev. and Mrs. E. S. Williams	223
C. H. Mason	224
G. B. Cashwell	225
Downtown Dunn, North Carolina	226
Dunn's Cotton Market	226
Seymour, Seated with Bible	241
Lee Hall	242
Iva Campbell	243
Mrs. A. G. Garr and Lillian Denny	244
S. D. Page and F. M. Britton	244
Azusa Street Missionaries, Leatherman, Hezmalhalch, Ryan	245
A. A. Boddy and Thomas B. Barratt	246
Smith Wigglesworth	246
"Summer Solstice" Cartoon	260
New Testament Church Cartoon	261
Della Cline	262
Apostolic Faith Mission	262
The Devil's Bubbles	263
Misc. Critical Articles	264
Seymour, Seated, Looking Forward	265
A. G. Osterberg and Owen "Irish" Lee	266
Phineas F. Bresee	266
The Azusa Street Mission	292
Letterhead	292
Charles F. Parham	293
Burning Bush Cartoons	293
Frank Bartleman	294
The Eighth and Maple Mission	294
Elmer Fisher	295
The Upper Room Mission	295

The Sign on the Azusa Street Mission	296
Rachel Sizelove	296
Mr. and Mrs. R. J. Scott	297
Julia Carney	297
Mr. and Mrs. Edward Doak	297
William and Jennie Seymour	298
Marriage License	298
George Eldridge	299
Elder and Mrs. Covington	299
William H. Durham at Tent Revival	300
R. E. McAlister	300
Train Trip to Chicago	316
The Cummings Children	317
Mrs. Tom Oddy	318
Indianapolis Baptismal Service	319
Mrs. Oddy at Baptism	319
Baptismal Cartoon	320
Glenn Cook	321
Murphy League Hall	321
Charles W. Lowe	322
A.F.C.O.G. Doctrine	322
The Older W. J. Seymour	338
Boddy's Photos	339
Gee's Photo	340
Later Photos of the Mission	340-341
Missionary Frank Bartleman	342
Frank Bartleman in his senior years	342
Seymour's Grave	343
Thirtieth Anniversary Flyer	344
Thirty-ninth Anniversary Flyer	345
Fiftieth Anniversary Photo	346
Fiftieth Anniversary Flyer	346
Azusa Street Sign	347
Seymour Stained Glass Window	348
Los Angeles Plaque Dedication Service	349
Ribbon Cutting	349
Memorial Plaque	350
The Cry for Revival	352
"The Comforter Has Come"	354
Larry Martin	376

About the Author

Dr. Larry Martin has given more than 45 year in gospel ministry. He has spent almost twenty-five years pastoring churches in Oklahoma, Texas, Florida, and Tennessee. While still in his teens, Martin launched his ministry career as a traveling evangelist. He returned to evangelism from 1997 until the end of 2004. For three years he pastored in Pensacola, Florida and then answered the call to a new missionary/evangelistic venture in early 2008. He continues in that work.

Believing as Wesley, that the world is his parish, Doc Martin has travelled in more than fifty countries. He has taught in Bible schools, preached in mission churches both large and small and led mass evangelism crusades where as many as 40,000 have professed Christ in one event.

Martin has attended eleven different institutions of higher education. He is a graduate of Cameron University, Oklahoma Missionary Baptist College, Southwestern Oklahoma State University, and The Assemblies of God Theological Seminary. His last degree earned was the Doctor of Ministry degree at Austin esbyterian Theological Seminary in Austin, Texas.

In 1994, Martin was chosen as the president of Messenger College in Joplin, Missouri. He also served the college as the Dean of the School of Lifelong Learning and as a professor of theology and missions.

From 2001-2004, Martin served Brownsville Revival School of Ministry in Pensacola, Florida as Academic Dean. He taught a number of courses in the college and was a regular speaker at the Brownsville Assembly of God Church.

Also a free-lance writer, Martin's articles have appeared in *Charisma, The Remnant, Ministries Today, Pulpit Helps, The Missionary Voice, The International Pentecostal Holiness Advocate, The Pentecostal Messenger, The Pentecostal Minister, The Message of the Open Bible, The Pentecostal Leader, The Church Herald and Holiness Banner, The Brownsville Report*, and *The Church of God Evangel.*

Martin, considered by many to be an authority on the Pentecostal revival at Azusa Street, is the author of *The Life and Ministry of William J. Seymour* and editor of The Complete Azusa Street Library. He has written or edited *In the Beginning*, and *We've Come this Far by Faith*, histories of early Pentecostals and the Pentecostal Church of God, *For Sale the Soul of a Nation, The Topeka Outpouring of 1901, Have We Lost Our Mind* and has edited and/or contributed to several other works.

River of of Revival Ministries, Inc. was founded by Martin and he continues to serve as president of the ministry.

Martin is married to Tajuana Jo, a full partner in the ministry. The couple have two children, Matthew Dallas who lives in Cape Girardeau, Missouri and Summer Jo who lives in Pensacola.

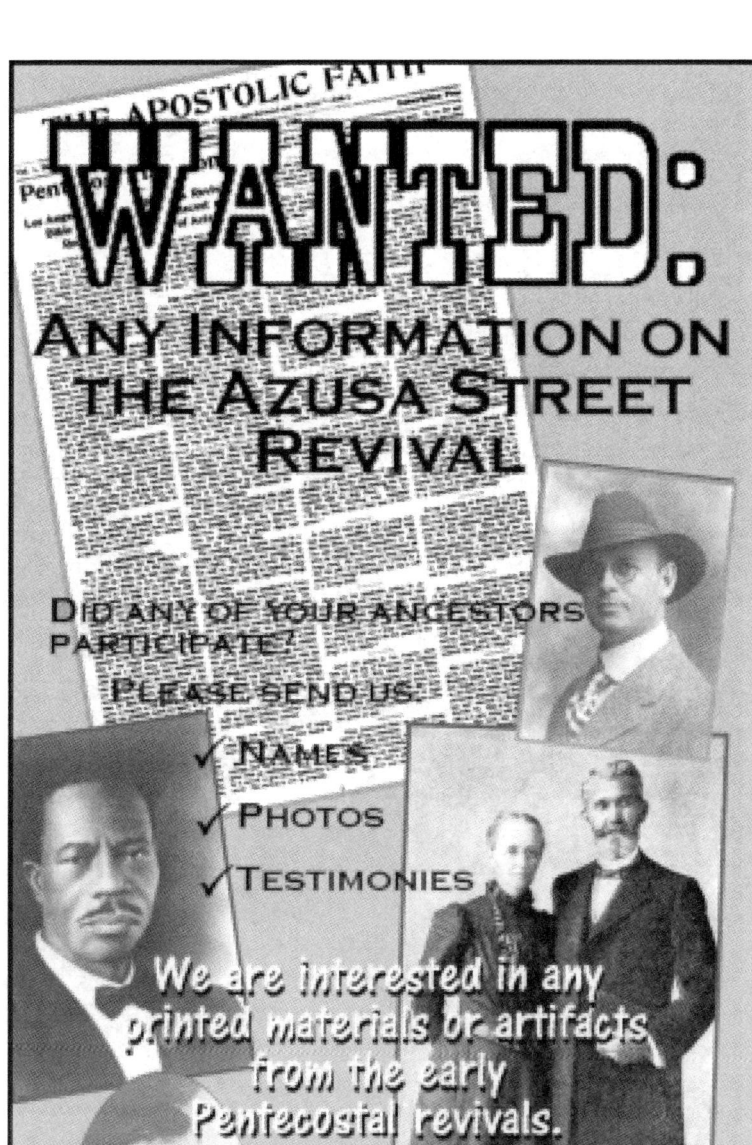

VISIT US AT WWW.AZUSASTREET.ORG

Other titles from Christian Life Books:

The Topeka Outpouring of 1901: 100th Anniversary Edition

Edited and Compiled by Larry Martin

This book is a must for all students of Pentecostal history. Dr. Martin has compiled a series of eye witness accounts of the revival that started the Pentecostal movement. Included are stories from each of the major players, academic critiques, and newspaper articles. This edition contains several never published accounts and photos. 257 pages.

The original edition is also available. It tells the same story, but with less detail and at a lower price. 128 pages.

"... through faith, though he is dead, he still speaks." Hebrews 11:4

"CARRIED BY ANGELS"

LEONARD RAVENHILL
1907 — 1994

"ARE THE THINGS YOU ARE LIVING FOR WORTH CHRIST DYING FOR?"

Christian Life Books is honored to make available classic books by Leonard Ravenhill. Each book, in its own way, will convict you and draw you to a closer walk with God. No one in the Twentieth Century, prayed more, believed more, or worked more for revival in America and his native England than Leonard Ravenhill. Speaking from the grave, his words are as powerful today as when the ink fell from the pen of this anointed man of God.

Logging some 150,000+ miles a year and often speaking with over half-a-million young people annually, Winkie Pratney has wide experience in youth work. His technical background in both science and the popular music culture has given him a unique insight to the particular needs of a media-dominated technological society, and his constant monitoring of youth trends combined with continual feedback from young people themselves has helped him interpret these for those with a vital interest in the welfare of the young. Besides annual leadership training seminars he has for three decades helped challenge and inspire young people to holy and happy living.

A frequent featured speaker and guest on national television talk shows, his audio and video-tape lectures are carried by many effective outreach ministries as part of their training. Winkie has authored more than twelve books including youth manuals like the best-selling *Youth Aflame!*, *Handbook For Followers Of Jesus*, books on contemporary and historical issues like *Devil Take The Youngest*, *Dealing With Doubt* and evangelistic and apologetic works like the contemporary devotional theology *The Nature And Character Of God*.

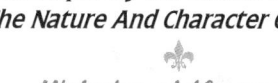

Histories of the world's greatest revivals!

Biographies of the revivalists!

Proven principles to change the world!

When the question Is asked: "What hinders revival?" one of the simple answers is this: We do not have men and women who are prepared to pay the same price to preach the same message and have the same power as those revivalists of the past. Without these firm believers, the community can never be changed... We say we want revival. But who today is prepared to live a life of absolute obedience to the Holy Spirit, tackling sin in the church as well as the streets, preaching such a message of perfection of heart and holiness of life—a message feared and hated by the religious and street sinner alike?

This Book Should Be Mandatory Reading for Every Serious Christian Worker!

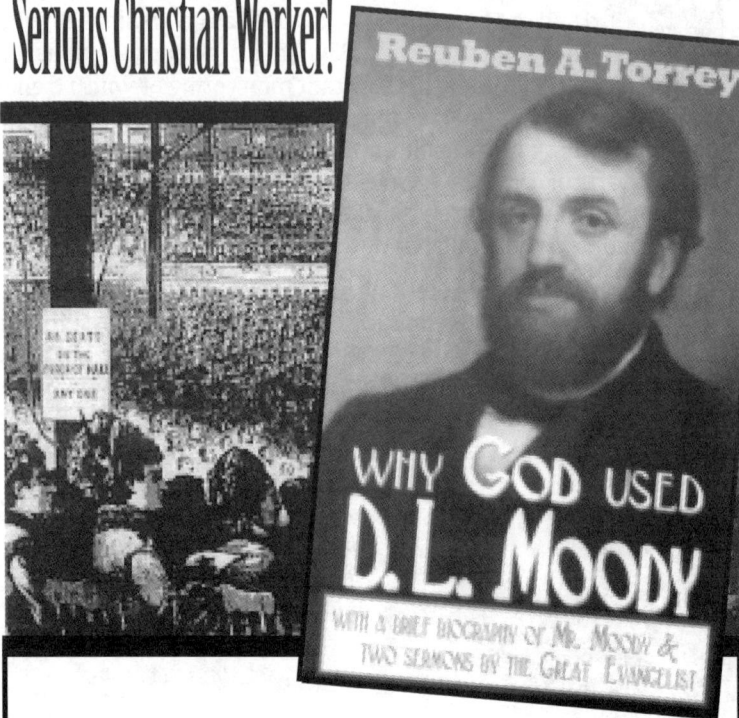

D. L. Moody was the greatest evangelist of his generation, perhaps of all generations. He personally preached to more than 100 million people before the days of mass communication or transportation. Tens of thousands were converted by this anointed servant of God. Although mostly without formal education, Moody also wrote books, established churches and founded schools that are still training men and women for ministry.

R. A. Torrey, one of Moody's closest friends is uniquely qualified to tell the world of Moody's secrets to success with both God and man. This book will challenge and inspire every reader whose heart is praying for a closer walk with God and more effective Christian service.

Christian Life Books has added a brief biography of Moody and two of his great sermons to this reprint. It is sent out with the prayer that God will use others as he used Dwight L. Moody.

Has the Church Gone Crazy?

Dr Larry Martin explores the contradictions between Western Christianity and the faith of the New Testament. Fascinating reading for anyone searching for true biblical faith.

Check our website for more titles.

www.rrmi.org

THIRTY MINUTE SERMON SERIES

The World's Greatest Sermons from the World's Greatest Preachers!

Sinners in the Hands of an Angry God. Jonathan Edward's fiery revival sermon is now available in a 32 page pocket booklet. This may be the most famous sermon of all times. When originally preached, *Sinners in the Hands of an Angry God* stirred New England to a Great Awakening.

The Lost Christ. One of the best sermons ever preached by one England's greatest evangelists. Gypsy Smith travelled the world proclaiming the good news of Jesus Christ and warning even the most faithful church members that they, too, can lose Christ.

Repentance. Billy Sunday was one of the greatest preachers in America's history. He left a profitable career in baseball to become an evangelist that preached to tens of thousands in the nation's largest cities. "Repentance" is one of his classic sermons.

Ask Your Christian Bookstore to
Stock these Great Books on Revival.
Available Only from Christian Life Books!

The Topeka Revival of 1901

The Brownsville Revival

Other Great Books for your *REVIVAL* Library

CHRISTIAN LIFE BOOKS
P.O. BOX 36355
PENSACOLA, FLORIDA 32516
www.rrmi.org & *www.azusastreet.org*
info@azusastreet.org

Some Good News

"And a certain rich ruler asked him saying, Good Master, what shall I do to inherit eternal life?" Luke 18:23

Ever since time began, man has been searching for a redeemer, one that could save them from fear and death. Many years ago, a rich man came to Jesus asking what He must do to be saved, and though centuries have passed, men are still looking for the same answer.

As a church, we are sometimes guilty of adding to the scriptural plan of salvation until we make it sound hard and unreachable. WE analyze God, and describe Him in such intellectual terminologies, that we put redemption over the heads of most ordinary people, leaving them in spiritual darkness. However, there is nothing any simpler than the BIBLE plan of Salvation. Here is is presented in five steps.

1 REALIZE YOUR NEED FOR SALVATION

"For all have sinned and come short of the glory of God." Romans 3:23

As ministers, we can beg, plead, and threaten, but a man will never come to God, until he realizes his need. I have met many people who were convinced that their good works were sufficient to warrant salvation. Not so! The Bible says our own RIGHTEOUSNESS is like filthy rags in God's sight. Read John Chapter 3, Jesus told Nicodemus he must be born again.

2 REALIZE THAT JESUS IS YOUR SAVIOR

"Neither is there salvation in any other; for there is none other name under heaven given among men, whereby we must be saved." Acts 4:12

After realizing your need for a Savior, you must recognize who that Savior is. God never said we could have eternal life by believing in Confucious, Mohammed, Buddha, a guru, or Hare Krishna. Neither a church, nor a preacher, can save you, you must turn to Jesus Christ, the Savior of the world

3 CONFESS YOUR SINS

"If we confess our sins, he is faithful and just to forgive us our sins, and to cleanse us from all unrighteousness." 1 John 1:9

Thirdly, you must confess your sins to God. Tell Him that you realize your wrongdoings, and you see His forgiveness. Many times we can apply James 4:2 to our salvation, "...Ye have not, because ye ask not."

4 BELIEVE THAT GOD HAS SAVED YOU

"But as many as received Him, to them gave He power to become the sons of God, even to them that believe on His name;" John 1:12

The first three steps to your salvation are tangible, the fourth is invisible. You must reach out in simple faith, sometimes without feelings, and believe that Jesus is the Son of God, and that He has forgiven your sins. Jesus said if you asked you would receive; so if you have asked, believe salvation is yours!

5 ABIDE IN CHRIST

"If ye keep my commandments, ye shall abide in my love; even as I have kept my Father's commandments, and abide in His love." John 15:10

Salvation is just the beginning of a brand new life. To really be saved, you must follow Jesus everyday. There may be trials of your faith, but abide in Him, and His grace will be sufficient for you.

If you have not yet accepted Christ as your personal Savior, bow right where you are and pray this simple prayer:

> "God, I know that I am a sinner, and that only you can be my Savior, I am asking you to forgive the sins of my old life, and give me a brand new life. By faith I believe that you have saved me, and now give me the strength to abide in you." AMEN

Plrese write us and tell us about your decision to follow Jesus.

You can invite Dr. Larry Martin to teach on the life of Bishop Willam Seymour and the Azusa Street Revival at your church, conference or event. Dr. Martin, a missionary evangelist, is a leading authority on the historic revival and the editor and publisher of The Complete Azusa Street Library. He is also available for revivals, crusades and church services Please visit our websites or send us an email for more details:

drlarrymartin@azusastreet.org
www.drlarrymartin.org
www.azusastreet.org